ered by Rall and found interesting insights into religious questions concerning faith, theology, and the responsibility of modern Christianity. The analyses undertaken have contributed to a greater understanding of this figure.

ESSAYS IN AMERICAN THEOLOGY:

THE LIFE AND THOUGHT

OF

HARRIS FRANKLIN RALL

ESSAYS IN AMERICAN THEOLOGY:
THE LIFE AND THOUGHT OF HARRIS FRANKLIN RALL

by

W. J. McCUTCHEON

*Chairman, Department of Religious Studies,
Beloit College*

Philosophical Library
New York

Copyright, © 1973, by Philosophical Library, Inc.,
15 East 40 Street, New York, N. Y. 10016

All rights reserved

Library of Congress Catalog Card No. 72-190198
SBN 8022-2085-1

Printed in the United States of America

TO MY WIFE, KATY,

WHOSE PATIENCE ATTESTS HER LOVE

TABLE OF CONTENTS

	Preface	ix
Chapter		
I	A Biographical Sketch of Harris Franklin Rall	1
II	Theological Methodology in General, Rall on Ritschl in particular	21
III	The Theological Methodology of Harris Franklin Rall	46
IV	Religion vs. Christianity	74
V	Theology and Trinity	104
VI	Christology	130
VII	Soteriology	149
VIII	Anthropology	163
IX	Ecclesiology	176
X	Eschatology	197
XI	Harris Franklin Rall's Image, Impact, Immersion into "American" Theology	209
	Annotated Bibliography of Harris Franklin Rall	236
	Appendices	248

    A. Lecture Notes, 1919-1950
    B. "Which Way Theology?"
    C. Pastoral Prayers
    D. Anthology of the Cross
    E. Selections from *"We Believe"* and "Dr. Rall Answers"
    F. Speaking Schedule

Footnotes		314

PREFACE

After rereading this book, after having written it, I can only conclude that two or three notes must be made apparent at the beginning. With these keys available the book will prove itself more valuable than without them. No attempt is made herein to present the biography of Harris Franklin Rall. Of course, an opening chapter designates his place and his particular academic history in America and abroad. Also, throughout the book mention is made of his importance to the Methodist Episcopal Church through his activities in her life. But quite consciously, I have avoided detailing any of the life of that church and his particular personal contributions to the Methodist Federation of Social Service, or, the Fundamentalist-Modernist Controversy, etc. At best I have tried to include various mentions of his critical impact upon these groups without falling prey to the temptation to develop these workings in detail. Especially would this be true of his impact during his teaching career upon the outstanding leaders of that Church. I have added as appendices several documents that allow the reader to begin to sense the person of Harris Franklin Rall. Why avoid such a biographical approach? Foremost is the fact that I think the masterful job on that Church and hence Rall's place in her life has already been written.[1] I am tempted after this work to begin a general history of the religious climate of America during the first forty years of this century, with focus upon the inter-war period, 1919-1939, as that particular history has yet to be documented and written.

1. Emory Stevens Burke, gen. ed., *The History of American Methodism.* 3 Vols. (New York-Nashville: Abingdon Press, 1964).

Another aspect that becomes apparent in this book is found in the very selection of Harris Franklin Rall himself rather than in Douglas Clyde Macintosh, or William Adams Brown, or other "major" theologians. Why *Rall?* The genesis of the approach arose out of my present involvement in current consultations of church union and racial and social identity questions in our city. It came afresh to me that to truly understand the American experience one has to forego and abandon notions of generality and universality to comprehend American history and reinvestigate the specific and particular[1] Such is the case in all areas of cultural history and I now suggest intellectual history of this land. By research after this fashion, the historian is more likely to retain the integrity of the period visited, in its own way, and further to check the temptation to force the previous period's thoughts into present methodological and fundamental frameworks. I know this to be the case because of my personal odyssey as a scholar in America: the completion of the dissertation and then the realization that what you discovered belies the material from which and by which you made your discovery. On this see my own confession in relation to the "Chicago Theology" of the inter-war period in chapter XI !

1. E.g., Henry F. May, "Shifting Perspectives on the 1920's," *The Mississippi Valley Historical Review*, Volume XLIII, June, 1956 to March, 1957, pp. 405-427; Barton J. Bernstein, ed., *Towards A New Past, Dissenting Essays in American History.* (New York: Random House, 1967). Franklin L. Baumer, "Intellectual History and Its Problems." *The Journal of Modern History*, XXI (September, 1949), pp. 191-203. Also, cf. Charles A. Barker, "Needs and Opportunities in American Social and Intellectual History," *Pacific Historical Review*, XXI (February, 1951), pp. 1-9; John L. Greene, "Objectives and Methods in Intellectual History," *The Mississippi Valley Historical Review*, XLIV (June, 1957), pp. 58-74; John Higham, "American Intellectual History: A Critical Appraisal," *American Quarterly*, XIII (Summer Supplement, 1961), pp. 219-33; Rush Welter, "The History of Ideas in America: An Essay in Redefinition." *The Journal of American History*, LI (March, 1965), pp. 599-614, R. Richard Wohel, "Intellectual History: An Historian's View," *The Historian*, XVI (Autumn, 1953), pp. 62-77.

The function of what I have just said is apparent in the selection of Harris Franklin Rall for analysis to begin to understand theology during the first decades of this century. Theology, that is, in America, as most prevalent among the majority of Americans. In other words, I try to make to case that it is *denominational* theologians, those who taught in the church's seminaries and were the literal church fathers of the ministers of the land, and those who also wrote in the numerous journals read by the millions in the church, who best serve as indices to a time. Since the 1940's and the Great War (!) Protestants have shifted grounds for the theological sources as have the Jews since the Holocaust and the Roman Catholics since the Second Vatican Council. So, in our time *movement* theologians, those whose denominational connections are unimportant, become paramount for an understanding of theology now. Not only Rall should be studied for an understanding and appreciation of early 20th Century Theology in America, but as well many similar theologians in order that a more accurate *intellectual* history of the past be discerned.

The final aspect that I discovered in the research for this book is the rather, to me, startling misreading that has been afoot among American church historians; namely, still suggesting that the father to American liberal theology earlier in this century was Friedrich Schleiermacher. No one can question that Schleiermacher is *the* most important modern Christian theologian (even Barth admits that).[1] But that is not to credit him with being the major or even most important input into the unique experience of American theology. Just as Sydney Mead has argued that America has gambled with a new form of the church,[2] and uniquely so, I will argue that American theology itself need not be seen as a European stepchild but that it too is a

1. Karl Barth. *Protestant Thought from Rousseau to Ritschl.* (New York: Harper and Row, Publishers, 1959).
2. Sidney E. Mead. *The Lively Experiment, The Shaping of Christianity in America.* (New York: Harper and Row, 1963).

unique understanding of the gospel. Further, the one single most important influence for the first half of this century was not Schleiermacher but Albrecht Ritschl, who acknowledged his indebtedness to his master, but greatly modified his theological method and content. It is Ritschl who must be seen as most helpful as the genesis of a unique American theology in these years. And, no one ranks with Harris Franklin Rall as (1) his interpreter to America, and (2) his "developer" (what an American term!) of themes tinged within a Ritschlian framework. When one reads the thoughts of Harris Franklin Rall he hears Ritschl in American dress (or suit), conformed to a quite unique American experience. One can find great enlightenment in placing together the major works of the three (Schleiermacher, Ritschl and Rall) and tracing their developments and implications.

I cannot pass by without proper acknowledgements: to Mrs. Rall for delightful conversations and some materials by her husband; to my seminary and graduate school professors, particularly David Shipley and Sydney Ahlstrom from whom I learned to see and perceive; to Garrett Theological Seminary for access to documents of Professor Rall's and for a teaching assignment in The Theology of Rall; to a family who amidst conversation of growing up absurd were willing to listen to an aging theologian whose words sounded absurd on young ears.

CHAPTER I

A BIOGRAPHICAL SKETCH
OF
HARRIS FRANKLIN RALL

The beginning of any life commences prior to conception. Harris Franklin Rall was born in Council Bluffs, Iowa, February 23, 1870, the son of Otto and Anna Steiner Rall.

Some time in the fifteenth century, an Italian ancestor bearing the name Rallo, following northward the German count whose attendant he was, settled in Wurttemberg. There the name became Germanicized as Rall. A faculty colleague, Irl Goldwin Whitchurch, said of Rall: "One who knows the quickness of mind and gaiety of spirit (I can think of no better descriptive term) which mark this modern theologian will find it as easy to trace the influence of his Italian ancestors as of the generations of Germans who have left their stamp in the rigorous ordering of this thought."

Otto Rall emigrated from Wurttemberg at the age of fifteen. He settled in Pittsburgh during the decade which preceded the beginning of the Civil War. There he met Ann Steiner, who had come with her widowed mother from the Swiss canton of Graubunden on the upper reaches of the Hinter-Rhein, and had settled in Pittsburgh on the invitation of her father's cousin, the church historian Philip Schaff. Otto Rall and Anna Steiner were married in 1860. Otto

Rall entered the ministry of what was then the Evangelical Association, later the Evangelical Church, now part of the Evangelical United Brethren Church. Otto and Anna S. Rall established a home like that both had known in their youth: warmly evangelical, with a touch of mysticism, marked by a simple and devout piety.

His boyhood there, Harris Franklin Rall later wrote, was "a potent influence" in his religious life. His minister-father had little formal schooling but, a respect for scholarship and an ambition that his children should have what he lacked. Young Frank Rall was influenced more by his father's religious evaluations than his theological ideas: "religion was fellowship with God in vital experience, a sound ethical emphasis for which there was to be no substitute, and a deep appreciation of the Church, not as a sacrosanct institution, but as a fellowship and a living instrument which had the right to the unfailing service which both my parents gave it."

Otto Rall had a conservative background, but, in his son's eyes, an essentially liberal spirit. He saw too clearly where the realities of religion lay to be disturbed by the progress of Biblical criticism or the controversies about evolution. His children went to state institutions of learning at a time when pious folk talked of them as 'hotbeds of infidelity.'[1]

In 1887 Rall enrolled in the State University of Iowa from which he received a B.A. in 1891 and an M.A. the ensuing year. During this part of his student life, he credited Professor G. T. W. Patrick with functioning as his mentor, who gave him, not so much a set of conclusions as an example of open-mindedness and of order and lucidity in thought and expression.

When I went to the University of Iowa as a boy of seventeen, I had some real understanding of what religion was and a deep respect for its reality because of the genuinely devout lives of my father and mother. I had some general convictions, but religion had not been identified with a dogmatic system. I had a respect for scholarship and no fear of the truth, and neither my university course nor my later work at Yale and abroad brought me any severe crisis.[2]

Rall's relationship to Yale University proved fruitful both during his four years of study at the Divinity School, 1892-96, and following graduate work in Germany, his one year as lecturer at the Divinity School. (He later returned in 1931 to present the Nathaniel W. Taylor Lectures). In New Haven he studied under Professors Samuel Harris and George B. Stevens.

It is significant to note several aspects of theology at Yale during these closing decades of the nineteenth century. Few historians identify "Yale Theology" in any unique way, such as is characterized in studies on the Princeton Theology, or The Andover Liberals, The Oberlin Theology, or even The New England Theology of earlier decades.[3] Nor are its major theologians ranked in stature with either earlier professors (Timothy Dwight, Nathaniel Taylor) or later professors (H. Richard Niebuhr, Douglas Clyde Macintosh and Robert Calhoun). Roland Baiton, Professor-emeritus of Ecclesiastical History, Yale University, divides the curricula at Yale Divinity School into three categories during the period from the Civil War to the latter decades of the nineteenth century and the inauguration into the curricula of the "new disciplines:" church history (1861), social ethics (1891-92), Christian missions (1897), and sacred music (1897).[4]

Theology, Bible, and Homiletics were the "established disciplines." (The latter does not directly relate to this study and can be treated lightly). The theological tradition at Yale has been dealt with at length by many historians. Of particular interest to this biographical sketch of Harris

Franklin Rall are the careers of Professor Harris and Professor Stevens, neither of whom can be esteemed for his originality in theological writing. Samuel Harris had assumed the Dwight Professorship of Systematic Theology in 1871 following pastorates for some fifteen years and teaching Systematic Theology at Bangor (Me.) Seminary. Harris' professional writing did not begin until 1883 at the age of 69, and it was largely intended for local pastors.[5] (Note: Rall will emulate this same pattern in his numerous writings: the market of the local pastor.)

Three comments demand attention on the teachings and style of Samuel Harris. The first by Charles A. Dinsmore:

> As a theologian he belonged to no school, but occupied a transitional position between the old dialectical theology of New England and the more modern methods of thinking. Naturally conservative, he was open-minded to the scientific and critical information of his time and he embodied much of it in his thought. He taught that God, the Absolute Reason, is progressively revealing himself in the universe for the perfection of the individual and the establishment of the Kingdom of Christ; and that man, because under the influence of rational motives he can determine the ends to which he will direct his energies, is a free moral agent, and makes a supreme choice either of God and all rational creatures or of himself only as the object of trust and service. The choice of self is sin. The love that is required in the law of God is the free choice of the will to trust and serve God and one's neighbor. Thus sin is selfish choice and love is primarily an act of the will. More than any of his predecessors Harris was a convincing interpreter of the instinctive powers of the mind, which he claimed, apprehends five ultimate realities: the true, the right, the perfect, the good, and the absolute. These intuitions give man a real knowledge of

the universe in which he lives and ample light for the direction of his choices.⁶

Frank Hugh Foster, historian of New England theology, concluded the theological position of Harris in a somewhat different manner. He placed him squarely upon the general ground of New England theology, favoring the Trinity, the deity of Christ, original sin as native corruption, the Edwardian doctrine of the nature of virtue as benevolence, the moral government of God, the governmental theory of the atonement, regeneration by the use of means, and rejection of imputation.⁷ The significant aspect of his theology, Foster reports, is that Harris begins at new starting points, and with new methods and principles. He likens him to Sir William Hamilton of the Scottish School.⁸

The final comment, which bears directly upon the thinking of Harris Franklin Rall, is proffered by Professor Bainton. He judges that Harris projected one of the first attempts at an American culture religion. From Puritan theology onward, American theologians discovered the plan of God, if not his Kingdom, developing upon the American continent. At the time of Harris' writing, the world did appear reconciled. The war had concluded; slavery had been abolished; the Union had been saved. Educational reform was a-budding and the popular will-to-good was emerging. Thus America, and democracy, for Harris, as later for Harris Franklin Rall, provided the locus for the coming of the holy commonwealth.

> God has always acted by chosen peoples. To the English-speaking people more than to any other the world is now indebted for the propagation of Christian ideas and Christian civilization. It is a remarkable fact that in this day [1874] that the thinking of the world is done by the Christian nations; that the enterprise and energy of the world are mainly theirs. They alone are colonizing, and by their commerce and enterprise push-

ing their influence throughout the world. So also the political condition of the Protestant nations is that of constitutional government, popular education, and a growing regard for the rights and welfare of the people.[9]

Professor George B. Stevens abandoned the parish ministry after successful graduate study at the University of Jena. His thesis ("The Rational Grounds of Theism") met with exceptional acclaim and he was granted his doctor of divinity in 1886. From that year until 1895 when he was appointed to the Dwight Professorship of Systematic Theology, succeeding Samuel Harris, he held the Buckingham Professorship of New Testament Criticism at Yale Divinity School. Bainton says of him, "Both chronologically and theologically he lay between the older luminaries and the new."[10]

Most of Stevens' writings fall within what is now called, "Biblical Theology."[11] (Even though at Yale, Professor Frank Chamberlin Porter held a specific chair of Biblical Theology). Several themes in these publications find expression in Harris Franklin Rall's later writings on the New Testament. Stevens deciphers the Gospel of John as an interpretation of the life and teaching of Jesus as being derived and subsequently shaped by a long life of Christian thought and experience. In his last book, *The Christian Doctrine of Salvation,* written one year prior to his death in 1906, he pleads that we distinguish "between the contingent thought-forms of the first Christian thinkers and the essential religious life and fundamental Christian certainties concerning God and the experience of salvation, which they were seeking to expound".[12] Bainton judiciously concluded that, "In his final book Stevens was still the Biblical theologian, though one has the feeling that he was not so much deriving his theology from the Bible as discovering in it those selected strands which met his needs."[13]

One article of interest by Stevens was his comparison of Horace Bushnell and Albrecht Ritschl, written a year after

Rall's lecture on Ritschl at Yale. Stevens notes how Bushnell and Ritschl stand unlike in their appearance, vocations, and in their writings. Yet, the affinity between their theological results appeared striking. There was no direct relation between them. Stevens ascertained a kinship of spirit and method in their separate theologies: "... both insisted that Christianity was a religion and not a system of transcendental metaphysics, and both sought to interpret the New Testament and Christian history in accord with this presupposition."[14] Stevens then details this affinity in four areas: (1) the limitations of theological knowledge, (2) the Trinity, (3) the person of Christ, (4) the doctrine of atonement. Bushnell in his theory of language and Ritschl in his neo-Kantian epistemology show that "... a fully rounded system of speculative theology is quite impossible; both lay strong emphasis upon the religious, as contrasted with the merely logical and theoretic, character of theological knowledge."[15] Each believed that only revelations expressing the external nature of God might be uttered. The eternal background of the threefold revelation is undefinable. Bushnell declares (1) the divinity of Christ is to be found in what he is and does for men as the Revealer of God and Savior from sin, and (2) the nature of the indwelling of God in him is a mystery on which theological metaphysics throws no light. Stevens claims these are the chief points of the Ritschlian Christology.[16] In other words, the Christian estimate of Christ is founded in history and in experience. Each built his doctrine of the atonement upon the love of God, although Bushnell leaned more to the governmental view. Stevens concluded that these two men had brought to the American theological scene signal service: in defining the nature and limits of theological knowledge, in exposing the unclearness and the contradictions in the doctrine of the Trinity, and in insisting that theology is not a kind of dialectic, but a science of the Christian faith, an interpretation of religion. "The true task of our time is to Christianize theology — to reconstruct it into accord with that highest revelation of the mind and will of God which is given in Jesus Christ."[17]

Merle Curti has noted the important shift in American graduate training in the latter decades of the nineteenth century. Not only was there continued enrollment in European universities, but the direction of that study was channeled from England to the continent, particularly to Germany.

> The little stream of students that sought the German universities in the second decade of the nineteenth century had broadened until, by the sixth decade, it numbered 300; by the seventh it had reached 1,000; and by the ninth, more than 2,000. In that decade the tide began to turn, inasmuch as American graduate faculties had now become sufficiently well established to provide admirable training at home. The stream nevertheless continued; in all, some 10,000 Americans matriculated in German universities between the War of 1812 and World War I.[18]

Harris Franklin Rall received the traveling Hooker Fellowship from Yale University in 1897. During the following two years he studied at the University of Berlin, 1897-1898, and at the University of Halle-Wittenberg, 1898-1899, and at both places concentrated upon philosophy and theology. He received a doctorate in Philosophy *magna cum laude* from Halle in 1899 having written, and published, his dissertation on Leibnitz, written under Alois Riehl.[19]

Rall's choice of German theologians proved remarkable. At Berlin he studied *Dogmatik* under Julius Kaftan, Pedagogy under Friedrich Paulsen, Christian Ethics and the History of Ethics under Otto Pfliederer, and *Einleitung* of the New Testament and *Einleitung* in Church Teachings under Adolf Harnack. Without question Hegel and Schleiermacher were the great figures of German philosophy and theology of the nineteenth century. Subsequently, Albrecht

Ritschl established a distinctive school of theological thought under which Kaftan, Pfleiderer and Harnack fell sway.[20] Rall's indebtedness to these professors as well as his criticisms of them, and especially Albrecht Ritschl, will be treated in the last chapter when consideration is given to the importance and impact upon American theology of Harris Franklin Rall. Suffice here to categorize the particular emphases of these three professors at the University of Berlin.

Julius Kaftan had been educated at Erlangen, Berlin and Kiel, and began his appointment as professor of apologetics and philosophy of religion at the University of Berlin in 1883, following ten years of teaching systematic theology at the University of Basel. Albrecht Ritschl acknowledged his indebtedness to Kaftan, particularly to his *Das Wesen der Christlichen Religion,* which appeared approximately fifteen years earlier than Rall's residence in Berlin. Kaftan was directly responsible for Ritschl's modification of Schleiermacher's methodology. In a letter to Harnack, Ritschl concedes, "In the doctrine of religion and revelation, Kaftan has provided occasion for me to express myself more clearly, and I have done so with interest."[21] In *Das Wesen,* Kaftan had criticized Schleiermacher and Ritschl for interpreting religion solely in terms of the feeling of dependence, however absolute, upon God. He proposed that the idea of God and his power is the primary theological category. Crucially, that which moves man to such dependence rests upon the good or the value which man hopes to obtain from the Deity. Mueller records of Ritschl's response to such criticism:

> Not only in the larger sections *[The Christian Doctrine of Justification and Reconciliation]* which were revised do we find the term 'dependence upon God' avoided, but also in thirty-three other instances scattered throughout the book where it is used, we find it replaced by other expressions such as: operation of God,

> ...relationship to, stance toward, or belonging to God...in accordance with the divine dispositions (Fügung).[22]

In 1897, the year of Rall's arrival in Berlin, Kaftan published his eight volume *Dogmatik*. Its appearance was welcomed by critics for two reasons: the availability of a first hand knowledge of the Ritschlian Theology, and because

it was by Ritschl's "...ablest disciple in the systematic sphere...."[23] Kaftan describes his position:

> The proper and main business of evangelical dogmatics is to exhibit the knowledge which accrues to faith through appropriation of the revelation of God attested by Scripture. In the discharge of this task it is completely determined by Scripture and the Church's Confession, and in effecting this it renders to the church, in respect of preaching and teaching, an absolutely indispensable service.[24]

Kaftan develops this thesis in relation to his theology, methodology and other normative Christian doctrines. Methodologically, he contends for Ritschl's "corrective" of Schleiermacher, as to safeguard the validity of Christian knowledge and continuity of the Christian religion. "This he accomplished, it is contended, by vindicating for the knowledge which comes by faith the character of real knowledge, and also by subordinating Christian doctrine to the objective and stable norm of the revelation of God, which culminated in Christ."[25] And to this position Kaftan gives his adherence, only urging more explicitly than Ritschl the trustworthiness of faith.

> By faith, and especially Christian faith, is everywhere to be understood knowledge in the proper sense of the term. For knowing means the appropriation or

formation of judgments with the accompanying presupposition that they are true, i.e., that they correspond to the reality given externally to the subject. But this the religious man assumes in respect of his faith, so that the latter has for him the validity of full and actual knowledge. If this assumption becomes precarious religion itself totters, and if it is abandoned religion is at an end.[26]

In his theology, Kaftan reflects the Ritschlian protest against metaphysics. Thus, he abandons the classifications of God's attributes, especially those which attempt to describe and relate the so-called immanent attributes. The trinity is relegated by Kaftan to problematic status for speculation and his personal opinion labelled by Paterson as related to the old heresy of Sabellianism. The Chalcedonian Christology is credited with value for the "Greek Church," but of little consequence for the purified evangelical theology. Eschatology is circumscribed to but twelve pages. Paterson praises Kaftan on a point which Rall later emphasizes throughout his career:

> It cannot be denied that there is here an honest and consistent attempt to develop and press home the truth which Paul opposed to Jewish legalism — *viz.*, that we are saved, not of works, but by grace on the ground of faith in Jesus Christ. And this being so, it may be strongly held that the Ritschlian theology renders a much-needed service in recalling other schools to a juster sense of the perspective of Christian doctrine.[27]

Otto Pfleiderer taught at Tübingen from 1864-68, the university at which he had studied from 1857-61. In 1870 he became professor of theology at the University of Jena and five years later joined the faculty at the University of Berlin.

Out of the mass of Pfleiderer's writings, two critical emphases need be noted here as they reflect themselves particularly in the later writings of Harris Franklin Rall: (1) Pfleiderer's defense of the non-miraculous origin of Christianity. In 1905, he wrote a very influential book, *Christian Origins,* in the preface of which he warns that those who feel satisfied by "the traditional church-faith" perhaps ought not to read the book. It may hurt their feelings and confuse them in their convictions, two results Pfleiderer prefers to avoid. Nevertheless, he has concluded that there are many truthseekers for whom "the traditional church-faith" has become outmoded, and who wish to discover the eternal and the temporal in the origin of their faith, from the standpoint of modern science. For them he wrote *Christian Origins*.[28]

In the Introduction, Pfleiderer sketches the background of the recent historical conception of the origin of Christianity, from the Deist movement of the seventeenth century through the mystic-poetic interpretation of Bruno Bauer. Out of the welter of sometimes supplementary, sometimes contradictory, biblical studies, Pfleiderer concludes that any idea of the origin of Christianity as resultant of one person, coming from anywhere, cannot be sustained. To be sure, the impulse to the formation of the Christian congregation must have centered in the event of Jesus, but social environmental forces were at work as well. He credits Ferdinand Christian Baur with applying to the history of Christianity the correct term, "evolution."

The origin of Christianity is to be thought of as a developing process, in which various other factors were working along with the life-work of Jesus; these united and adjusted themselves gradually but not without inner contradictions and struggles.[29]

The significant underlying presupposition of Pfleiderer locates in later discussion related to the method by which the above definition was reached. The historical origin of Christianity, according to Pfleiderer, *can only be maintained,* when prior theological claims or church dogmas no longer rule and the theologian employs the same principles and methods as any other historian. Further, *only one* presupposition can be followed: "... *the analogy of human experience,* the similarity of human nature in the past and in the present, from the causal connection of all external happenings and inner psychical experience; in short, from the law-abiding order of the universe which ever conditioned all human experience."[30]

Pfleiderer nevertheless endeavored to crystallize out of the fluid evolution what he adjudged the essence of Christianity. He urged the abandonment of the older dogmatic assertions as mere phenomena of a deeper reality which he then defined as the specific manner and way in which man experiences his relation to God and the world and the feelings which become established in him as a permanent emotional tendency, held in common by many people. Within such an anthropological context, he next asks a series of rhetorical questions in an attempt to isolate the emotion uniquely Christian: the expectation of the speedy arrival of Christ of the early eschatological church? the courage of the Crusaders? the mortification of the monk? the duty of the Protestant in performing ethical duties? No, none of these. The focal point must be Jesus, granted the obscurity of the origin of Christianity, and granted also the confusion of biblical tongues about him. Essentially, Jesus is like nineteenth century man, bearing no unique metaphysical relationship to God. His consciousness of divine sonship attests the characteristic essence of Christianity.

> We may therefore consider the consciousness of divine sonship — this salient new feature in the personality of Jesus — at the same time the characteristic essence of the Christian religion, its distinguishing mark

from all that is pre-Christian and extra-Christian, and the nucleus of all specially Christian utterances concerning God, man, and the world.[31]

Love, is the essential religious relation.

The theologian's task then, according to Pfleiderer, rests with extrapolating doctrines in accord with such an essence. God is portrayed as Father or Holy Love who arouses in the Christian an impulse to love. Man is pictured in the highest idealism united with sober realism.[32]

Christ is given a central position among the geniuses and heroes of history.

> For at a time when the ancient world did not know what to make of its hitherto existing ideals, and was facing spiritual bankruptcy, Jesus perceived the new and most exalted ideal of man — sonship of God — through the revelation of the eternal λογος in his inmost heart. He represented it in his life and teaching typically and evidently, with impressive and educating power for all who were willing to receive his message. Finally he surrendered his life for its realization in a community of the children of God — that new spiritual Kingdom of God, — which took the place of the carnal hopes of the Messianic Kingdom of the Jews. Therefore Jesus is rightly called the Redeemer and Saviour of men, $K\alpha\tau'$ $\epsilon'\xi o\chi\mu'\nu$, and his life-work the work of redemption or the revelation of salvation, $K\alpha\tau'$ $\epsilon'\xi o\chi\mu'\nu$. His appearance was the turning-point of the times, and his work was the decisive victory of liberating truth and love over the power of darkness and the impure spirits of sin and error, in the bonds of which humanity had been held captive. By his death, which was at the same time the victory of his cause, the victory of the divine

principle in humanity was decided forever and guaranteed for each of his successors.³³

The eschatological Christian task, then, is to found a new world for the whole world, or, as Rall will continually suggest, to Christianize the world. One cannot repress seeing implicit in this prolegomena that slogan which comes later to identify much of American Protestant liberalism: "A God without wrath brought men without sin into a kingdom without judgment through the ministrations of a Christ without a cross.³⁴

Less need be written about Rall's third German professor, Adolf von Harnack, in the light of extensive and intensive research on his thought and its importance to Protestant Theology since the nineteenth century.³⁵ Two brief statements are in order. Glick proves conclusively that Harnack's basic orientation, a fundamental reorientation of prevailing theological opinion, was firmly set by the beginning of his teaching at the University of Giesen in 1879. That orientation is set forth in two pieces of correspondence in the years 1873 and 1874.

> The practical demand which I feel, if I may be permitted to speak of such a thing, amounts to this: to give to the system of dogmatics such form that it will deal first with that which is the original standard and foundation, and to be certain that everything else will actually appear as derivative, and never again can be ascribed as having any other value. Through our usual arrangement presently, a fateful error is suggested, and undeniably it produces much harm. If one prefixes to the valid doctrines of justification and redemption all the sections concerning God's essence, the Trinity, and Christology, the misunderstanding that the latter conditions the former

certainly arises, while the fact is precisely the reverse, that we attain to the latter only through the former. The fact that anyone — and there are many — can still doubt Christianity because they doubt the Trinity (better, perhaps, there are still many who put a justifying garment on their unbelief), is ground enough to build the edifice from the beginning up, not from the abstract to the concrete, but from earth to heaven.[36]

To be sure I am of the opinion that we must learn to strip off from the forms of our Christian belief much which through habit and custom we believe to be united with its inmost being. I am convinced that we must learn to do this in order not to come into conflict with the truth, but I believe I sufficiently estimate how many hot battles one will have to fight, and how bitter and hard on the conscience such conflicts are.[37]

Paul Tillich reminisces about Harnack in retelling his acquaintanceship with him.

He himself once told me that in the year 1900 the main railway station in the city of Leipzig, one of the largest in Central Europe, was blocked by freight cars in which his book *What Is Christianity?* was being sent all over the world. He also told us that this book was being translated into more languages than any other book except the Bible. This means that this book, which was the religious witness of one of the greatest scholars of the century, had great significance to the educated people prior to the first World War. It meant the possibility of affirming the Christian message in a form which was free from dogmatic captivity and at the same time very much rooted in the biblical image of Jesus. But in order to elaborate this image, he invented the formula which distinguished sharply between the gospel of Jesus and the gospel about Jesus. He stated that the gospel about Jesus does not belong in the gospel preached by Jesus. This is the classical formula of liberal theology; the gospel or message preached by Jesus contains nothing of the later message preached concerning Jesus.[38]

To trace the career of Harris Franklin Rall upon his return to the United States is to delineate his dual role of systematic theologain and theologian of the Methodist Church. On his return in 1899 he studied at Yale University and lectured on the outline and significance of Ritschlian theology. These lectures represent one of the first presentations of Ritschl to an American audience if not the English-speaking world.[39] Rall taught at and was president of Iliff Shool of Theology in Denver, Colorado, from 1910 to 1915 when he became professor of Christian Doctrine at Garrett Biblical Institute in Evanston, Illinois, where he remained until his retirement in 1945. Rall was ordained into the ministry of The Methodist Episcopal Church in 1900, and held his first pastorate that year in East Berlin, Connecticut. For the next decade he divided his pastorates between Trinity Methodist Church in New Haven, Connecticut, 1900-1904, and First Methodist Church (Lovely Lane Chapel, where the "Christmas" or organizing conference of The Methodist Episcopal Church was held in 1784) in Baltimore, Maryland from 1904-1910.

Professor Rall intensely fulfilled his role as a theologian to the Methodist Church. His impact on that institution will be treated in detail below. Here it must be noted that the range of his service to the church spanned from preaching in its pulpits (cf. appendices 3 and 4), to actively participating in the life of the Church on the General Conference level. He served as treasurer and vice president of the Methodist Federation of Social Service in the days of the leadership of Profesor Harry F. Ward and Bishop Francis J. McConnell. For several years he wrote studies for and lectured before the Annual Supply Pastors' Institutes. "Dr. Rall Answers" (cf. appendix 6) appeared in the official journal of The Methodist Church for several years. Many of his publications were written specifically as study guides for local congregations. In the revision of the Methodist ritual in 1916 he played a major role as Secretary of the General Conference Commission charged with this task. In 1937 he represented The Methodist Church as a delegate to the World Conference on Faith and Order. Horace Greeley Smith in his memoriam relates how Ernest Fremont Tittle, renowned Methodist preacher, sought and received approval of a Quarterly Conference of the First Methodist Church, Evanston, Illinois, to appoint Harris Franklin Rall to the post of official adviser to the Senior Minister. In his nominating speech Tittle confided that for more than two decades he had gone continuously to Rall for advice on clarifying some difficult theological question, for counsel on controversy over social issues when "freedom of the pulpit" was at stake, and for assistance in the more delicate problems of administration in the church. Rall was so elected. Smith recounts, "So far as can be learned, he was the first and the last man ever to hold such a title in the entire history of the whole Methodist Church."[40] Lastly, it was as professor of Christian Doctrine at Garrett Biblical Institute that Harris Franklin Rall made his greatest impact.

The theological history of American Methodism and Rall's significant role in it, has been treated extensively elsewhere.[41] In 1944 Professor Rall had occasion to reflect upon the significance of theology specifically at Garrett and the place of Garrett in the total church emphasis of the twentieth century. He traced the history of the teaching of theology throughout the previous ninety years, beginning with John Dempster, Miner Raymond, and Milton Terry. His acquaintance with the former rested upon one lecture on divine Providence, given in 1854.

Rall depicted it as "... a vigorous, rather dogmatic assertion against the beginnings of naturalism of the one God who ruled all things as he had created all, but not of the problems we associate with this theme: God in the individual life, God in history, and the problem of pain, of evil in the heart, of evil in the history of man."[42] Of Miner Raymond he summarily wrote of his large three volume work: vigorous, scholarly, dogmatic. Milton Terry was foremost a biblical theologian. "BUT IT WAS NOT A READY made dogmatic system which was determinative for him — Nor was it the letter of the Bible. He saw Christ as the center of the Bible and its point of orientation. And he saw personal religion and religious experience as the chief concern of the Bible."[43] Rall also had occasion to list professor Irl Whitchurch, whose arrival at Garrett in 1921 marked its recognition for need in professorial leadership in philosophy of religion, philosophical and Christian ethics, and in the psychology of religion. Dr. Georgia Harkness' appointment in 1939 heralded one with wide contacts in the church, and "... matching scholarship in theology with a fine religious insight and both with an unusual ability at clear and effective presentation."[44] Rall finished his emphasis on theological teaching at Garrett by simply cataloging in appreciation various short-term and interim professors: Dr. Davidson, Nels Ferre, Paul Ramsey, Elton Trueblood, Edward T. Ramsdell, Robert Cushman, Wilhelm Pauck, and a "Frank of Presbyterian."

Professor Rall in sentimental yet calculating style subsequently lists Garrett graduates who had been shaping the church then and who had received their theological training at his hand: Bishops F. W. Warne and E. Robinson of India, Lee of Malaysia, and Springer of Africa; teachers Don Holter, Hsuing, H. Lew, Fujinaga, Chyung; the numerous universities and colleges staffed with Garrett alumni, including Hamline, Baker, Morningside, and several "Wesleyans", Yale, Northwestern; church administrators Davidson, Bollinger, Ehrensperger, Eiselen; preachers Throckmorton of San Francisco, Roy L. Smith of Los Angeles, Stanley McKee of Riverside, California. "Nor should I forget the men working among the colored people, like Dick Schermerhorn and others at Atlanta, and in the Colored Methodist Church at Atlanta, men like Bishop Hemlet and President Fountain."[45]

> But when I think of the marching feet of Garrett, my mind dwells first and most upon this great empire of the middle west and upon the ministry of the average church, the pastors in city and town and countryside. There is where the great many of our men go and these men are our joy and pride. Here is the strength of the Christian Church in this land, and here is the real strength of the leaders of tomorrow. Throughout these states, from the Alleghenies to the Rockies. The paths are not always easy for these marching feet. They have led to wide prairies of the northwest, and the dust bowl of Oklahoma and Kentucky. But the men have marched on in the spirit of the young man of long ago, and they have shared hardship and poverty in these last years with the people to whom they have gone. If religion and democracy are to be preserved for the world when it is being threatened with destruction in its ancient home, then the names of these Garrett men must be writ high among those who serve not the church alone but all humanity.[46]

The ending of most lives concludes with dying. Such is not the case with Harris Franklin Rall, who died October 13, 1964.

Chapter II

RALL ON RITSCHL

Rall, after having received the Hooker Fellowship at the conclusion of his studies at Yale Divinity School under George Barker Stevens, spent the years 1897-99 at the Universities of Halle and Berlin. Although not studying directly under Albrecht Ritschl, Rall acknowledged that Ritschlian theology, albeit from its master not systematically outlined, was still in its ascendancy during these years of study under Friedrich Loofs, Julius Kaftan, M. W. T. Rieschle and Adolf von Harnack. Upon his return to the United States, Rall spent an entire year at Yale as student and lecturer and during the Spring of 1900 lectured to the divinity school students on "Theological Method and the Ritschlian Theology"[1] thereby providing one of the earliest exposures of Ritschlian theology to America. He began his lectures by noting some of those fundamental questions which must precede the positive construction of a theological system, such questions as the nature of religion, the character of religious knowledge and its ground of certainty, the sources of theology and its seat of authority. He then circumscribed his lecture to contemporary Germany and specifically to Ritschlian theology, because "... ever since Schleiermacher we have been going to school in Germany in theology, and the whole history of theology and philosophical thought in Germany for this century has a direct and profound significance for us."[2]

Citing the current theological unrest Rall detailed current solutions to the quest for "... new forms of doctrine in which to express the abiding Christian faith."[3] There are those who view no task at all. What is needed is not a system of doctrines, but a theology of the Bible. The professorial chair of Systematic Theology could be abandoned in favor of Scriptual Exegesis and Biblical Theology. The historical approach which fathered this view of "Back to the simple Jesus" also provided the inner inconsistency of this approach for two reasons: "Biblical theology can give you a sum of ideas, it cannot give you a unitary system of thought or belief; and, the Bible is primarily a book of life, not of doctrine."[4] (It is needful to note at this early juncture that these cited reasons of inadequacies of the biblical approach will continue throughout Rall's career and will be central in his rejection of those later "German" theological writings associated with Karl Barth).

The second proffered solution to theological methodology came from those whose cry was for an "undogmatic Christianity." "We do not want church creeds (*viz*, theological creeds), and we do not need systems of theology." Religion is a matter of absolute feeling and the essence of Christianity is the ethical. "Not by creed, but by deed." Rall then quoted Felix Adler:

> Every attempt to settle problems of faith has thus far signally failed, nor can we hope for better results in the future. Certainty, even with regard to the essential dogmas, appears to us impossible. We do not therefore deny dogma, but we prefer to remit it to the sphere of individual conviction with which public associations should have no concern.... Religion does not even necessitate the belief in a personal God.... The feeling of the sublime is the root of the religious sentiment.[5]

Rall objected that such sentiments might be appropriate for some men, but not for the Christian. To such a religion consisting in pious feelings (an undogmatic religion), Rall counters that Christian faith not alone impels one to reflection and to expression in terms of rigorous thought, but that disciplined thought belongs to its essentiality. Therefore, Christian faith must be expressed in doctrines which include necessarily a conception of this Worldground as personal God, with a particular world view, and a view of Christians in this world.

> Christian faith implies thought, ideas. It impels to an expression of its belief. In the church this must be the expression of a common belief. It becomes here the guide and norm for instruction of those within and proclamation to those without. This is dogma, or creed. No Christian church can fulfill its function without this, or ever has done so. Cf. Harnack, *Thoughts on the Present Position of Protestantism*, p. 58 "We must never abandon the endeavor to add a new creed to those which already exist, a creed which shall contain the essential articles of the saving Faith as a standard for the office of the ministry and the guidance of the Church."[6]

Rall adds, the religion which consists in feeling and still implies opinions will give way before the positive position of science and philosophy which contradict it. The church needs then a theology. In his lecture Rall proceeds to cite the reason for the then current vacuum in theological doctrine as *Zerfahrenheit*, or a lack of any common positive world-view.

He notes the historical-critical method as a third method which he feels engages almost all contemporary theologians. The old focus of interpretation was coded inspiration, the new as revelation, historically conditioned. But, he points out, such a hermeneutical hiatus issues in methodological problems for the theologian. The important point for us, he writes, is that we should recognize the problem involved in this change. The first problem that meets us here is the question of the method of interpretation and inspiration of the Scriptures. The old method was very simple: the Bible is a textbook of doctrine, equally inspired in all its parts. The theological task is to excerpt its doctrines and arrange them in a system. Usually the theologian already possessed his system, and thus his task was to buttress each doctrine with an array of proof-texts, taken without regard to their source, context, or original historical significance. That method is dead, but the changed condition remains unsatisfactory by simply paying attention to the historical meaning when quoted, or using the results of biblical theology. The problem goes deeper. If revelation be progressive, a commonly held presupposition, where is the standard by which to order its various stages in regard to their value and authority for us? If that theory which made each word equally binding, is relinquished, how does the theologian discriminate between the essential and incidental, what is to act as guide in the interpretation of the Scriptures? If the mere words of the canonical books are not authority, where lies our authority? And, if these books are but historical products, and the canon itself is the same, where is the basis for an authority in them? And, what is still more important, if these books are submitted to historical criticism, to decide whether they be trustworthy or not, does not our whole faith hinge upon historical inquiry? [Sic] Can we ever find Christian certainty, and at best shall we not have to say that some new conclusion may overthrow our faith, or some central doctrine of it?[7]

An associated methodological problem for the "historical question" theologian, is that of the norm by which he is to adjudge the content of theology. Rall concluded that "... there is no absolutely unbiased historical study," and that theologian must accept, relate and interpret the facts according to his own tastes. "His method is that of psychological analogy, and here the personal equation cannot but play its part."[8] He noted that evolutionary form was the common form of the philosophy of history at the end of the century. He saw how the insistence on absolute continuity in progress and on an unbroken chain of causality might rule out factors vital to the Christian conception. "History, says an English writer, is only possible on the presupposition of the absolute continuity and homogeneity of experience, and that presupposition is uprooted and annihilated by the presupposition of Revelation." (R. W. Macan in *The Resurrection of Jesus Christ* as quoted by Gardner, *Exploratio Evangelica*, p. 136). Says Pfleiderer, speaking of the conceptions of the incarnation, the miraculous birth, and biblical miracles, and the like, "These are the beautiful conceptions,... but this is not history, intelligibly conceivable history. All this undoes the conception of history from the bottom." (Gifford Lectures, II, p. 23).[9]

The final criticism Rall sets to the historical method insofar as it informs theology is coined in the question: "What is the relation of the historical to the ideal, and does the historical have a significance above the ideal, or principle, which it expresses? How can a historical fact or person have absolute and permanent significance for us? Can we rest our faith on that which is historical and subject to historical criticism?"[10]

Next, Rall considers theological reconstruction under the guidance of evolution as found in the writings of Dr. Lyman Abbott and Dr. Newman Smyth, contemporaries of his and exceedingly influential leaders in the American Church. For the former, evolution is explained as divine immanence plus continuity of development.[11] The second writer finds the key to theology in biological study.

> It springs from the profound conviction that the one theological task which waits to be accomplished is a thorough and comprehensive demonstration of the fact, which the disciple of old perceived, that the Life was manifested in Christ, and hence it was proven true that his essential words meet and match the great principles of life which have been hidden in nature's heart from

the beginning. (It will be shown how naturally, and as the appointed heir of all things, Christianity wins and wears the crown of life....) The next reconstruction of theology will be a vital one: it will result from a deeper knowledge and a truer interpretation of the sacred Scripture of Life, which the hand of God has written in nature. The coming theologian, therefore, the next successful defender of the faith once given to the saints, — will be a trained and accomplished biologist.... Each organic form will tell him the story of its origins, and the least living cell will unveil the secret chambers of its divinity. (*The Place of Death in Evolution* by Newman Smyth, pp. vii, viii).[12]

Rall shows his impatience with such a theological methodology by referring to the craze of evolution and theology as comparable to an epidemic of the measles, and wistfully longing for its abatement! The fundamental weakness of the approach, as he judges it, is its total inability to speak to those spiritual dimensions of life.

Such spiritual dimensions are the presence of freedom and moral responsibility, the perception of moral and religious beliefs and ideals, and the recognition of our obligation toward them. This is the life of which Jesus was the Master, this is the thing of value which is at stake with our Christianity, and this is the thing of which the biologist himself will tell you that he can, as such, have no knowledge whatever. It is simply playing into the hands of naturalism to confuse such distinctions. [Rall: To this I may add a word in anticipation of a later discussion: whatever incidental aid may come for defense from other sources, the positive and ultimate apologetic of Christianity must always be a Christian apologetic, which will find the defense of Christianity on the same high plane of the ethico-spiritual on which Christianity stands.] For another suggestion as to the reconstruction of theology, cf. Gardner, *Exploratio Evangelica*. He thinks we "must look to progressive intellectual principles...for the way to modern doctrinal reconstruction." What he means by these principles is really certain modern philosophical conceptions. He cites three: (1) the sense of law; (2) the thing of evolution (meaning the philosophical theory); (3) new metaphysics and new psychology (neo-Kantian scepticism and the voluntaristic psychology).[13]

Yet another methodical approach for theology, the fifth outlined by Rall, was that of neo-Hegelian idealism as illustrated in the writings of President William DeWitt Hyde of Bowdoin College. Such theology appeared to Rall but a return to the old, uncritical, speculative method with its *a priori* foundations, and in large measure passing over the historical and critical questions of the late nineteenth century. At this point in his lectures, Rall sets forth his test of theological method: "Is Christ really authoritative for us in our theological thought, or do we ground our theology on a speculative philosophy whose principle Christ may illustrate and corroborate?" Baring his personal "antimetaphysical" Ritschlian stance, he implores:

> There are two things that we need to look squarely in the face. The first is the fact, that, in this day we cannot take for granted any philosophy, and the cocksureness of omniscient neo-Hegelianism will not take the place of a sure and critical grounding of its system. And we need to face the question, secondly, whether we can afford to rest the certainty of our Christian faith upon any one philosophical system, or risk its contents by imposing such a system upon it. On both points the history of the Hegelian theology in Germany is instructive.[14]

After discarding these five theological methods, each indicative of a prominent place in the American theological scene, Rall introduces the Ritschlian counterproposal with added personal revision. Ritschl holds that religion is *not* primarily a concern with the thinking, but of the *feeling* and the *willing* personality. Religious knowledge is never merely theoretical, but always rests on propositions which express the value of meaning *for us,* i.e., on judgments of worth.[15]

Experience is the source of religious knowledge: a thing can be known *only* in what it does, and God can be known only insofar as he works upon us or does something for us. But this experience has an objective correlate, the historical revelation recorded in the Scriptures, and herein is the source of theology. More restrictedly, the source for theology is the confession of the first Christian community, in which we find the full significance of Christ for us. As Christ is the channel through which God comes to us, so every doctrine must be gained and judged in relation to him: theology must be christocentric. The meaning of this statement shall be better understood, if some of its negative implications as seen by Ritschl are included. Theology can use only what is given in experience; therefore all theoretical considerations must be excluded, and Ritschl opposes all so-called proofs for the existence of God and theistic philosophy in general. No philosophy! If all knowledge is given with the experience of what a thing does for us, then it is idle to ask what God is, apart from our experience, or to try to construe a knowledge of him in *a priori* fashion. Therefore, no metaphysics! If God is known only through positive revelation, and the supreme revelation is in Christ, then he is the sole source for Christian theologians. Therefore, no natural theology! To this should be added Ritschl's constant cry, No mysticism! For mysticism he connects on the one hand with a false philosophy, the neo-Platonic, and condemns on the other hand on the general principle that all true religious experience must have a necessary ethical aspect, must be experienced in moral conduct.

Ritschl's uniqueness for theology rests not in the separate ideas or principles in any system. Rather it lies in his ability to see the significance of certain ideas and their combination into a unitary view, and then their subsequent application to the whole of doctrinal thought. (There follows in Rall's introductory lecture a discussion of Ritschl's delineation of the nature of religion into four types, intellectualistic, moralistic, metaphysical, feeling, and a subsequent brief outline of Ritschl's theology.) He criticizes Ritschl's delineations as too narrowly tied with ethical presuppositions and argues that Christianity alone exhibits their harmonious unity.[16]

The relation of the ethical to the religious is the primary question of theology, Rall opines. Ritschl said it was the master question. It must be solved first by recognizing as the ground and norm of morality the divine character itself, which is revealed to us as a personal ideal in Christ. And the great problem of the relation of an external authority to inner freedom is also solved in the Christian life, when the spirit of Christ is no longer an external standard but becomes an inner principle and an inner life, our highest aim and joy, as well as our holiest obligation. But the first, the philosophical problem, Ritschl cannot solve, because, like Kant, he lets ethics stand apart on its own footing, and denies a general moral law and moral world-order divinely founded. And the second, the personal problem, he cannot solve because he lacks the true conception of the inner, religious spirit-life.

At this point of criticism we find the first statement as to Rall's methodology, and that which will in largest measure mark the theological methodology of the significant number of American theologians until the impact of Karl Barth in the early 1930's: theology will issue from social and personal salvation and the recognition of a *personal ideal* in Christ as *both* the ground and norm of morality. Such a new motif in America is heralded by Rall's clear reporting of *tete de tete* between Albrecht Ritschl and Julius Kaftan, Rall's immediate teacher of Dogmatics.[17] Kaftan corrects Ritschl here and puts the position thus: "The religious world-view consists of judgments of being, is knowledge in the real sense, resulting from the knowledge that God is and what God is. But its inner relations are different from those of other theoretical knowledge. At its base there lies, not an objective apprehension of the world and the elaboration in thought of the impressions thus won, but an inner experience which consists of judgments of worth." (*Dogmatik*, 29.) Rall even goes to lengths in this lecture to score Ritschl's lack of discussion on pneumatology as related to theological method, an oblique methodological correction employed by H. Richard Niebuhr some three and one-half decades later.[18]

In his explication of Ritschl's theory of religious knowledge, Rall concludes that for Ritschl (and for Rall) "... the subject matter of theology is the knowledge that is given in faith, i.e., religious knowledge, or the knowledge of faith." Such "knowing" has two marks: it is practical or, as Ritschl puts it, it rests on judgments of worth, and secondly, it is experiential, or realized in the experience of what God does for us. From this, Ritschl (and Rall) concludes as to method: no metaphysics, no philosophy. Teleology and not ontology becomes the base of his methodology. What Ritschl (and Rall) means here is a denial for theological method of considerations of divine substance and cause; the materials of theology are given in religious experience. Also, Rall asserts, faith is not a special form of knowledge, e.g., the acceptance of truth upon authority. Is rests neither upon external authority nor upon purely rational consideration. The appeal to faith is the appeal to our innermost convictions, *ethical and spiritual.* "It comes to us, to men who must act, who must set something as our highest good, who must have our ideals. It sets before us its highest good, its ideals."[19] Rall also desires to move beyond what he calls "Ritschl's halting view" of the reality of the objects of faith. He would have the objects of faith possess objective existence. From judgments of worth, theology does conclude judgments of being. "The true and the right and the good by their very worth convince us that they are the most real of things, so real that we stake the interests of our whole life upon this faith." In support of this Rall cites his agreement with William James in his *The Will To Believe*.[20]

Rall concludes his lecture on Ritschl's theory of knowledge by denying or at least separating himself from Ritschl's claim of exclusion of metaphysics in the religious knowing. He writes, "We must proceed to consider the objective being of God, and we must go beyond the predicate of love." One need not subscribe to the Absolute, but one *can* use the idea of the Supreme as a common datum of religious man. What revelation in Christ supplies is the content for this conception and it subsequently determines its religious value for us.

Yet, in another sense, the theoretical cannot be dispensed with. Whatever its special grounds, religious knowledge is real knowledge, and it must be worked over in the same way as theoretical knowledge and by the same mind. That mind cannot stop at isolated facts, but of necessity will combine and interpret and deduce. We do right when we start in our conception of Christ from below, from the religious experience, from what he does *for* us. We do well too if we discriminate between that which is directly implied in faith and is necessary for this, and that which we may conclude, or the opinion to which faith itself may untimately impel us. But it is natural and inevitable that we should go further and ask as to the nature of Christ in his being for himself and his relation to the Father, and we know how this impulse is seen already with John and Paul.[21] Metaphysics as pantheistic idealism, to be sure, must be avoided, but engagement in the pursuit of theoretical knowledge following from moral action cannot be avoided.

Never did Ritschl conclude that religion, *ergo* theology, rest solely upon a subjective basis (as did Percy Gardner and Auguste Sabatier).[22] The objective correlate of faith is revelation. In Christianity, revelation means God coming to man in Jesus Christ, thus providing the source of theology.[23] The two central ideas that Rall emphasized were the analysis of religious knowledge of salvation and secondly, its source lying in revelation. Religious knowledge is knowledge of salvation because religion itself is practical. It is moral and spiritual being. Under this first head was implied the thought, that, as religion is practical, religious knowledge must relate itself to experience. Further, as being practical, as concerning things of worth, it appeals not to theoretical considerations primarily, but to faith. Under the second head came the emphasis on the historical revelation in Christ, and on Christ as the principle of knowledge and the seat of authority.

> I may sum all this up by two words, theology must be soteriological and christocentric. Or I may make this plainer by concrete statement: in Christianity I am concerned, not with abstract knowledge about God and the world and man, but with the definite question of God in his saving purpose for me, and the knowledge that I desire concerning God and the world and myself will all be related to this central great question. This is what we mean by a soteriological theology and it rests on the conception of Christianity as a redemptive religion. Further, this saving purpose of God is revealed and realized in Jesus Christ, through whom I come into the desired relation to God, by whom the new life is mediated, and therefore this theology must be christocentric.[24]

Rall in his outline addresses himself to methodological issues. On the theme of Scriptural authority, Rall recounts Ritschl's Christocentric hermeneutic and feels hopeful that it will somehow develop as a useful option between the inerrant view and that which judges Scriptures by the norm of man's own inner consciousness. Why use Scriptures as a ground for theological questions? No *á priori* theory of inspiration will suffice; for Rall rejects it on the grounds of the absence of inner witness and contrariness to the frame of reference (he means ethical here) of the God-man relationship. The point of departure, rather, must be the *fact* of revelation. "We, as Christian theologians, do not start from some universal world formula, which we have construed by philosophic or any purely theoretical means, and under which we try to subsume the truth for which Christ stands. Rather it is the truth in Christ from which we view the world; we know God as seen through him, and in him we find the meaning of things and of our own life." Scriptures are the bearers of this revelation to us. As to how one is to read and understand this Bible, again one cannot proceed from *a priori* judgments.[25]

The writers of the New Testament are not mere recorders of the revelation. The revelation in Christ was completed in their life, their experience, in themselves. That completed revelation of the living Christ comes to us in their words, their confessions. There is, therefore, a vital, organic relation between the revelation and their very words. And when we have believed in Christ, when we have found him through their record and testimony of faith, then we learn, not through a theory before held, but by this experience and in this new life, what these writers mean for us, what truth they bring to us, how much they are our teachers, as well as pedagogues to lead us to Christ.[26]

A second methodological question demanding an answer centers on the ultimate seat of authority. The answers generally fell within the class of the individual and the subjective experience of the external and what Rall calls the legal. He ascertains that recent biblical studies preclude any longer the claim for Scriptures as sole and supreme authority in themselves; they contain the theologian's authority, namely, Jesus Christ, for the authority cannot be something apart from the substance. "The authority that Christ has for us as *theologians* rests ultimately upon the authority that he has won over us as *believers*."[27]

The conviction as to his divine nature, when it is a real faith conviction, follows upon the power that he wins over us, and does not precede and ground it. It is the inner, the direct appeal that Christ makes to our hearts and consciences, that makes him the authority supreme for us. He rules our thought, because he rules our whole life. His authority is not outer and legal, but inner and personal. And its ultimate ground lies in this, that in him we know that God has come to us. None other than God can be the supreme authority for faith, and Christ is God to us.

Subsequent questions on "which Christ" are recognized by Rall (The teachings of Jesus vs. The Christ of full faith) and he, while appreciative of the return to the "fleshly Jesus," implores the Yale students to the latter, the authority of the full Christ. He opposes the view that scientific criticism can reduce the accoutrements of the faith, and, in effect, present the "real" Christ. He says that such an approach is impossible. The source of authority cannot be located in the teachings of Christ, but in the Christ of history, especially that of apostolic times. He finds in this teaching one of the decided merits of the Ritschlian theology. It is not with general ideas that we have to do in Christianity, not with general notions about God's nature, or a moral world-order, or man's immortality, or the natural divinity of human nature. What we have in Christianity is God known to us in Christ, and known in his redemptive purpose for the world. That purpose Christ shows to us, and in that he reveals God to us (as ground and norm). In himself he brings the new life, and into that life he inducts us by and in a personal relation to himself. He himself in person, and not merely in the principle that he represents, has abiding significance for us in our life in God.[28]

If Ritschl is correct, namely, that the great work of Christ was redemptive, his induction of men into this new relation to God, this new life in God, and that the completion of this work was in his death and resurrection, then certain conclusions of deepest import for the question as to the real Christ follow. We can see how with this most important point the teachings of Jesus could at most deal only in anticipatory suggestions. It would have been in utter contrast to his whole method had he done more than this. What men should think about his person and what they should say about his work, all this Jesus trusted to the future, as he did with more than one other deeply important question. With him teaching joined hands with life, and he did not separate them in order to anticipate future conditions and future needs. Then it becomes clear, too that we must go to the first disciples, if we would know the full revelation of the real Christ. Only in what he did *for them* and in what he became *to them* was his work and his revelation completed. And it was only as these disciples spoke out of this new life and new experience, that men could learn the "real Christ" in all his meaning for our life. And may we not conclude further, that he became to them, in their faith, what it was in his purpose that he should become? Here then is our seat of authority, not the Christ of history as against the Christ of faith, nor the Christ of faith as apart from the Christ of history, but the Christ of history as apprehended by faith and as proclaimed in the faith of the first believers. To the records of the life of Jesus on earth we must always go, that we may scan here the lineaments of the face of our Lord. To this story, as evangelical believers, we shall always cling.

It is not the Christ as teacher alone who is supreme authority for us, not the historical personage merely, whom historical study may disentangle from the Gospels, but the full and whole Christ of the New Testament, the Christ teacher, the dying and risen Christ, the Christ as living Lord and Saviour, apprehended in faith, experienced in his presence and power by his disciples, and proclaimed as Saviour to the world. In other words, it is the Christ of faith, who is the real and the historical Christ as well. In summation on biblical and hence theological hermeneutic, Rall restates an old formula, *testimonium spiritus sancti internum*, as the only way in which theologians can use the Scriptures in their methodology. Since theology is really but the explication of what is immanent in faith, the organization of theology must align itself to the two regulative community principles: the "practical" or soteriological and the Christocentric and the two constitutive ideas, those of reconciliation and the kingdom of God. Rall charges Ritschl with, in fact, departing from his elliptical "two foci" methodology by concentrating almost exclusively upon the single constitutive idea of the kingdom of God. Instead, Rall suggests that the former constitutive idea (reconciliation) gives us the thrust-point of approach for theology.

> We do not merely wish to learn what task God has for us. Before we begin to practice the righteousness of the kingdom of God, something must precede. We need the strength that comes from a loving trust in God. We need to know that our own sinfulness is not an insuperable barrier to our approach to him or to that loving trust. And only in this new relation, on the ground of this faith in the loving Father who is world Creator and Ruler, can we have that perfect confidence, that faith in providence, which will make us independent of the world and strong for every task and trial. These truths are vital to Christianity. This is preeminently its religious aspect, and these truths we may sum up under the general thought of the salvation in Christ, or the redemption through Christ. I cannot, therefore, follow either Ritschl or these disciples of his in making the idea of the Kingdom constitutive for theology. I agree with the principle which Bornemann[29] lays down, and which he follows, that we must seek to know God's being and will from his activity, from what he does, from his self-revelation. But I should make the redemptive work of Christ as evinced in his life, his death,

and his presence in the Church central and supreme as the source of this knowledge, rather than the teaching concerning the kingdom.[30]

The consideration of the possibility of a single conception or single doctrine which can be constitutive for theology next draws Rall's attention. Quoting Dr. Fairbairn, *The Place of Christ in Modern Theology*,[31] as his example of the position — the single constitutive principle of the Fatherhood of God — Rall argues that the implicit adherence in this position of the distinction between a formal and material principle for theology cannot be maintained (such as the formal principle is the Bible, the material principle the gospel or justification by faith.)

> The authority for faith must lie in that which *is* [italics added] the substance for faith, its object and its content. The Bible has authority for us in that it *brings* the gospel, i.e., Christ, and it has no authority aside from this.... Even of Christ we must say, it is not his consciousness conceived abstractly, taken by itself, that is normative for us. It cannot be. That would be contrary to the nature of the Christian faith. The object of that faith is not the consciousness of Christ any more than it is a collection of writings. It is the Christ in whom we see the loving grace of God in whom we believe. But it may be said, when you have believed in this Christ, when you believe that in him God is incarnate, that in him the mind of God has entered the world, then his consciousness must express for you the absolute truth of God. I admit such a conclusion, but I see no reason for thus moving round a circle, for putting the abstract principle behind the concrete and given reality. You might as well say, the mind of God is the true source of all truth, and therefore of theology. The principle would be incontestable, but fruitless. And so this principle is formal and barren. Certainly the consciousness of Christ

is back of his words and work. But it is his words and work that are given to us. And what is all important for us, in these we know that *God* is given to us, that he is revealed in his loving purpose, his purpose of redemption. Christ as the revelation of the Saviour God is the material principle of theology, *as he is its formal principle:* in him is the substance of faith, and for this reason the authority for faith. We know him, as we know any person, by what he does. He becomes our Savior and Lord not by the ideas which he sets forth, but by that which he does and represents in his person. The person, the life, the work, these are the things immediately given. In them are the immediate objects of faith, in them the norm and source of theology. The ideas are never given immediately, or objectively, or independently of these live and personal realities. And I apply to Dr. Fairbairn his own principle, the primary, not the derivative, can alone be constitutive for theology.[32]

Rall adjudges, notwithstanding the appropriateness of "Father language" to express our conception of God, that in such a position and term, the full content of Christianity will not be found. The term "Father" is figurative, amenable to all forms and types of culture and for its content is dependent upon the ethics of its users. Contrarily, the Christian conception of God is not simply of God the Father, but of God as the Father *of our* Lord Jesus Christ. Fatherhood of God cannot be used as the sole constitutive principle in addition because it omits "adequate aspects of truth.... And, chiefly, it is the thought of Sovereignty which is essential to the true conception of God, and yet it is not included here.... Now if you take the idea of Fatherhood in any strict or definite sense, the other aspect of sovereignty or righteousness is not included."

After reviewing briefly other possible "single constitutive principles" for theology (e.g., the Incarnation, justification by faith), Rall concludes that none is to be found and there need be none in order to develop a unitary and organic theology. "What is needed for this is a unitary center and a unitary point of view." Christ is the living center of our Christian world view. The Christ who is this center is the Christ in whom we believe, not merely the Christ whose ideas we accept, nor whose world-view we try to adopt. He constitutes the center of our faith and of our world-view. He must be for theology what he is for faith. Christ himself must be the living principle and the organizing center. We need a Christocentric theology. Then the further question comes of our conception of Christ. It is really the same question before discussed, what Christ is our authority, to which Christ do we return? The answer is, the Christ of faith, that is the historical Christ apprehended in faith as the living Christ and Savior. It is the Savior Christ. Here are Rall's regulative principles, theology must be Christocentric and soteriological.[33]

As to an analytical review of Ritschl's apologetics, Rall notes the two-fold questions involved, namely, those dealing with the ground of Christian belief and then the manner in which I can assert and defend a Christian world-view against other views.

In reference to a general apologetic he believed that the defense of the faith must be in the practical reason that can attain to the conception of God. The theoretical reason cannot give us the real conception of God nor can it defend or destroy it. Within the practical sphere the conception of God is necessary as an answer to man's practical needs as spirit; that it is necessary, if he is not to reject the inescapable dicta of his moral self-consciousness, and if he is to hold this latter in a unity with his knowledge of the world. The proof of experience accompanies this practical necessity. The conception of God and life thus attained is received and realized in active obedience and approves itself as true in this life experience. The question of individual certainty Ritschl only touches upon, but he relates this to the conviction of the personal faith in Christ.[34]

Rall then reviews in some detail what he considers the "best Ritschlian" exposition of apologetics, Julius Kaftan's *The Truth of the Christian Religion*. Looking at Kaftan's apologetic as a whole, he notes as its general position: The supreme question of knowledge (that of the ultimate cause and purpose of the world) is practical, not theoretical. Its solution cannot be theoretical, whether scientific or speculative, first because the problem is practical, second because it transcends the sphere or capacity of this sort of knowledge. Having next determined what the rational idea of the highest good is, and found it to be ethical and religious, and not primarily theoretical, a matter of knowledge, he finds: that such an analysis agrees with what Christianity offers in the idea of the Kingdom of God. This implies the acceptance of the Christian revelation in which it is given and the conception of atonement by which it is made possible. The ultimate problem of life and knowledge can be solved only from the practical standpoint, and Christianity commends itself by being the most perfect solution. As regards a theoretical solution, on the one hand, such is impossible; on the other, to remand the problem to philosophy would be to exalt knowledge above the ethico-spiritual as superior in value and authority, as the highest good. This general standpoint the Ritschlians all occupy. They unite in this quasi-scepticism over against philosophy, and they set forth Christianity as the absolute religion in that it gives the perfect answer to this problem.[35]

Following the appreciative summary of Kaftan, he approvingly continues with Wilhelm Herrmann's, *Christian Communion With God*.[36] We might sum up Herrmann's view thus: Our Christian certainty rests upon an experience that is bound up with the person Jesus Christ, whose spirit and life convince us of their reality, whose character makes possible for us the belief in the supremacy of a living God and the triumph of the good, who leads us into loving fellowship with that God, and through this solves for us the problem of the moral life. It is the proof of experience with a strong christocentric character. Closely allied to this thought of Herrmann's are some words of Harnack, who does not, it is true, picture that deep religious experience of which Herrmann speaks, but who brings out in his own unequalled manner the significance of the life and character of Christ for the certainty of belief.

> The Christian faith is not... the gentle illumination of earthly life or an easy submission to its toils and hardships. No — it is a decision for God and against the world. It is an eternal life that is in question, whether in and above nature and its happenings there is a kingdom of holiness and love, a city not made with hands, whose citizens we should be. And joined with this message there goes the summons for a change of heart and a denial of self, and we feel that here is a question of either or, which must decide our inner life. Is victory possible in this struggle, and is there indeed a higher reality at stake, over against which the world is nothing? Or are we deceiving ourselves with our feelings and premonitions? Are we perhaps after all shut in wholly in the circle of unfree nature, in the circle of our earthly being, and fighting a miserable fight with our own shadows.[37]

Then, in an altogether too quick a manner, Rall states his own soteriological and christocentric apologetic, "... that as Christ is the center of the Christian faith, so he is the greatest apologetic of Christianity.[38]

As the heart of Christianity is in the ethical and the religious, so here its defense must be. But all the inner worth of Christianity, its incomparable content of truth and ideals and life, all this is summed up and set forth before the eyes of men in Jesus Christ. His character, his spirit, his life, and that which he can become to men today who will open their hearts to his great message, this is central for the positive apologetic of Christianity. It is this apologetic that you will find with men like Bushnell[39] and Dr. Dale[40] and this is the current that sweeps through the strong words with which a Robertson[41] and a Phillips Brooks[42] commended the truth of Christianity to the hearts and minds of men.

As to the persistent problem of *which* Christ, a problem then engaging to major theologians of the time, Rall agrees with Ritschl that it is the Christ who is met in the historic Christian community within which one stands as it recites the picture of the biblical Christ.[43] As to the threat presented by the new historical criticism, Rall assures, first of all, not to fight an imaginary situation. Historical criticism has not imperiled one of the essential traits in the picture of the Christ that the Gospels give and in whom the apostles believe. Second, it is one thing if historical criticism reaches results that contradict the conception of Christ held in faith. It is another thing if it declares that these records are not all or in the main first hand historical sources, original documents, such as the strict historian can accept as basis for scientific history. The first alternative does not hold and will not occur. Where such results have been set forth, it has been where dogmatic preconceptions and a surreptitious philosophy have donned the garb of historical criticism, and have exceeded the bounds of the latter. As regards the latter alternative, Rall concedes that it in large part obtains, but adds, it is another thing to prove that this is false, and the inner grounds for the faith in Christ, which must always be decisive, are sufficient for belief that the picture which these documents present in its heart and essence is trustworthy. Finally, he notes that one of the urgent needs of today is a criticism of criticism. Historical research often carries with it a complete ready-made philosophy, which, with the most charming philosophical naïvete, it assumes as a matter of course. We need to ask as to the fundamental principles and presuppositions of historical study, and we need carefully to determine its task and prescribe its limits.

From this point of view I cannot wholly agree with what Harnack says, when he declares that historical study must determine who and what Christ was. I do not minimize the importance of this study. It is through the Jesus of the gospels, the Jesus that walked upon earth, that we know the Lord of our faith. The Jesus of history is not to be separated from the Christ of faith. And yet, when once he has won my faith, then he becomes a larger and a more content-full reality than he was before. Then I accept that which upon pure historical study I could not accept. Is there in the records of the New Testament material which strict scientific scrutiny might accept and deem sufficient on purely scientific grounds to prove the resurrection of Christ? I do not hesitate for my part to say, No. And I am willing to say that as to other miracles of the Bible. But my faith in Christ makes the belief in those records possible for me, and compels me to the faith, that, though he died, he rose again and liveth. I do not say that this is a bald conclusion of faith. It has its rational grounds for me, alike in the records of these events, and in the subsequent history of the early church. But the compelling ground is not scientific. In the same way I accept the apostolic proclamation of the living and the reigning Christ as they knew him in life and experience. Here are determinate elements for my conception of Christ which fall outside of the method that Harnack suggests.[44]

Secondly, as more stress is to be laid on the ideal, the ethical and the spiritual, so more place must be given to the testimony of that life and experience in which higher things are tested and realized. Here is where Dr. Dale's argument comes in, by which he finds an independence even over against the historical.[45] Thirdly, with an emphasis upon the ideal and the experiential, a far greater place must be given to the person and character of Christ. Such lines as those suggested by the writers mentioned today are crucial. And we may call up here Bushnell's chapter on the Character of Jesus and Ullmann's treatise on the Sinlessness of Jesus.[46] Fourth, in harmony with what has been said, the best defense of Christianity and best commendation of it will be secured by the positive setting forth of the truth of Christianity, not philosophically or theoretically, but as the gospel of life and love, as that which perfectly meets the deepest needs of human nature. Such an apologetic will be practical, will be christocentric, and will put before men the challenge that Christ does: He that willeth to do his will, shall know of the doctrine whether it be of God. Finally, there comes up the important question, as to the part that philosophy and theoretical considerations are to play in apologetics. There are two positions that have been taken here. You may declare with the Ritschlians, that all this is to be ruled out absolutely. With that I cannot agree. And that position is not adhered to by the Ritschlians. You may say that science does not conflict with theology. But the opinions of scientists do, and historians and philosophers set forth views inimical or fatal to our faith. Moreover we are all under the impulse to organize our knowledge into a whole and to hold it in a harmonious unity. And none of us content ourselves either with practical faith, or single, observed facts, but press on to conclusions, and theoretical conclusions. All this involves for us as individuals and as theologians a use of the theoretical reason. On the other hand, I do not agree with a position like that held by Professor Orr, nor with his actual method of apologetic as illustrated in his work on *The Christian View of God and the World*.

> If apologetic is to be spoken of, this surely is the truest and best form of Christian apology — to show that in Christianity, as nowhere else, the severed portions of truth found in all other systems are organically united, while it completes the body of truth by

discoveries peculiar to itself. The Christian doctrine of God, for example, may fairly claim to be the synthesis of all the separate elements of truth found in Agnosticism, Pantheism, and Deism, which by their very antagonisms reveal themselves as onesidednesses, requiring to be brought into some higher harmony.[47]

In what must be seen as one of the earliest American interpretations of an introduction to Ritschlian apologetics or Ritschlian theological method, Rall portends the future lines which theoretical and philosophical considerations for theology would take and concludes they would be through a critical study of the theory of knowledge, a central concern of American theology in its liberal era of the first decades of this century as well as contemporary times. It is instructive to the historian to trace these methodological motifs in America in the interwar decades and in particular in Harris Franklin Rall throughout his distinguished career as teacher, church leader and social prophet. One can do so only, however, by first frankly acknowledging that for Rall the focus shifted from methodological concerns *per se* to issues he considered more essential to the life of the church: evangelism, stewardship and what can be called "religion and Christianity." Insofar as his energies were expended in these latter areas, he did touch upon fundamental theological stances. Rall nevertheless, did engage in three fields of inquiry directly connected with methodology: biblical interpretation, apologetics with natural and social sciences in particular, and in theories of knowledge.

CHAPTER III

THE THEOLOGICAL METHODOLOGY OF HARRIS FRANKLIN RALL

A. Biblical Interpretation

Separated by thirty years and spanning a major theological revolution which included radically new biblical interpretation, are Professor Rall's two books on biblical understanding: *New Testament History* (1914) and *According to Paul* (1944).[1] Prior to the earlier publication, Rall made evident, through his preaching and writings, his opposition to what would in the 1920's have been called "biblicism" and his qualified endorsement of the newer historical method (later we will note his sharp criticism of this method as exemplified by Ernst Troeltsch). Fundamentally, Rall in his methodology of religion, defined as life in its highest aspirations (truth, beauty, goodness) and most especially in the latter, the ethical sphere, insisted that the Bible and its contents be measured against its impact on these areas of life:

> And not only is the Bible a book of life, a revealment of the living God in the life and faith of man; it is only through life that we can apprehend its truth. This great word of Jesus is fundamental for the theologian, as it is for the seeking disciple. If the Bible were a mere textbook, then the mere reason could understand it, and any skeptic could be an equally good theologian with the Christian. But Christianity is not a philosophy. It

is an experience and a faith; its truth is truth for faith and experience and its theology must be experiential.²

From this axiomatic stance, Rall never moves throughout the thirty years. To avoid misunderstanding and to charge Rall with "life-mysticism," let it be added at once that Rall, following Ritschl, merely argues for a two-fold exigency of biblical interpretation. One, its authority and hence its viability can be circumscribed only within the historic community that recognizes its importance and not by any located data from that *present* community (cf. below on the problem of historical relativism), be they creed or dogma of a preceding era of that community. Secondly, Rall is *not* making of the Scriptures an anthropocentrizing of human needs, etc. (cf. below his acidic comment on Troeltsch). Rather, he agrees with Ritschl in saying that God's action toward man in Jesus Christ *must* meet man within his own context and not one foreign to him. Scriptures are sacred because they are confessions of those who most immediately stood in the presence of God in the flesh.

New Testament History was written as a college text, and with "The Bible itself [is] the only book needed."³ Significant to the methodological problem under review is the structure of the book: first, it is a historical study. Rall contends that to understand Christianity one must go to the greater movement lying back of the Bible, the Church, and doctrine. He certainly is not calling for the *grundmotif* of Ferdinand Baur, e.g. (Cf. Hefner, *Op. cit.*, pp. 14ff),⁴ of *Idee* or *Geist* to which Christianity gives illustration. Rather, that which grounds the Bible, the Church, and doctrine is the current of Life, "... which was at once the greatest revelation of the divine Spirit and the greatest movement of the human spirit that mankind has known."⁵ At issue for the Church is what its Founder taught and did and the origin and development of the "world brotherhood" that came out of the little company of Jews that followed him.

Rall, in the structuring of the text on Scripture, evidences his awareness of and dependence upon the then contemporary historical-critical method. A check of the bibliography alone indicates acquaintance with current scholarship with the suggestion that if one could afford but one additional book, it should be a Dictionary of the Bible. Of equal significance is the Ritschlian flavor in methodology, i.e., that the Bible does not bear its own inner witness but relies upon and is judged by "life" for its authenticity. What Rall means by "life" is but the practical and personal as against the theoretical and metaphysical categories.

When writing the second book, *According to Paul*, (The Ayer Lectureship of 1942), Rall again indicates his timeliness to current New Testament criticism and its focus on theological inquiry. The mid-1930's serve as a focal point for a measurably new theological climate in America, with fresh interpretations of Biblical hermeneutics (not then so labelled) as well as radical · reorientation of systematic theology and social ethics.[6] Accompanying such a revolution was a new emphasis upon Pauline Studies, with Karl Barth's *Romerbrief*[7] and Anders Nygren's *Agape and Eros*[8] serving as symbols of the times. Rall stands aside from Barth and his influence in this study as well as in other writings. Perhaps it is better to note here the full scope of his reaction against the theology of Karl Barth.

Professor Rall welcomed the Barthian theology as a corrective to the helplessness identifying the post World War I American Society. However, he cautioned those who would see in Barth a new Messiah, that "Barth does not have the solution to our problems (his theology ends in Calvin's), but we need him to see better what those problems are."[9] Rall's criticism of the Barthian movement centered in two probing queries: how does the "Wholly Other" reveal himself to man, and, how is the saving relationship maintained between God and man. "Barth's emphasis upon God is one thing, his doctrine of God is another. The emphasis is not as with the prophets and Jesus upon the ethical, but primarily upon the metaphysical. Characteristic is the fact that it is death rather than sin that is most stressed."[10] Rall viewed Barth's doctrine of God as dualistic and as stemming from Hellenistic rather than Hebraic philosophy. But he insisted that Barth never resolved the dilemma of how revelation takes place within this dualism. "So far from being of aid here, through his conception of God and the world, he tends to make incredible the revelation which he asserts, and in no case shows how that revelation enters human life."[11]

More critical than this, yet allied with it, was the piercing criticism Rall directed toward Barth's undercutting of the basis of the Christian hope of salvation. Rall believed that the heart of the God-man encounter was the salvific act of God toward man. He was critical toward all systems which ensconced this central motif. His prime question always was: does this doctrine speak against or in any way slight the salvific act of God; if so, it cannot and must not be believed. Rall determined that Barthianism was such a doctrine.

> Barth, I fear, has no adequate answer for our questions. It is well for the preacher to say God, but we must go farther. How can we know God? How can we be sure of Him? How does God move in this world? How does he enter savingly into our life? Here Barth fails us. His teaching is more calculated to emphasize our need than to meet it. It is not a theology that Wesley could have taken to his colliers, or that we can use with common folk in our churches, or that will meet these pressing questions of the modern mind. It is well to lift up God, especially in this day when man has been so satisfied with himself. But the Christian evangel proclaims not the God high and lifted up, but the God who draws near. In his effort to stress the first, Barth has set such a gulf

between man and God that he cannot give place to the second.¹²

Rall reviewed Barth's *Credo* and noted that "Especially should those in the Methodist tradition see how his position rules out large areas in that gospel of Christian experience, of saving help, and transforming power for which the Methodist movement in particular has stood."¹³ To this end is quoted a paragraph written by Rall in answer to many student and alumni queries from "Which Way Religion" printed in the *Garrett Tower* in January, 1935:

> Are we going back to Calvin by the way of Barth? No. A divine determinism that fixes every event, including the fall of man and the damnation of the non-elect, a God who is arbitrary will and authority before he is moral goodness, the denial of human freedom and responsibility — we are not ready for these. We are not ready for Karl Barth: for the dogmatism that marks his method, for the agnosticism that leaves God finally unknowable, for the dualism that sets God and man so sharply against each other that God cannot really enter into human life, that rules out a real doctrine of the indwelling and transforming Holy Spirit and denies Methodism's insistent belief in salvation as moral renewal, nor for its assertion that religion has no message for the social order and can furnish no power for its renewal.¹⁴

In particular, Rall charges Barth has no theology of the third article of the Creed:

> That is true despite the longer discussion of the Holy Spirit in Barth's *Dogmatik*, Vol I, Part I. pp. 470-489. Hence he can find no place for a union of God and men by which man in any measure is made over by

the Spirit of God into the likeness of Christ, into the spirit of a true child of God through the dwelling in him of faith and truth and love, wholly the gift of God and yet at the same time the true life of man. The Spirit in us, so far as this life is concerned, means for Barth our recognition of the word when God speaks to us. But even this seems dangerous to him, destroying in a measure the creatureliness of man, so he hastens to add that in reality we do not know or recognize God's word to us; it is God (the Spirit) who thus knows. God, as it were, hears himself speak. Beyond that is the vigorous insistence that 'everything which can be said about man's receiving the Spirit, being driven by the Spirit, and filled with the Spirit, is in the meaning of the New Testament an eschatological expression;' that is, it is viewed as belonging to the *eschaton,* the end, to another age, not this. What man has here he has in faith, which means as a promise. It is not in the least degree fulfilled or accomplished in the present. We have it only as the expectation of what is to be. 'We assume this future completion because it speaks of God's act, though the hands which we stretch out to God are empty.' Does he mean that, except for a hope, our hearts are empty, too? There seems to be no place in Barth for salvation as sanctification, that is, as a real making over of the believer.[15]

In *According to Paul,* Rall established the basic Pauline outline to be a series of polarities over the entire range of theology. That of eschatological hope and present fact affords an example. Throughout the New Testament, Rall sees salvation as proffered in the future, yet coupled with this is the recognition of the fact that the forces of that new-age were already at work. Paul frames his theological understandings within this hope in the eschatological form of his Jewish heritage, and, "Side by side with this he sees what God is doing now in saving his people and he rejoices in it though he thinks of this as only for a brief period before the end." That eschatological — or apocalyptic, as Rall labels it — hope is ensconced with "the lawless one" or "the one that constraineth" and other first century language descriptions. But he admits that his own eschatological outlook, albeit more modest than the first century detailing, must "... assert the continuity between the historical and that which lives beyond history." It is precisely at this point of continuity that Rall judges the entire Barthian movement to be in error stating that relationship with God now established cannot be circumscribed within this stark dualism of the movement. In an apparent strange inconsistency Rall disparages Barthian dualism under a methodology he earlier had criticized Ritschl over: a cultural relativism. It was a weakness in Ritschl to allow morality as the basis of this theology. Rall argued then (1900) that ethics stemmed from the direct relationship of the individual to God. Now, (1944) in criticism of Barth, he argues for continuity, but from the basis of cultural value.

> They [Barthians] emphasize the sovereign power of God and stress direct action, and tend to destroy any creative meaning. But it is the values won in history that are to be conserved in the world beyond history, values won in the free and convinced response of man to the word of God's redemptive love through the surrender of human life to the rule of this spirit of love. No destructive final conflict, no exercise of sheer power, not even of divine omnipotence, can of itself create such values, or, in other words, be the means of salvation.[16]

Rall lists in his commentary on Romans 9-11, no long, detailed exegesis, but rather a recognition of several intertwining elements which can be separated, in his opinion, only at a misreading of Paul. The failure to note this dual play of the religious motive and the apologetic motive has wreaked undue emphasis upon divine sovereignty, absolute predestination, total depravity and strict determinism. Rall summarily argues on behalf of restoring these dual motives — the religious and the apologetic (to use Ritschlian categories, the moral) or, the indicative and the imperative — in the following manner:

> Religious speech will always include an element of paradox, that is, of statements that stand in apparent contradiction. It must not be strained after, as has been the modern vogue, where in the reaction from the superficially rational, paradox has been assumed to be the hall mark of truth. Paradox belongs rather to form; the essential matter is the fact of the polarity of life. It is not that life is irrational or that we have a contradiction of mutually exclusive principles; it is rather that there is in all concrete existence, from lowest to highest, a certain duality of movement or of forces. If there were direct opposition it would mean deadlock; actually, though it involves a certain tension, it is rather the condition of life and growth. All this is exemplified in the problem with which Paul was struggling, that of divine sovereignty and human freedom. We all know the duality of human life that is here involved: on the one hand a sense of dependence, of an all encompassing Cosmic Order, of a Power that rules our life; on the other, the consciousness of individual and autonomous being, a life set apart from all else as by 'a salt, unplumbed, estranging sea,' and a power to determine our reaction toward that which is without, of which Augustine and Calvin themselves freely take account when they entreat and exhort or when they assert moral responsibility. And here the relation of the ethical to the religious comes to a head. Knowledge of the truth as that which reveals the meaning of our life, freedom of choice and action, and consequent responsibility, these

are the core of the moral life. The awareness of a higher Power, the feeling of dependence, the sense of awe and reverence and absolute obligation, these are at the heart of religion. Taken separately, the one may lead to passive fatalism, the other to moralism or shallow activism, deficient alike in respect of adequate goal and of power of attainment.[17]

B. Apologetics

A second index to measure Rall's theological method is provided in his apologetic criticisms against the major methodological thrusts of (1) the historical method and (2) Behaviorism associated with the writings of J. B. Watson and Albert P. Weiss.[18] These are singled out because they appear influential not only during those times in which Rall writes, but also as important methods in the social and behavioral sciences today.

Rall wrote little directly upon theology and evolution, but he did contribute a paper entitled "Faith in God in An Age of Science" to a collection of essays by Garrett professors published in 1928. Having assayed the factuality of the "new universe" presented by science, he jocularly scorns those fellow theologians who adopted evolutionary naturalism and "could not distinguish between an abiding faith and its changing form of expression." Joyfully, he reports that in the latter years of the twenties, "science-olatry" was passing and the proper limits of science were being recognized.

> The world with which, after all, we are most concerned is the world of persons and values, of man and God, of love and truth and beauty and goodness and justice. There is no fault here with which science is to be chided; it is doing its proper work.[19]

At the same time, the world in 1928 (The Scopes Trial still

in everyone's mind) was coming to a clearer definition of religion as a conviction, an attitude, and a life.

> It is a conviction that there is a world of higher reality beside this world that we see, a world of the Spirit, of God; and it is in relation to that world, religion believes, that the true life of man is found. Religion is an attitude toward this world and toward life, an attitude of reverence, of truth, and of loyalty. And religion is a life, a life that expresses this conviction and attitude and that is lived out in relation to God and world and man. Religion as we have seen, must express itself in forms, in Church and creeds and Sacred writings and the rest, but these are not religion itself. And we are learning to make that distinction.[20]

Rall, interestingly, restates a typical response to evolution located decades earlier in the writings of John Fiske[21] and others; i.e., evolution is not simply continuity, but change, the appearance of the new, the higher, the teleological, the purposive. In addition, science is "friendly" to theology in its presuppositions of unity and order in the universe moved by one power which is grounded in reason. Indeed, praise should be given to the natural sciences as to advances in social sciences. Such studies can but abet an understanding of the world in which God operates salvifically. Evolution, in particular, affords greater appreciation of the "deeper spiritual meanings in the order of nature." It is not for us a soulless mechanism, or a blind and inexorable inevitability. It is the divine way of working, a way that has a far deeper wisdom than any primitive faith in causal intervention. "The laws of nature are the thoughts of God." Science has also reduced the theologians' dogmatic pronouncements of the sheer power of God to the playing down of his goodness. Theologians humbly turn to the world and "see the actual method of God is that of growth, with toil and conflict and pain.... Gone is the God who works from aloft by some easy word of power. In his place is the vision of a God who dwells with men and walks their path of labor and pain."[22] Rall does not concern himself with the evolution controversy as such, because, as we have already noticed, in his view scientific inquiry by its own definition does not concern itself with the religious and moral responsibilities of man.

Little scholarship has been accomplished in tracing the influence of European historical methodology upon the American theological scene in the late nineteenth and early twentieth centuries. Perhaps the Darwinian hypothesis and the new social application of theology overshadowed the explicit writings on historical method. Perhaps such writings were in publication but yet to be discovered and analyzed. In the March, 1910, issue of *Methodist Review,* Rall commends the place of the historical method in the Church as beyond question.

> It is linked with the surest progress of our intellectual life. It has the respect for facts which marks the scientific spirit, the age of realism, as against the age of speculation. It brings out the modern sense of individualism. It gives expression to the idea of development, which in some form is inseparable from our thought today. It has magnified the personal and spiritual as against the mechanical and external. It has enforced upon systematical theology a respect for the actual and has made it more biblical. It has aided the appreciation of the real meaning of Christianity by lifting above the dull level of the letter the mountain peaks of prophetism in the Old Testament and of gospel in the New.[23]

However, the question he writes, is not the right or value of the historical method, but its final meaning for theology.

> And now, in the name of this supreme science, the supernatural is ruled out, not as a conclusion, but as a

premise, and the whole movement makes for an interpretation of Christianity as a philosophical idealism, against its conception as a positive historical revelation and a divine redemption. Here is our issue: Have we adopted a new conception of Christianity by taking the historical method?[24]

Rall then criticizes those he labels the left-wing Ritschlians, whose writings reflect not only the adoption of the new historical method, but who, in such an orientation in fact, propose a new conception of Christianity: Johann Friedrich Hermann Gunkel of Berlin; Johann Franz Wilhelm Bousset of Göttingen and Giessen; Wilhelm Heitmueller of Göttingen; Paul Wernle of Basel; Heinrich Weinel of Bonn and Jena; William Wrede of Göttingen and Breslau; Ernst Peter Wilhelm Troeltsch of Bonn, Heidelberg and Berlin and in part Otto Pfleiderer of Jena and Berlin (although he was Hegelian in theology and opposed Ritschl). Each started his writing on Christian theology within the general idea of religion, and concluded:

> We must study not a dogmatic revelation but religion, and religion wherever it is found. Christianity cannot be separated from all other history. As historical, it is part of the greater whole of human happening. As religion, it is simply the flower and consummation of the movement of religion which is as broad as human life.[25]

The leader of this school was Ernst Troeltsch of Heidelberg, whose theology is summarized by Rall as denigrating the old, dogmatic method with its desire to find an absolute authority for faith.

> Now it [method] seeks it [authority] in a supernatural history, which is different from all other history. This history is conceived as an absolute revelation, and

this revelation is set up as authority. The whole is regarded under the idea of a redemption which is worked from without. This position, says Troeltsch, is impossible for anyone who accepts the historical method. History must criticize, it can never give you absolute certainty. History sees everything in relations. You cannot pick out some fact or fraction of history and give it absolute value. Every such part belongs to a larger whole, is dependent upon it, inseparable from it. The dogmatic method is an impossible attempt to rise above the limitations of history, out of the one great stream of history to separate some single current and give it a supernatural source and an absolute value. Instead of this, as historians we must study religion as we find it everywhere among men, and Christianity as part of a larger whole, that we may find at last, as the fruit of this universal movement of the human spirit, the ideals and values in which we are to believe.[26]

Rall reasons that this position assumes as its starting point not a conclusion or even a summary of detailed results of historical study by which conclusions subsequently are set forth, but the exclusion of the supernatural, the opposition to the idea of a positive revelation and of Christianity as a divine redemption, and a hostility to a Pauline Christianity. Understanding that his task as a critic was to ask these deeper questions, e.g., What are the true principles of the historical method? Do they involve these conclusions? Is the historical method to be sole and final? Rall carefully examines the three principles of the historical method as proposed by Troeltsch: criticism, analogy, and correlation.[27]

While acknowledging the value for theology of these principles, he maintains that each in its use by this school foreshortens the methodology of Christian theology. To be certain, the theologian must be critical of all source materials, but for this school, criticism

> means that no fact of the past can be absolutely established, and that therefore the historical can never be the basis of Christian certainty or yield an authority for Christian faith. To this larger question of the relation of faith and history we must turn later. So much can be said here: What is really involved is not the divorce of history and faith, but the limits of historical science, which can no more ground our faith than can any other science.[28]

Again, we can best understand the past insofar as it is analogous to that which is happening elsewhere and in the present. But analogy here means something different for Rall:

> Troeltsch speaks of the 'omnipotence of analogy' which 'involves the similarity in principle of all historical occurrence.' Here is not the analogy which helps us to understand the past, but the analogy which determines what the past could have been. It is not a key but a norm, a law. It is evidently the idea of the uniformity of nature that comes into play here. The religious nature of man is everywhere and always the same, and will always manifest itself in the same manner. These laws of the religious life, or analogies, the historian must trace out, and this will determine his interpretation of other religions. The writings of this school are full of this use of analogy. It is applied with a wealth of learning and the greatest industry. Its purpose is generally the same: to bring down the higher to the level of the lower, to use the primitive in order to determine what the advanced must be. It is applied in two directions, which may be considered separately. The first has regard to those forms

and ideas in which religion expresses itself. It is refreshing to hear these men protest against super-refined literary criticism and the overemphasized study of the doctrinal or intellectual side. The first business of the theologian, they declare, is the study of religion. Unfortunately, their conception of religion neutralizes this advantage. Religion appears as a sort of native force with which men are endowed, and which has its own natural laws of development by which it comes to expression everywhere in the same forms of cults, the same myths and ideas. Nominally, they admit the supernatural element. Indeed, they reproach us with narrowness in limiting this to one religion. In reality, however, religion is not God disclosing himself to man and lifting man into the fellowship of holiness, but the evolution of a native force working out according to its own necessary laws. We can understand now how the principle of analogy is applied. We know how it has been used where men juggled with the phrase of evolution. The highest religions are explained by the primitive in which they find their source, and the primitive forms, in turn, give us the rule for interpreting the higher. Thus Troeltsch declares that 'the primitive religions give the foundation and the means of explanation for all the more complex forms, forming the fruitful womb for all new religious forms and the substratum which persists under all higher religions. Heitmueller's monograph on the phrase 'In Jesus's Name' is a typical illustration. From every source of primitive faith and superstitious practice he brings together the illustrations of the belief in the magical power of the name and its use in incantation and prayer. The heaping up of these analogies is to prove that we have in the Christian phrase such a magical survival. In the same way this writer takes up the question of Paul's view of the sacraments. Primitive religion is full of its sacrificial meals. Christianity has the same in the Lord's Supper. The lower must again explain the higher, and the principle of analogy must serve to prove identity. And so Heitmueller proves that for Paul the sacraments have a magical efficacy which lies in the form or act itself. Gunkel's work on the Religio-Historical Interpretation of the New Testament gives illustration for the great events of the life of Christ. He searches out the analogies in other religions for the stories of infancy, for baptism and temptation, tranfiguration and resurrection, as well as for many other ideas in the New Testament. There may not be a single instance in which he has a case strong enough to stand alone, but the heaping up of these analogies is meant to convey the same general idea: the primitive is the source of the later, and the lower must be used to teach us what the higher means.[29]

Rall's primary contention, of course, is that religion is not to be classified by mere language forms or cultic practices; rather religion is a matter of the new spirit which can use any form of language, filling these forms with new meaning. The attempt by Troeltsch is seen as an effort at a naturalistic scheme of things "... which can conceive no history without its general laws of happening, to which all things must be leveled down. Is not all this a misconception of what history means and of what historical studies should be?"

The rationality of natural science rests upon the power to reduce events to general laws. If you do that with history there is nothing left. Science has no place for the individual, history lives upon it. The scientist must leave the individual aside. The plant interests him, not as an individual plant, but as one of the species. Even a chance peculiarity would concern him only as it illustrated a general law. The historian considers not what is the same, but what is different, not that which simply repeats, but that which happens once. It is the individual with which he deals, the individual in the realm of personality. The modern historical school under the influence of the ideas of natural science is misusing the principle of analogy in the search for general laws. It is failing in its first task, the study of the individual and the appreciation of those personalities who make history and who are more than illustrations of general laws. It has so over-emphasized the idea of continuity in history as to change it to the principle of identity. It has failed to see that the meaning of human history is in the forward look and the forward step, and not the ceaseless round in which nature repeats itself.[30]

The third principle — that of correlation — seems also to be conceived on the naturalistic order. It corresponds to the principle of the conservation of energy and the correlation of forces.

Is God really present in this history — acting, directing, self-revealing? Is he not only in this history but more than this history? Or is the divine here simply the sum of human forces, everywhere the same and everywhere pressing on in the same blind fashion? It is the question of the real personality of God and of his transcendence.[31]

Rall does not doubt for a moment that community and social forces are integral to the modern idea of history. Indeed, he claims Christianity itself is a historical religion centering in Jesus of Nazareth and can be understood only in specific relations. There is only one history that dogmatic theology can make impossible and that is that history where all things are joined together in a strict causal relation and where all development proceeds from a self-sufficient unity of immanent forces; namely, the historical method as announced by Troeltsch. The questions of correlation for Rall, then, include these:

> Troeltsch speaks of the 'mutual interaction of all phenomena of the historical-spiritual life, so that no change can occur at any point without preceding and succeeding change at some other, so that all occurrence ... must form one stream in which all and each belong together.' What this means is made more clear by Troeltsch's protest against what he calls the dogmatic method.[32]

Rall is *not* saying that this historical school stands for naturalism, for a merely causal explanation in history. He *is* saying that their protest against the supernatural is consistent only from this standpoint. And, further, the historian can only study events in their relations; he cannot declare such events as causally determined by those relations.

> That is not history but dogmatism, the popular philosophy of a naturalistic or pantheistic evolution. It is not implied in the historical method.... Correlation, then, does not mean causal dependency. It is true that naturalistic science, as such, cannot consider the miracle. But historical science has no right to suppress either the significance of human personality or that direct play of divine personality which we call the supernatural.[33]

Illustrative of this position criticized by Rall are the then historical studies regarding the Person of Jesus Christ and Paul's Christology. How can one explain the Person, the Resurrection, the early Church's faith in his Resurrection, etc.? Turning from the internal witness of Jesus and the early church, Gunkel, for example, can explain the resurrection through comparative studies of religion and can conclude that such an idea must have come to the disciples indirectly from paganism through Judaism.

> That the resurrection occurred on Easter Sunday at the rising of the sun points to the Oriental celebration of the day, the turning from winter to summer in the Babylonian religion.... The Christology [of Paul] was not so much formed to sound the mystery of his person, as though Jesus were primus and the Christology second; rather, the souls which longed for the nearness of God, which had need of a son of God appearing from heaven, transferred to him these ideals of their hearts.[34]

Or, again on Paul's Christology, Wernle estimates this theology to have originated not within the early historic Christian community but from

> ... the transfer of a bold speculation to the historical person of Jesus .... Jesus came to the Greeks in the form of a dramatic myth. Again they [early Christians] had the story of a god, and from the most recent time. This conquered the world.[35]

The specific errors in this approach, according to Rall, are two: an inverse of putting the pyramid on its apex, or to put it another way, the basis of Paul's Christology is other-than-the-total-impression of Jesus Christ, whose personality dominated the early disciples. On such a precarious apex the whole massive pyramid of Christianity is balanced, that Christianity which not only conquered the old world but which was never more agressive than in the twentieth century. Rall concludes that in answer to man's religious quest, such neo-Ritschlians offered a longing set for a faith, a myth turned into a creed, an hallucination founding a theology, and the greatest Person of history misunderstood and displaced by this creation of his disciples. Secondly, to repeat, the historians of this school by definition preclude the activity of a transcendent God who can come into the historical movements of men.

What does the historical method imply for theology? Summarily, the principles of historical study do not rule out the supernatural. Only a naturalistic scheme of mechanical causation could imply that, with a pantheistic idea of a kind of spiritual conservation of energy and correlation of forces.

> The world of history is the personal world. Even human personality will break through such a scheme. The law of the personal world is not quantitative equivalence, not cause equals effect. Its mark is not sameness, but difference. To recognize this leaves play for human personality, but equally so for the divine. There is no more rationality in the exclusive immanence of pantheistic evolution than in Christian theism.[36]

One further point demands attention: that of historical relativism, or, the relation of history and faith. Within any articulated methodology, theology must deal with the rather difficult question of the present within which it now seeks expression as determined by or connected with that which is not by definition a part of the present consciousness of the community. Rall reads this historical school as denying that the faith of the present — any present — can locate a ground for certainty in anything historical. It precludes any possibility of offering an Absolute as authority for present commitment. In lieu of that one intervention in history of God's direct and final revelation in Christian history, evolutionary idealism of a pantheistic trend is substituted. Troeltsch is quoted as positing instead of special revelation, "Reason ruling in history and progressively revealing itself." In this, revelation becomes practically equivalent to man's religious intuitions. . . .

> History is thus the 'unfolding of the divine Reason.' It is an 'ordered succession, in which the central depth and truth of the spiritual life of man mounts upward out of the transcendent Ground of the Spirit, in the midst of struggle and error of every kind, but yet with the logical necessity of a normally begun development.'[37]

Rall labels such writing as modified Hegelianism which he defines as a development through immanent forces according to rational necessity. This necessity is grounded in the World-Spirit, and these forces are God. He hedges on criticizing this position, but does suggest, that the position has nothing to do with rigorous, scientific historical statement. Rather, a leap of faith has been taken and the historian has in fact joined the dogmatic defenders against which he has been fighting. Secondly, such an optimistic view cannot be sustained in the history of Western culture. Lastly, this position, a very influential one at the turn of this century, has in unwarranted fashion minimized the meaning of personality. For this school, the relation of faith and history becomes one of identity whereby present history becomes the ground and norm for faith and hence the source of theology, and not Jesus Christ as recorded in the New Testament. Faith, for Rall, can neither rest upon philosophy, as Kant proved, nor on historical science. Such a conclusion does not lead to a "present" or "mystical" foundation, for the relation of history and faith can be found singly in the authority of the early Church's confession that in Jesus Christ God was livingly present.

> The historical is not a problem for our faith, but a foundation without which it were not faith enough

for the storms of life. Religion is more than an inspiration, an ideal, a program, an evolution. It is more than man reaching up to God. It is God coming to men. In the faith that God has so come in our history the human heart will find its rest and strength, as it ever has. And in that truth, that has won the ages past, we shall find our conquering evangel for the days to come.[38]

A third measurement of Rall's methodology can be viewed against Behaviorism. As early as 1913 this psychological position became introduced into America through J. B. Watson. In 1930 Rall contributed an article "What Does Behaviorism Mean For Religion?", in a book he did entitled *Behaviorism: A Battle Line*. Labeling it a weasel-word much like evolution earlier in his career, Rall recounts the attractiveness of this new popular "in" among the intelligentsia: to wit; "... the desire to be considered scientific, 'the revolt' from the intellectual, the emphasis on the 'practical,' the unwillingness to think about ultimate questions." First, he wanted to sharpen his criticism of this method by classifying it into radical Behaviorism, which is an implicit philosophy and the strictly psychological Behaviorism, which is a method of study. The latter Rall welcomed as he earlier had welcomed evolutionary theory and the historical method. All sciences are to be sought as aids toward a clearer study of the development of religion and the knowledge of human behavior which can afford the greatest appropriation and expression of religion.

It is in what he calls the "crude behaviorism" of J. B. Watson that Rall takes issue. Interestingly the same charge is laid here as he formerly laid to Troeltsch and the school of the historical method: Watson departs from the practice of descriptive analysis of behavior by asserting value judgments and thereby introducing a form of a "religion". Indeed, well aware is Rall of the place accorded religion by Watson.

The origin of religion Watson finds in the laziness of certain men who wanted to get their living without work and so invented such superstitions as the belief in the soul and the supernatural. The successors of these medicine men are the priests and preachers of today, and the soul superstition as a religious survival vitiated all psychology until Mr. Watson appeared. Religion is the incubus of which humanity must be rid before progress is possible.[39]

Behaviorism's simple investigation is limited to the study of man as a unity, a stimulated, responding organism. Rall contends that Mr. Watson, however, leaves this proper scientific sanctuary when he becomes "... a prophet, a preacher, an evangelist, a man with a faith and a program. He is a dogmatic metaphysician.

He declares that there is no reality which cannot be thus observed. He denies that what the senses observe may indicate a reality that is not physical: 'The behaviorist cannot find consciousness in the test tube of his science.' It follows necessarily that there is no consciousness, no rational self, no intelligence, no ideals, no purpose in man's conduct, no beauty, no moral goodness, no God. There is, of course, no argument here; Behaviorism ceases to be a scientific method and becomes a dogma.[40]

It is not without surprise to read that Rall will consider Behaviorism as a religion insofar as it deals with salvation. For Rall, religion is salvation. The source of salvation for Watson cannot be any higher power, but the planned manipulation of stimuli. With this understanding in mind, Rall concluded that Behaviorism was not only a "religion," but indeed was hostile to traditional religion by ruling out the idea of God, the "higher goods of life," the evidence of any fellowship between God and man, the trust of loyalty and good among men as above physical stimulus and response, the ethical responsibility uniquely to be ascribed to man, and the hopes of any social reality let alone that symbolized by the Kingdom of God.[41]

In conclusion, we can see that in the development of his theological methodology throughout these years, Rall indicates an openness to the major discoveries in the fields of social sciences, and historical method and Behaviorism in particular. He has already abandoned anything resembling the "old" whether it be inerrancy of the Bible or metaphysical abstraction. He welcomes newer thought insofar as it can remain useful in the apologetic task of the theologian to better know his sources and the community before whom he is writing, speaking and reading. Rall castigates any methodologies as they leave their utilitarian frameworks to become in fact optional "religions." What is instructive for the historian is the question as to his rejection of the revolutionary "new theology" of the 1930's, whose concern was equal with his as to its Christocentrism and Soteriology as being the primary foci for theological methodology and whose sources were also those of the Scriptures in general and the New Testament in particular. The reason for this rests upon that which Rall foresaw as the next line of theological inquiry as early as 1900: theories of knowledge. The question of knowing was fundamental to Albrecht Ritschl and likewise those of the Ritschlian School, notably Julian Kaftan and Wilhelm Hermann.

C. Theories of Knowledge

Ritschl rejected the Platonic and Lotzean theories of knowing the theoretical in favor of that of Immanuel Kant in the "practical" realm. Kaftan carefully and exhaustively described knowledge as the perception that this or that is so. Still further, knowledge is in principle communicable and can always be a general possession. Finally, knowledge is directly measurable upon our practical action. The source then, for Kaftan (under whom Rall studied) of all our certain knowledge is in the last resort, *Experience*. "For if knowledge is the apprehension of what is real, it is by experience and experience alone that we become acquainted with what is real."[42] It is true that distinctions of perception arise in experience such as those sensuous, those mental and historical, and interactions among them.

Ways of knowing, the locus of certainty and authority, identify the major foci of Rall's concern with theories of knowledge. He follows the Ritschlian school by continually favoring practical knowing which must issue in moral action. It is interesting to note, however, that throughout his professional career, Rall in no way modifies beyond amplification his earlier remarks. What he reiterates in 1914 in *A Working Faith* tends to be repeated as late as 1940 in *Christianity*.

> This third way of knowing [sense and logic] then, is the most important. You may speak of intuition of what you will. It is not simply a theory of knowing, but a theory of what is real. The real things in life are the vital and personal, and we know these not by mere feeling or by mere intellect. We know them by daring and living.... Can we know the personal God?.... First comes a conviction, an intuition, some sense that these are real. Then comes a venture, a surrender to these as that which is worthwhile. Then comes the knowledge that is given in the actual commerce of life, something far broader and richer than our first vision, at its best something big enough to satisfy our life and strong enough to hold it.[43].
>
> ...We may first summarize our position in regard to knowledge: (1) Knowing is not a special activity or 'faculty' of man; it is an aspect of the total process of living. Life at every level, from amoeba to man, is a matter of relations, relations that require constant action and

adjustment. The world acts upon man; man acts upon the world. In this experience man comes to know his world.... (2) Such knowledge is not absolute ... it is in their behaviour that things are truly known; a thing is what it does.... (3) It is a mistake to think that we have a direct knowledge of the physical world while our ideas of the spiritual world are a mere guess or unfounded wish. There is no knowledge of any kind without the mind's work of interpretation.... Yet my knowledge is not less true knowledge because it is subjective, because these are *my* precepts and *my* ideas, and because in shaping them I have used analogies from my own experience. What else could I use? ... all our thinking is necessarily anthropomorphic.... (4) The great error against which we must constantly guard is that of an artificial separation ... separating man from his world.... As regards the knowledge of God: (1) The knowledge of God, like all other knowledge, must come by way of life. It will be the knowledge of acquaintance, not the knowledge of information, knowing God and not merely knowing about God. Religion will therefore hold the primacy here, not theology or philosophy, not tradition or authority.... (2) Religion has its own ways of knowledge and they are determined by the nature of its subject matter, God. There are underlying principles that will hold good here as in all knowing. Observation and experiment, reflection and criticism are as much needed here as elsewhere; but if religion is a matter of life, of active commerce with the object that is known, then the nature of that object will determine what the relations are through which it can be known. If men have found that faith and moral loyalty are conditions for the knowledge of God, then that fact is not altered by the other fact that these attitudes and ways are not required of the biologist.[44]

The nature of the object of the knowledge of God (the

foregoing quotation) has determined the ways in which man will come to such a living knowledge. It is true that man is dependent upon God's mercy at revealing himself; it is also true that man can assist or prepare himself for appropriating this in his search for God. God has revealed himself secondarily through nature, through conscience, through human relations those depth experiences of life, through his activities in history, and supremely through Jesus Christ.

> .... [to] practise the righteousness of the kingdom of God, something must precede. We need the strength that comes from a loving trust in God. We need to know that our own sinfulness is not an insuperable barrier to our approach to him or to that loving trust. And only in this new relation, on the ground of this faith in the loving Father who is world Creator and Ruler, can we have that perfect confidence, that faith in providence, which will make us independent of the world and strong for every task and trial. These truths are vital to Christianity. This is preeminently its religious aspect, and these truths we may sum up under the general thought of the salvation in Christ, or the redemption through Christ. I cannot, therefore, follow either Ritschl or these disciples of his in making the idea of the Kingdom constitutive for theology. I agree with the principle which Bornemann lays down, and which he follows, that we must seek to know God's being and will from his activity, from what he does, from his self-revelation. But I should make the redemptive work of Christ as evinced in his life, his death, and his presence in the Church central and supreme as the source of this knowledge, rather than the teaching concerning the kingdom.[45]

To know God is to have fellowship with him and this can be sought by the help of others or in human fellowship: to place oneself in the historic community of those who claim to have "found" him. Worship, or spiritual awareness, is a second way: to situate oneself under the experience of the inexplicable, to entertain the mystery of the holy. There is the path of action: to plunge oneself into the needs of another and come to the realization of God's presence.

American scholars have long credited Friedrich Schleiermacher as the most significant influence upon the emerging American theological scene of the early twentieth century. The evidence seems to be mounting that it was Albrecht Ritschl who claims that place. If such a reevaluation becomes commonplace, Harris Franklin Rall must stand as one of his initial interpreters to Americans. Ritschl's theological themes as expressed by Phillip Hefner resound in Rall's theological methodology: The centrality of the question of reconciliation for theology, the fundamental category of theology as personal and religious ("Upon what basis can the individual be reconciled to God?"); the central theological schema of soteriology, Christocentrism as ecclesiology (the necessity of the historic community as the bearer of the Jesus Christ Event);[46] the testing of reconciliation by faith interpreted as trust ("This is the distinctive test of reconciliation with God, that one also becomes reconciled with the course of events that God brings to us, no matter how hard a blow these events deal us");[47] the Church as a fellowship, matched by commitment and faith rather than doctrine; the task of theology as that of describing the action of God in the life of the Christian believer as he lives in the Holy Spirit, or, to say it differently, the material of systematic theology is the consciousness of the Church;[48] the criterion for judging phenomena from Schleirmacher's *meaningfulness* to the category of *adequacy*;[49] the necessity of placing Christian faith and theology within the "vitalities of life,"[50] to use Hefner's catching phrase, and thus insisting in theology on turning away from abstraction and using life as its primary datum.

Chapter IV

RELIGION vs. CHRISTIANITY

The closing decades of the nineteenth century in Europe and the opening decades of the twentieth century in the United States were marked with theological ferment. Research in biblical hermeneutics, philology, "comparative" religions and history of religions brought pressure upon the theologians to carefully delineate the apologetic nature of denominations even more specifically. (Methodism, in the case of Harris Franklin Rall).

Rall early in his career, in his Yale lectures of 1900, summarized the Ritschlian position on the nature of religion. (Cf. above, Chapter II; pp. 9ff) Religion is not creed, not theology, but life and faith. Initially, to speak of religion is also to take into consideration history itself, within which one can raise the question of the prevalence, the manifestation, and the structures of the various religions. Albrecht Ritschl had devoted himself to historical investigation and sought to locate within history his methodological principle. Rall does not so direct his attention, but does condition his analyses of religion by recognizing the necessity of placing religion within history and secondly, by affirming that one's view of history helps to determine one's content of religion. The first of these is to be documented throughout Rall's career in his rejection of abstraction (e.g. creeds, doctrine), mysticism, or feeling of absolute dependence as constitutive of religion. In his last publication, *Religion As Salvation*, Rall reviews the prevailing interpretations of history and government, endorsing democracy as a great social philosophy with its world view of man as moral personal being and its "authority of truth and justice and good will."[1] Not only here but more emphatically in earlier decades, Rall implied parallels if not dependencies between Christianity and democracy.

The Nature of Religion in General

"Bread and love and religion have been the three impelling interests of man" writes Rall in his Bross prize-winning book of 1940, *Christianity*.[2] Here, as in his commentary on Ritschl some forty years prior, Rall illustrates religion as rising out of man's existential concern. He claims for religion the satisfaction of and provision for the three basic needs of humanity: the signification and significance of the daily events of life, the fulfillment of basic urges in all men, and the assistance toward having the good triumph over the evil, the higher over the lower, or, the wholeness of our divided selves.[3] He is then careful to denude such an operational definition of any inner or psychological anxiety or any intellectualizing search for explanation. On the contrary, he claims religion deals with impulses demanding self-assertion and self-achievement inseparable from all of life but which take new and distinctive forms with man. He quotes with approval Ritschl's declaration that the circle of religion was not described by two points, God and man, but by three, God, man and the world. He claims that Ritschl, a pragmatist before William James, continues to exert a strong influence in modern theology, and sees the "historical-psychological" approach associated with the name George Albert Coe as the same basic approach. "Religion then, is concerned with man's achievement of values in this world, or over against it, through the help of God."[4]

The second source of religion is man's awareness of a world of higher order "... an unseen world in which are found the meaning of his life, the higher goods for his attainment, and the ultimate forces upon which his life depends."[5] Rall insists that this aspect is as necessary for understanding the nature of religion as is that of the "functional" source. Religion is a response to that which man perceives as beyond him and which offers him "salvation" or protection and safety in a hostile environment. Such a source can be and is experienced by different men in diverse ways. What is significant is that man always perceives this power as beyond any observable or measurable data; it transcends nature itself. Awe, reverence, wonder, fear, fascination and a sense of ultimate dependence combine, "... and are called forth by man's feeling that he is in the presence of something more than himself or his fellows or the world of things, a Power that has supreme meaning for his life."[6] That which separates religion from magic or superstitious fear is that in man which senses in this higher world not merely power and mystery, but "... meaning and goodness as well, something to which he can aspire, in which he can trust, before which his soul must bow."[7]

Essential as are these two sources of religion — man's needs and that which both evokes faith and responds to it — they count nothing without the third aspect; the active and reciprocal relation between man and this higher world. Again, Rall states that as man lives his life, he constitutes religion. "In Hocking's phrase, it [religion] is a 'revolution of the will, as determined by a radical insight.' It is a two-way relation. From man's side it means insight, reverence, aspiration, worship, and surrender; from the other side it means for man salvation, the transformation and completion of life by help from above."[8]

It becomes increasingly clear from this statement as well as his other writtings on this subject, that Rall adheres to a view of *homo religiosus,* or, man is a religious being by nature. I think it unfair to claim an identity between Rall and contemporary phenomenologists of religion (e.g. Mircea Eliade and Joachim Wach) for he quotes Soderblom to the effect of a radical bifurcation in man between the sacred and the profane. Nevertheless, he seems to imply that man is by nature a religious being and not one who could be seen as either neutral toward religion or as an areligious being to whom the igniting of the religious search must be attributed to the Wholly Other. To put the matter another way, in defining the nature of religion, Rall is encapsulating the source of religion *within* the capacities or at least the fundaments of man. Differentiation within religion in general of smaller identifiable sub-religious cultures (e.g. Christianity, Buddhism) will be along the lines that will exclude revelation as fundament.

If religion in general is thus circumscribed by human adaptation, it is *man's* inner attitudes that the historian must use as his criteria for further study of *homo religiosus* and he ought not pursue any source beyond man's constitution (e.g. Scriptures, statements of the historic community) for those criteria. Rall follows such a line of thought in his careful delineation of those marks of the "religious man:" awareness and insight into the deeper meaning, the higher values, the hidden forces of the world; awe and reverence of that which is other as well as like himself; a trust and religious faith (*supra*), the

> '... conviction of a steadfastness, a certainty, an uninterrupted interconnection in the fundamental relation between value and reality.... Faith is akin to faithfulness and presupposes faithfulness in its objects.'[9]

Rall employs two references of noteworthiness in America to emphasize that religious man exercises the spirit of aspiration, adventure, and the creative spirit in religion. The first is to Alfred North Whitehead.

> 'Religion,' says A. N. Whitehead, 'is the vision of something which stands beyond, behind and within the passing flux of immediate things; something which is real and yet waiting to be realized, something whose possession is the final good, and yet is beyond all reach;

something which is the ultimate ideal and the hopeless quest. The vision claims nothing but worship; worship is surrender to the claim for assimilation, urged with the motive of mutual love. The worship of God is not a rule of safety — it is an adventure of the spirit, a flight after the unattainable. The death of religion comes with the repression of the high hope of adventure.'[10]

The second notation is to Joseph Wood Krutch. Rall encourages the reader to comprehend religion better by judging it against its opposites. Against that spirit which apprehends and aspires the highest, there is secularism, which views the world statically and materially and has little desire to possess and enjoy it. Less common is the profane spirit which knows the holy only to trample it under foot. There are those whose confidence has gone, who have turned from faith to despair, saying with Krutch that "... since life has lost all high meaning, nothing is left us but to die like men since we will not live like beasts."[11]

The Function of Religion

Given this definition of religion, its function can almost be dismissed in a word or two. "The function of religion can be nothing less than to secure for man the highest and fullest life."[12] Rall admits the difficulty of this definition, its possible perjuring, its acceptance of the totality of man's life so that "religion" can be described as any man's highest value. The perplexity of the issue for him, however, rests with the fact that even being open to such proliferation, religion still survives. That is to say, why, with all the possible avenues open to man to secure the highest and fullest life (e.g. logical rationality, mystical insight, emotional satisfaction) why does man still desire religious community? That which both attracts man to religion and bids him stay is the knowing relationship man establishes with another Power that proffers him wholeness, or unity, or what Rall calls right relations between self and the other, the self and the universe, the self and other persons, and even self with one's own self. Stated as such, there appears no clearly-wrought defense of one specific religion's claim of finality for itself in fulfilling the "highest and fullest life."

Yet Rall suggests as the criterion in the defense of Christianity that it does offer the *most complete* fulfillment. To defend this appraisal, he employs the concept of polarity in his methodology in the manner that he reasoned Paul used it, with particular reference to Romans 9-11. Polarity may be defined as "two poles or parts at which certain properties are the opposite to one another, as in a magnet."[13] Rall has already engaged this principle in his "push-and pull" definition of the nature of religion (the "push" of man's needs and aspirations, the "pull" of that beyond which beckons him to respond). Divinity and unity, freedom and order, the calculable and the unpredictable, dependence and assertion are all seen as one inclusive of, or at least only understandable by, the fact of the other. If there is any evidence of a duality, it will be confined to a duality of process and not the material. Rall uses this principle of inclusiveness to criticize the emerging "continental theology" of the 1930's, as noted above.

Polarity signifies, then, not a duality of beings, but a tension between opposites which can bring about action and progress. To this must be added that such tension includes interpretation, or "mutual completion."

> The problem of the pull of opposing forces or interests is not solved by the familiar formula of 'both-and', nor yet by the principle of alternation which Hocking has developed finally in relation to the demands of action and rest in religion. Something more than addition or alteration is involved here. The opposing aspects or tendencies of this duality are not only both needed for individual life and progress, but each demands the other for its own completion; and if each be pursued far

enough, and explored in its fullest meaning, it will lead, like a straight line in Einstein's curved universe, not simply away but back again. Rest brings the call to action and is the spring of action. Thus there is a constant pull between the individual and social in religion, as in all life, but neither comes to real expression without the other. So obedience, as Paul insisted, is the way to freedom. It is as if you stood at either pole of our earth and found the other by digging deep enough.[14]

Lest there be any confusion, it must be made clear that for Rall polarity is not merely another word for paradox. Remember, earlier Rall delineated his understanding of the use of paradox. There, in his commenting on Paul, he noted paradox as integral to religious language, but limited its place to form not being, (*supra*, chp. III) Nor does Rall wish to be understood as restating a Hegelian dialectic,

> ...the immanent and unceasing procession, the opposition of thesis and antithesis is constantly being resolved in the unity of the higher synthesis, a proof of which man is the spectator. This is rather the pull of forces remaining in tension, going to constitute that life of man at whose heart is the need of constant decision and action.[15]

The specific polarities are easily purveyed in the terms of individual and social, solitude and action, worship and moral responsibility, permanence and change and a polarity in one's experience of God with awe, reverence and fear on the one hand and fellowship and nearness on the other. Pertinent to his thought, Rall quotes at length from Friedrich Heiler:

> The alternation of childlike speech and mystical silence, of prayer and meditation, of 'Thou' and 'He,' of 'personalism' and 'impersonalism,' gives to the soul's communion with God a constant tension and an inexhaust-

ible fruitfulness. The living God is both *Deus absconditus* and *Deus revelatus*, the God who dwells 'in light inapproachable' and who becomes visible in human form, the impenetrable darkness of mystery and the bright light of revelation, the all-consuming fire of wrath and the helping, saving, self-giving redemptive love. For that reason true communion with God must include the polarity of personalism and impersonalism, and the life of devotion must move back and forth between the confident 'Thou' of prayer and the awed 'He' of contemplation.[16]

The interesting fact to note is a pattern typical of American theologians prior to the decade of the 1940's. Having been highly critical of the historical method as symbolized in the writings of Ernst Troeltsch (*supra*), Rall employs this methodological approach in his attempt to spell out carefully the nature and function of religion in general. Consistent with his earlier criticism of the use of the method as an "olatry," he seeks criteria for his definition and assessment of religion outside the particularities of religion and its own truth claims. His sources include philosophers and social and behavioral scientists with no mention of historians of religion or cultural anthropologists, such as Friedrich Max Muller (1823-1900), E. B. Tylor (1837-1917), and James G. Frazer (1854-1941).[17]

In June of 1925 the American Institute of Sacred Literature issued a trilogy of courses including "The Religion of the Bible," in the teaching of which Professor Rall joined eight other scholars. Here he narrowed his broader concept of the nature and function of religion by looking with specificity at the Bible to test his earlier hypotheses. He began by stating:

> The purpose of this study is not to defend the religion of the Bible, nor even to argue about its value for our day. It is rather to point out what that religion is at

its best, leaving it to the individual student to see what it means for present-day faith and life. For truth here as elsewhere must shine by its own light.[18]

The religion sought in the Bible is that concerned with values. The search arises ever-anew out of the needs of men and rests on the conviction of an unseen world. Indeed, the test of the validity of this unseen world is its absoluteness; i.e., that the man who gives his absolute allegiance is rewarded by the certainty that he has "... found something in which he seeks his highest good, upon which he sets his final hope, and to which he offers his deepest loyalty."[19] Rall then classified Christianity under the headings of Religion as "Faith," Religion as "Fellowship," Religion as "Loyalty" and Religion as "Hope." American theological liberalism of the 1920's, and Rall included, is caricatured as immanental, to the exclusion of any attention to the transcendence of God. Two comments must be made here: there is some validity in the general caricature especially in popular theology, but in specific instances care must be exercised. 1) Rall, here and elsewhere, clearly argues on behalf of a "God who was above," meaning by this a transcendent, or, a Holy Other God of ontological power and moral power and majesty. It is true, he does not dwell upon that otherness, but this might be explained by his Ritschlian framework of value judgment or, as now would be said, existential ultimate concern. 2) Even the very term "immanence" is foreign to many of the theologians of the 1920's. Rall, under review here, shied from employment of the word in his Ritschlian anti-metaphysical position, thinking that its use would shift the context to philosophical and abstract discussion whereon the actor might easily become a spectator. In his discussion of Christianity as a religion of hope, Rall dwells upon the social and individual goals of hope. He judges his immediate theological predecessors as too concerned with inner experiences and matters of the world beyond. Nevertheless, he not only allows for such language, but advocates Spiritual presence as an index of personal hope. He then concludes with an interesting statement on future life. Of particular moment in the quotation is the stress upon grounds for faith and value orientation. The statement nowhere mentions "immanence," although the substance of the doctrine is clearly present, within a Ritschlian context.

What did Jesus bring? And what does the religion of the New Testament offer by way of faith in the life beyond and of grounds for that faith? The ground for their faith may be put in one word — God. These men believed in God, in the living God, in a God revealed in Jesus who called men to be his children. In John 14: I, 2, the answer is very simply given: 'Let not your heart be troubled: believe in God, believe also in me. In my Father's house are many mansions.' In Jesus' reply to the quibbling Sadducees, the same direct appeal is made to God: 'God is not the God of the dead, but of the living,' Matt. 22:23-33. Paul's use of the resurrection of Jesus points the same way. These men were convinced that Jesus had risen from the dead and appeared to many of his disciples. But they did not simply argue that because Jesus had risen, therefore the doctrine of life after death was proven. The resurrection of Jesus meant that God had put his seal upon him: he 'was declared to be the Son of God with power, by the resurrection from the dead,' Rom. I:4. Read I Corinthians 15. It is Jesus as the revelation of God, as the Christ of God, with whom Paul is concerned. The final ground of hope again is the faith in God, the God who raised Christ from the dead, the God who will raise us who are Christ's, the God to whom finally the Son himself with all God's children and all powers shall be subjected, 'that God may be all in all.'

And here we come to the second ground of this

Christian hope in immortality, and that is the Christian idea of man and his value. In Psalm 16, quoted above, there is suggested the idea of the worth of man to God. Jesus makes plain the value God puts upon man. It is not the indestructibility of the soul that counts with the men of the New Testament, not the idea of a soul force that must survive; it is the conviction that man is a being like God, that he is of absolute, value and of worth to God, that God's very Spirit dwells in him. So the idea of the worth of man rests back for its full meaning upon the faith in God, and so in the end it is the faith in God upon which all rests. That is the argument of Tennyson:

> Thou wilt not leave us in the dust:
> Thou madest man, he knows not why,
> He thinks he was not made to die;
> And thou hast made him — thou art just.[20]

Christianity, In Particular

In 1927, an exchange lectureship occurred between three leading Protestant theological schools of Chicago and Hebrew Union College of Cincinnati. These lectures were published in a compact volume containing the initial efforts of the exchange, and included the following articles: "The Meaning of Christianity" by Harris Franklin Rall and "What Is Judaism?" by Samuel S. Cohen. There appears little scandal in Rall's lecture and much continuity with what Cohen claims to be the essence of Reformed Judaism. Christianity is not to be seen selectively according to any "so-called theology of the New Testament, whether John or Paul" (*supra*) but is to be viewed as the community of those effected by the light of the eternal or, to quote Rall, those common people "with a new sense of the divine." The heart of Christianity is that new experience of the eternal that Jesus encountered and passed to his followers. Later we will consider separately those common bonds uniting Christianity: a God of trust, a way of life, a means of help, a substance of hope. In that year of the Scopes trial, Rall could list the two great Christian convictions as that of loving God (built upon the Old Testament) and God as Indwelling Spirit. Curiously enough, after concluding some words on the ethical test of the Spirit's presence and making curt comments on what he was want to call "institutionalized religion," he makes approving, albeit oblique, remarks about church renewal. Is he speaking of "continental theology?"

> There were, of course, always groups within Christianity who appreciated this doctrine in its vital and inner meaning, and there are indications of a larger appreciation of it today. Several influences are cooperating to this end. Perhaps the most important is the new appreciation of religion on the divine side, of religion as that which is given to men. We have watched in the last generation or two the persistent and very necessary attempt to ethicize and socialize religion, to interpret it in terms of conduct and of individual and social responsibility. This is the 'activistic' side of our religion which some critics consider the significant aspect especially of the Christian churches of America. There is a growing realization, however, that, necessary though this expression of religion is, religion itself must find its source and power in the life that is given of God. The increasing interest in mysticism points in the same direction, as does also the growing appreciation of the importance of worship, especially in those Protestant churches that have laid the emphasis upon expressional activities. These needs and interests are met by the Christian idea of the Spirit as expressing the conviction that God is not simply the being to be believed in and served and

obeyed, but that he is the strength by which we live, the very life of our life, the indwelling presence.[21]

Is Christianity absolute, is it final? Rall declares that the answer to these questions is *sic et non*. The former is affirmative in that Jesus made upon men an absolute demand because he brought absolute reality. (It is not true, of course, that God could act absolutely in history without regard for man's appropriation; i.e., the divine must always be relative to man's stage of development, to his response.) Christianity is not final, for within Rall's operational definition of religion,

> If God be one, everywhere seeking to reveal and give himself to men, and if man be one, everywhere the same in his fundamental needs, then we should expect analogies in all religions, common ideas such as those of revelation, salvation, sacrifice and communion with the divine.[22]

The question begs of an answer to the fundamental question of the significance and originality of Jesus. It is quite clear that for Rall the type of measurement can only be that of ethical impact of his life upon the early disciples. Futile is the attempt to locate originality in his teachings or even his editorializing of existing Jewish prophetic teachings, but rather originality is to be found in his teaching of great concepts in their simplicity, unity, thoroughgoing ethical character, and universality of appeal. For example, the heart of the Christian faith is his idea of God.

> It is no conclusion of philosophy, to be overturned some time when its premises are shown false. It is no inheritance of tradition unthinkingly accepted. It is a faith that dares to believe that the highest that man knows is supreme in the universe, and that man

must live in the light of that highest. His God is transcendent in power and goodness, calling men to reverence and awe; he is immanent as the ever-working God of redeeming love, calling men to trust and surrender. He is personal and man may have fellowship with him; yet the center of religion is never man but always God, always the God that is above man, the power to be trusted, the good that summons to obedience and calls to achievement. Supremely significant is his idea of God as redemptive good will.[23]

Rall continues to suggest that rather than understanding the uniqueness of Jesus in terms of discontinuity with Judaism, the reader should see him as Irenaeus portrayed him, "He brought all newness in bringing himself."[24] He suggests further that the modern theory of emergent evolution offers a suggestive idea of life consisting of the development of making new wholes, where elements are joined together to form a new unity, not by mere addition, but in such a manner a new and higher life appears which analysis of individual parts could never have suggested. In similar fashion, Christianity can be seen as a greater creative synthesis with the personality of Jesus as its abiding and creative center. Jesus saw for himself the truth of God, then it came to expression in his own life and then in the life of his followers. His originality rested on his living this truth of God and imparting it to his disciples. Rall completes his thinking with a quotation from the renowned German Biblical scholar, Professor Julius Wellhausen of the University of Göttingen.

'The Jewish scholars,' Wellhausen once commented, 'say that everything that Jesus says is in the Talmud. Yes, everything, and much more besides. How did he manage to take the true and the ethical out of this rubbish heap of legal scholasticism? Why did no one else do it?'[25]

The unity of his message, and then the unity of word and life in his person, overwhelmed the few surrounding him, and he, through their retelling of his power, became the dynamic, creative force of this new way of life. Saying this, however, does not preclude the fact that from him did emanate a religious force that transformed religion from ceremonialism and institutionalization to a living, creative moral force. "The religion of Jesus is for man as man."[26]

The underlying concept of this religion "for man as man" was Jesus' idea of God. Additionally, Jesus saw man filled with ultimate possibilities toward good; therefore every man was sacred in his being a human and not because, as Stoicism held, of powers of intellect. He believed in man, and,

> in his reverence for humanity, in his passion for justice, in his faith in men, in his summons to a common service for a common weal, Jesus is the deepest spring of the best that we mean by democracy. The teaching of Jesus is the foundation of the highest social idealism of our day.[27]

The goal of his teaching — he offers fulfillment for all the needs and hopes of men, he holds up a social hope, he includes the life beyond — has been challenged as to its originality and uniqueness. Was it not a mere variant of the religious movements of the day, notably, the mystery cults? Certain commonalities raise the question: the evil of life, a longing for deliverance, faith in some deity, and a need of a hero-God who died and rose to life again. That which contrasted Christianity from being another mystery cult, according to Rall, was its insistence (1) upon a stark monotheism, *i.e.*, Jesus was not a hero-God, but one through whom the living God had come to men; he did not seek worship of himself; (2) that Jesus was a historical being; (3) of the ethical superiority which is a central demand of Christianity. If, Rall suggests, finality is to be found in other-than-life-situations, in creeds, in institutions, in ceremonies, Christianty can never be elevated as the final religion. If, on the other hand, finality is to be understood in terms of life and its character of man always being in the situation of making decisions, and that in these decisions he always seeks the highest as he best understands it, then Christianity represents definite and final insights in religion. Of course finality thusly described, encourages growth in the understanding of these insights and is hence ever open-ended. "The finality of Christ and of what he imparts," says H. R. Mackintosh, 'can justly be called in question only when a loftier fact than holy love has come into view."[28]

In the 1930's, two facts confronted Christian theologians causing them to rethink the particularities of Christianity: the re-thinking of the missionary endeavors of the Church and the call to Christian unity. Symbolic of the former was the experience of Edwin Lewis, Professor of Systematic Theology at Drew Theological Seminary of the Methodist Church. Until the 1930's, Lewis' theology was best exemplified as dependent upon British Idealism connected with the name of Seth Pringle-Pattison.[29] Throughout the 1920's Lewis wrote with a singular idealistic philosophical context. In 1926-29 he worked intensively as editor of the *Abingdon Bible Commentary*.[30] He states that he literally ate and slept with the Bible. In his work as editor he read many of the manuscripts, did all of the proof reading, checked all Scriptural references, prepared the index of forty-two two-column pages. This involvement in the Scriptural records was the initial turning point in Lewis' thinking. He forcefully came to see that "The Creator appeared as the Redeemer." If this was true, and he felt it must be or else one finds himself in the midst of the confusion of naturalism, it could be only by revelation. "Creation and the incarnation are alike acts of God, and each has its meaning, but we know the act and we know the meaning because, and only because, they have been *disclosed* to us."³¹

The first publication by Lewis after this discovery of the centrality of revelation was *God and Ourselves* in 1931. This was a summary of prevailing naturalism which proffered little place for Christian revelation. In this book Lewis brought under criticism all such naturalism but does not radically emerge as a champion of the exclusiveness of Christian revelation initiating solely from God and finding response of faith in man. He spoke continually of the co-operative endeavor of revelation as man's discovery and God's initiation. "All that we mean by civilization, and eventually by the kingdom of God, is but the exhibition of this cooperative principle on an ever-widening scale."³² In his defense of theism, he dwelt at length on the sovereignty of God as the most rational and ethical justification for belief in God. He listed the following men as those who had not yet bowed to Rimmon: Hocking, Sorley, Temple, Inge, Pringle-Pattison, Knudson, Leighton, Streeter, Lyman, Heim, Barth, A. E. Taylor.

The final break with his past came for Lewis in April, 1933, in his review of *Rethinking Missions*, edited by W. E. Hocking. The book, a composite work of laymen representing seven denominations, reviewed the waning mission program of the Church. The motive of missionary endeavor, as set forth by the Commissioners, was to seek with other people a fuller knowledge of the love of God, expressed in those principles learned through Jesus Christ, and compounded with those elements in the non-Christian religions which were in kindred with the teachings of Jesus. The centrality of Christ was affirmed by the fact that his life was supremely given to manifesting the true meaning of religion in the midst of the severest tests.

> The essence of the law he states in the two great commandments; the essence of right conduct in the Golden Rule, the essence of prayer in the Lord's Prayer; the

essence of theology in the picture of God as Father; the essence of the social ideal in the vision of the Kingdom of Heaven among men.³³

Lewis stated that his personal admiration for Hocking still did not prevent him from attacking the book. "The threads that were still binding me to my former compromises were broken — not without some sadness of farewell — and I went a way I could no longer evade."³⁴ Lewis' attack centered not upon what was denied by the Commissioners but what was omitted by them. He understood them to state that Christianity was but one among many religions but with superlative features, "but in nowise entitled to claim or to practice absoluteness or exclusiveness: rather, while it has something to give, it must also be willing to receive...".³⁵ Lewis railed against this casuistic approach and argued for the absolute claim of the Christian evangel, insisting that such a claim was not mere rhetoric, but of the very substance of the essence of Christianity. He envisioned the goal of the Christian mission as bringing to commitment those without the pale of Christ. In one bit of oratorical flair, he sets in juxtaposition the omissions of the report and the clear understanding of the New Testament. His first pronouncement of his belief in the centrality of revelation of God in Jesus Christ — without arguing its truth or falsity — was:

> But, after all, the claim that in Jesus Christ God did something that he had never done anywhere else, and that what he did unites with an aggressive divine grace on the one hand and the tragedy of human sin on the other hand, and that Jesus Christ was not simply a supremely religious man and the first Christian but rather a fresh and original manifestation of the Creative will, so that yesterday, today, and forever he is *the Lord of Christians* because he is the means of their deepest experience, and that it is through him alone

that God purposes — and has eternally purposed — to reconcile all men to himself, meaning, to achieve the complete divine-human unity — this claim is not merely a matter of formal literary expression, but it is of the very substance or essence of Christianity.[36]

Harris Franklin Rall also sensed the necessity of rethinking the mission of the Church and reflected on one aspect of this, the authority of the Christian faith. In January, 1940, the same year of publication as *Christianity*, but written years after that book as *Christianity* consisted basically of the Nathaniel W. Taylor Lectures on *Some Studies in Religion* delivered at Yale University in 1931, he asked:

Just what is this authority that we claim? To what does it belong? With what right does it challenge these other claimants to man's allegiance and what is our attitude toward other religions?[37]

Rall discounts the possibility of a religion without authority, in this context at least, yet raises again a question to which we have already addressed ourselves, namely, the relation of history and faith. Granted the constitutive factor in religion is God, who commands our reverence and requires our obedience, then absolute authority rests only with Him.

When we preach to men it is in order to present God. The decision we invite is for God. It is God in whom we ask men to believe, not our Church nor our system of doctrine. We speak to men only because He has spoken to us and because we believe we have a message from Him that has come through His revelation in Jesus Christ.[38]

However, the problem emerges in the recognition of the human element which appears necessarily at every point where the more-than-human appears, namely, the historic revelation in Jesus Christ, the Scriptures which convey this revelation to men and the church through which the word flows. Just what is the significance of this human side that necessarily accompanies revelation? Rall outlines the three common responses: relativism, absolutism, and what he calls prophetic religion, or the inclusion and emphasis of both the human and divine sides of revelation. What is of special interest here is his implied criterion of judgment in his criticism of the absolutism of "Continental Theology," with reference to Karl Barth and specifically to Dr. Henrik Kraemer, whose book *The Christian Message in a Non-Christian World*, prepared the delegates for the ecumenical conference at Madras.[39] Barth, it will be recalled, holds that the revelation of Christ is the Christian supreme standard of reference but also other religions are to be characterized by *Unglaube*, unbelief. "They are 'not response but resistance.' They are 'overt or covert endeavors toward self-justification, self-sanctification and self-redemption.' "[40]

At the heart of the matter are, once again, the criteria of religion — how does one define them, with whom is one dealing fundamentally as *homo religiosus?* Kraemer puts the issue:

> Is our standard of reference (our authority) to be a general idea about the essence of religion, or are we to 'derive our idea of what religion really is or ought to be from the revelation in Christ?'[41]

Rall indicates his rejection of Kraemer's selection of the latter alternative along two lines: he questions Kraemer's source of judgment and his valuation of the source of Christian theology.

> As to Kraemer's own position, two questions need to be raised. First, is it not determined in the end less by the facts regarding what we actually find outside the

Hebrew-Christian succession than by the theological point of view shared with Barth, which so conceives God and man and the strict discontinuity between human and divine that all revelation is by a one-way road from God to man, in which human search and aspiration and insight have no real place; and that all man's ideas and aspirations outside Christianity are merely human, and therefore cannot represent truth or have moral or spiritual value? Must not the basic question be raised as to how we are to think of God and of His way with man in revelation and redemption?

The second question concerns the 'standard of reference,' that is, the seat of authority. Here we must distinguish between the revelation in Christ and the form in which the Church interprets and presents this. For Barth this word of God to man becomes in effect a hard-and fast theological system of a particular type. Kraemer presents it is 'biblical realism' and interprets this in a form that is more widely acceptable. But the facts must be faced that even so simple a formulation as Kraemer's is nevertheless a human interpretation, that others would frame the statement differently and that we cannot assume that any interpretation can be simply presented as the authoritative revelation. Whatever difficulty it affords our apologetic, we must realize that every Christian presentation, every specification of just what the 'standard of reference' is, involves a human element and therefore an element of the relative.[42]

Rall here is exercising an historical method approach of selecting common elements among the several religious options. There is nothing in this quotation to indicate that such a theological position is an erroneous biblical interpretation or even that it is incongruent to the church's understanding. The standard of reference, or seat of authority, is also scored as "biblical realism" which, although presumed by Kraemer to be common property of Christians, can be questioned as to its presumption (according to Rall) of the status of divine *ipissima verba*. On the contrary, Rall argues that *every* presentation of *every* specification of a standard of reference is unconditionally conditioned by the human element. It would seem that Rall misses Kraemer's (and Barth's) thrust when he says,

> Perhaps we shall then be more ready to find in non-Christian religions and in the lives of saints in non-Christian enviroment, together with the human and errant and sinful, some working of God seen in truth and righteousness.[43]

Kraemer would undoubtedly reply in question, what is the criterion of "human," "errant," "sinful," "truth" and "righteousness."

Methodism

The second event forcing theologians to reconsider their views was that of Christian unity and ecumenism. If the decades of the late nineteenth century and early twentieth century are to be noted as the beginning times of the study of comparative religions, the middecades of the twentieth century are to be noted as the beginning times of the study of Church unity. In order to so enter discussion on "one faith, one Lord, one baptism," theologians had first to review that which set them apart. Such a task was not a new one for Harris Franklin Rall. As early as 1910 he addressed the 125th anniversary of the organization of American Methodism, meeting in First Methodist Episcopal Church, Baltimore, of which Rall was pastor. He spoke more to the obligations lying ahead for Methodism while acknowledging the greatness of her heritage and her impact on the present times. What he calls the Creed of Methodism is not any formal utterance, but an answer to the broad question, "What is the Christian religion? What is the Christian religion for Methodism? It may be summed up in this phrase: a historic gospel, realized in experience and expressed in life."[44] The expression of life has been the positive emphasis of Methodism in at least three ways: in constant fellowship with God, in holiness, and in service, "and the modern spirit which tests religion by what it does for men has had no greater exponent than John Wesley."[45] In accordance with this last emphasis, Rall takes pride to note that just two years prior to that in that same city the General Conference of the Methodist Church adopted its social creed.[46]

Methodism, including John Wesley, was never anti-doctrinal, but rather forced the doctrine to assist matters of experience and faith.

> Wesley's conception of Christianity was as intensely ethical as it was religious. But of Wesley's emphasis on holiness, either on the religious or the practical side, there is no suggestion here. Specific illustration will make the comparison more plain. It is not enough, with the Articles, to speak of infinite power, wisdom, and goodness, of unity and Trinity. What Methodism proclaimed to men was the heavenly Father, holy and loving, offering to all men his grace in forgiveness and in the fellowship of a holy life. Methodism had no doubt as to the divinity of Christ. But its supreme faith is not expressed in a definition concerning one substance and two natures, but in the thought of him who reconciled them to God, their Saviour from sin, the Lord of their life. Methodism believed in the Holy Spirit, but its concern was not so much in any question of *filioque* as in the witness of the Spirit and his presence as the power of a new life. It had a message that convicted men of sin, but its deep sense of man's responsibility and freedom and the guilt of sin which rejects the love of God finds no expression in the Ar-

ticles on free will, or original sin, or sin after justification. The Article of the church speaks of doctrine and order, 'the pure word of God' and 'the sacraments duly administered,' but there is nothing here of that practical faith of Methodism for which the church was a spiritual fellowship and a missionary force.[47]

The immediate cause of this article "Do We Need a Methodist Creed?" was the proposal at the Methodist Episcopal Church, South, General Conference for the formation of a new Methodist Creed. Rall favored the adoption of same, hoping that it would always express the faith in "the living God redeeming the world in Jesus Christ."

Let it be said again, the proposal is not that of a new legal standard to be used as a club over the heads of men. And let us ask soberly, in this day when we are turning more and more to essentials and away from dogmatic omniscience in lesser things, when other churches are striving to cast off inherited burdens, is there any real danger that the Methodist Church, expressing its simple, spiritual, evangelical faith, should lead us back to bondage or to persecution? As for an era of strife, look at the free churches of England, Calvinistic and Arminian, Baptist, Methodist, and the rest, agreeing on a common catechism. Look at Methodism, Presbyterianism, and Congregationalism in Canada adopting a common confession. Does it seem that in the single family of Methodism we could not agree without strife upon the essentials which we have preached and by which we have lived all these years?[48]

As to its contents, he offers,

What the character of such a creed should be has already been suggested. It should be positive. We want no polemic here against Roman Catholicism or Calvinism. It should be modern, speaking the timeless truth in the language of the day. It should be evangelical, expressing that conception of Christianity as a gospel of redemption for which our church has stood. It should be vital, the creed of a religion of experience and life. It should be ethical, true to the spirit of our founder in setting forth Christianity as holiness in life and faithfulness in service. It should be simple and brief, for it is to be not a theologian's system, but the servant of the life of the church. It should not be speculative nor intellectualistic, for it should express Christianity as that which can be appropriated by faith, experienced in the heart, and manifested in obedience of life. It will be a Methodist creed, not controversially or narrowly, but only as Methodism expresses the truth of our common Christian faith. And so it will be a catholic creed. Finally, it should express those truths which the Spirit has taught us for the needs of these days: life as a stewardship as well as a probation; the meaning of brotherhood in life for those who say 'Our Father' in prayer; the character of the church as an instrument of the kingdom of God, and its missionary calling at home and abroad.[49]

Some fifteen years later, Rall more thoughtfully spelled out what he understood as "The Methodist Theology." In an article in *The Methodist Quarterly Review* of 1925, Rall delineated the historic position of Methodist theology, assigning its unique significance to John Wesley's conception of religion itself. Rall denoted Roman Catholicism as a doctrine of the church, Calvinism as a doctrine of God, and Methodism as a doctrine of religion. He proclaimed Methodism's unique note to be the revival of the "central question that has come to the fore at every great religious epoch, not the question of this doctrine or that point of ritual or organization, but of the nature of religion itself, of the true relation of man and God."⁵⁰ The uniqueness of Methodism was its stress on the individual over the institutional and on righteousness over ritual. Rall cited precedence for this in the prophets, Jesus, Paul, Augustine, and Luther. He then summarized Wesley's conception of religion as follows: "Religion is man's life in personal fellowship with God, known in conscious experience, received by the grace of God through his Spirit, lived in holiness of life and especially in that spirit of love which forms the Christian fellowship and issues in Christian service."⁵¹

Rall stated that in this conception of religion one finds not only the distinctive notes of the Methodist heritage, but also the bases for a continuing Methodist theology: free grace, religion as conscious experience, and an emphasis upon moral living.

But John Wesley did not forego other elements in religion. It is rather that the institutional (was there ever a better organizer than Wesley?), the doctrinal (his sermons, authoritative for Methodists, often deal with doctrinal themes), the ritual (he deplored the total lack thereof by American colonial Methodism) were secondary to his emphasis.

> Religion is 'no other than love; the love of God and of all mankind; the loving God with all our heart and soul and strength, . . . and the loving every soul which God hath made' (V. 6. The references given are all to volume and page in the familiar seven-volume edition of the Works). Religion 'is no other than the mind that was in Christ . . . wrought in us . . . by the power of the Holy Ghost' (VII, 315). First Corinthians 13, he declares, contains the whole of the religions (II, 279). Christianity is the system that describes this character as in 1 Corinthians 13 and the Sermon on the Mount, and tells how we may attain it (V, 756). Into the fellowship of his societies Wesley welcomes Anglicans, Calvinists, Quakers, and Roman Catholics.

> The acceptance of doctrines is not decisive. 'A man may assent to three or three and twenty creeds, . . . and yet have no Christian faith at all' (V. 757). Neither do wrong opinions disqualify a man. 'For opinions or terms, let us not destroy the work of God. Dost thou love and serve God? It is enough' (V, 245). 'To believe is, then, to walk in the light of eternity; and to have a clear sight of, and confidence in, the Most High, reconciled to me through the Son of his love' (V, 757).[52]

This definition alone can provide a basis for any Methodist theology.

> Here is the free grace which Methodism preached, for this religion is a life which God freely offers to all. Here is involved its emphasis on religion as a conscious experience, for this life is given to us through the indwelling Spirit of God and so is known by us as such. The moral emphasis is here, the summons to holiness which made Methodism a revival of Puritanism; for who can have fellowship with a righteous and loving God, or receive his Holy Spirit, except as he shares and lives God's own life of righteousness and love? But while Wesley emphasizes holiness constantly in terms of plain love and service and good works, the other side is equally present in his idea of religion. Religion is a moral fellowship which we must live out, but it is at the same time one that God bestows. Religion and ethics are both here and are one. Wesley agreed with Augustine: 'Command what thou wilst, and give what thou commandest.'[53]

Although Methodism, and Wesley never developed a systematic theological system, and hence, one can never say, "*This is* Methodist Theology!," Rall does see many distinctive emphasis following from such an understanding of religion. First, the idea of God. The Calvinistic conception of God was primarily one of power with one outcome from that theology dealing with divine decrees and irresistible power. Methodism, according to Rall, did not abscond this power, but insisted that the *character* of God was the substantive issue rather than his sheer being. The relation between God and man thus became primarily ethical and personal and free, the relation of Father and son.[54]

Another shift is traceable in anthropology. Man in Calvinistic theology was portrayed as totally depraved, to be saved only if predestined and elected by a sovereign God. Rall suggested that Methodist theology implied a man who could respond to the call of God with his free choice and who could receive the help of God in free *moral* fellowship. There came from Wesley, also, a new concept of Christian experience and life, a concept Augustinian throughout, insisting that man is utterly dependent upon God for all is a gift from God, including religion. So Wesley taught clearly that holiness and perfection were requisite of the one called Christian.[55]

Rall prophesied the direction future Methodist theology would go: the emphasis on the personal and ethical makes it natural for Methodist theology to move toward a more democratic view of God, ". . . with a stress on immanence while remaining far from pantheism."[56] Methodist theology would join in the then new movement of religious education.

> Conceive it as you will — prevenient grace, the work of the Holy Spirit, the benefits of a universal atonement — the only childhood we know is one in which God is present by his Spirit from the beginning, in which there are impulses and capacities to which we may appear in our work of Christian nurture.[57]

Methodist theology, with its conception of man, was in a

position to welcome any new light on the nature of man, especially from biology and psychology. Their insistence on the plasticity of human nature could be joined to the Methodist insistence upon the transformed moral person. The same can be said in that area of particular concern in 1925: evolution and theology. Rall concludes that the juxtaposition of a verbally inspired writing and scientific discovery was unfortunate and suggested an answer that the former be discarded in favor of

> ... a living God of mercy and righteousness whom the Bible brings to us, and it is the life of personal fellowship with his in likeness of spirit [that is to be sought]. It is enough that the Bible brings us this God and that we know him.[58]

Let us then turn to evolution and science for more understandings!

In considering Methodist theology, this paper has endeavored to interpret the spirit of Methodism rather than to make the traditions of the past a hard-and-fast rule for today. There is a danger here which was pointed out effectively by Bishop Hoss at the Ecumenical Conference of 1901. 'If Mr. Wesley could know the extent to which many of his followers have fallen into the habit of repeating the *ipissima verba* of his teachings as if they were a final and conclusive statement of the truth, he would turn over in his grave and groan; for he himself, far from being the slave of traditions, was the freest and boldest mind of his generation.' The Methodist theology of tomorrow will be open to the truth. We may need Wesley's spirit here: 'In our first Conference it was agreed to examine every point from the foundation. Have we not been somewhat fearful in doing this? What were we afraid of? Of overturning our first principles? Whoever was afraid of that, it was a vain fear. If they are true, they will bear the strictest examination. If they are false, the sooner they are overturned the better. Let us all pray for a willingness to receive the light.' This Methodist theology will lay stress upon the abiding presence of that Spirit of God who did not cease to guide his Church when the apostles or Church fathers passed away. It will remain a theology based upon the historic faith, upon the great conviction of Christianity that God has come to men for life and salvation in Jesus Christ; but it will do so in the freedom of the faith, the freedom that rests back upon inner conviction, that understands and proves by the experience of life, that knows but one truth, the truth of God, and welcomes it from every source. With such a theology, vital, experiential, Christian, holding up before the world the moral demand as well as the religious promise that is in Christ, the Methodist Church through its thinking, instead of emphasizing division, may help to promote that oneness of faith and life which the body of Christ to sorely needs in this day.[59]

CHAPTER V

THEOLOGY AND TRINITY

"'Today there is but one religious dogma in debate,' says Professor Whitehead; 'and that is what you mean by 'God'. This is the fundamental religious dogma.'"[1]

Throughout his long teaching career, Rall insisted that the doctrine of God was integral to his definition of religion; i.e., *homo religiosos,* man as a religious being, seeks out a Power greater than he before which he responds in satisfaction of his basic needs. Rall's theology must be viewed in two rather distinct classifications: that dealing with *character* of God and that dealing with the *being* of God in relation to the world.

The Character of God

In the Yale lectures of 1900, Rall carefully chooses his words to insist upon the knowledge of God in the development of a relationship with him through Jesus Christ.

> The heart of Christianity, as I suggested above, does not lie in the general idea of a Supreme Being, who is spirit and all-power, nor in the abstract idea of freedom, nor in the thought of immortality as mere persistence of conscious being. The supreme thing for Christianity is the character under which God comes to us, and the purpose which reveals that character. (In what I add here I leave Ritschl). You may philosophize about a Creator all-powerful as the great First Cause, or deduce an intelligent World-ground

from a teleological consideration of Nature. But all these can never give you that to which the Christian faith clings, the God of loving grace who comes to us in Christ. Nor can mere general considerations, whether of natural theology or of philosophy, ever lead us to that conception of religion as redemptive which is given us in Christ.[2]

Rall, later in the lecture, specifies that two central affirmations buttress the Christian religion: the individual and social aspects of the positive historical revelation in Christ. Writing about the former, he insists that the heart of religion not to be an *idea* about God, no matter how lofty, but a *relation* to God which implies such an idea. Indeed, Christ did not teach man about God, but leads men into a "right relation to God."

> In him we see the righteousness of holy love, and he brings us to a real consciousness of our sin and guilt. In him we see the loving grace of God and receive the forgiveness of our sins. Through him we learn to make this trusting faith our life attitude. We not only gain from him the ideal of life, but in the personal relation to him of loving trust we find the power for that life. And finally, in that loving appropriation of his will for our life we know ourselves one with the Father, and from this standpoint, and this alone, we gain the faith in the Providence that orders our life in itself and in its relation to the world. For the Christian, it is Christ that mediates this life, and always will.[3]

The other aspect central to Christian revelation is that God has a social as well as an individual purpose for man. (Cf. below for a fuller statement on ethics.)

> This social purpose is connected with the terms church and kingdom, and both are positive, historical reali-

ties. Here again we find that Christianity is not a matter of certain general ideas about God, but is bound to that which is historical. Here again we must say, in Christianity God is known through his purpose and through what he does. This kingdom and church Jesus established and his disciples carried out his thought. And the revelation of God through this purpose and this work makes this historical record of abiding significance for us.[4]

The immediate context of these university lectures must here be noted in order to more adequatly assess the impact and the importance of Rall's judgments. Several studies delineate marked emphases in theological interpretation in the United States in the latter decades of the nineteenth and beginning decades of the twentieth century.[5] Peace was made. Increasingly, American theologians believed that the heritage they had received and out of which they attempted to speak to a world now constructed on the results of modern physical science and modern historical study, no longer proved adequate either in its kerygmatic or apologetic function. The situation would be better described as anomie rather than animus. Secular and scientific man listened no longer. Peace was made through theological accommodation, as Langdon describes the times, ". . . because both the *basis* of traditional doctrines and the *content* of these doctrines seemed incredible to the intelligentsia of that age."[6] The former, the basis of the doctrines, had been tied to the infallible inspiration of the Bible. With the emergence of scientific investigations that repudiated certain fundamentals (e.g. the dating of the earth's beginnings), came the shift of warrant from the absolute authority of Scripture to some present facet of contemporary experience — rational inquiry, religious experience, or moral experience — and the gradual disappearance of traditional doctrines that contradicted the shape of that contemporary experience.[7]

In like fashion, liberal theology adjusted its content accordingly from themes of divine transcendence, human depravity, and miraculous revelation and salvation to themes of reality as singly immanent, and man's nature and destiny one with evolutionary process of development over time from relative chaos to the contemporary higher forms of life and culture. "The divine force, said liberal theology, whose immanent work in the process has brought about such progress toward higher, more coherent, more adoptive, and more moral goals, is what men have called God. . ."[8]

William Newton Clarke and Olin Curtis, the latter representative of the American Methodist theological heritage that also buoyed Rall, provide substantial indices of American theological liberalism. Clarke, Professor of Christian Theology at Colgate University, published in 1898 his very influential book, *An Outline of Christian Theology*. Interestingly, his prolegomena establishes theological teachings through revelation made in life and action, not in writing. Further, the self-revelation of God is complete only insofar as it becomes effective in individual men and ". . . in the larger life of man, else God would not be actually known by means of it, and it would miss the aim of revelation."[9]

Olin Curtis, Professor of Christian Theology at The Drew Theological Seminary, acknowledged his indebtedness to four men who had formed his theology: (1) Dr. Daniel Whedon, for his insistence "beyond possible doubt" that the necessitarian has no case in ethics, and almost no case in Psychology; (2) Thomas Carlyle, who compelled him to appreciate the ethical appeal of the prophets of the Old Testament; (3) Professor Borden Parker Bowe, who led him to see the cosmic significance of personality; and, (4) Bishop Martensen, who started his present conception of the organism of Christian doctrine.[10] Curtis subsequently develops this organism from a lengthy, nearly two hundred pages, prolegomena to dogmatic theology whose contents of Man and The Christian Religion resound off the foci of man as a responsible moral person and racial solidarity.[11]

No single aspect of the character of God better labels liberalism than belief in "the Fatherhood of God and the Brotherhood of Man." The following excerpts reflect in substance such a view of the first part of that phrase.

> That God must be the great servant of the universe is evident as soon as we remember that from him proceed all the wisdom, power, love, and patience that it needs or has ever needed. . . The universal Sovereign is the universal servant, and if he ceased to serve the universe would cease to be. . . But the truest name for God in his relation to his creatures is Father, . . . Transmission of life is the best human analogue of creating, and God's feeling toward his creation is best represented by that of a parent. . . If his creatures are responsive and obedient, his helpful and educative care is ever with them to lead them to their destiny of likeness to himself. If they are disobedient, and so misuse his gift of freedom as to practice moral evil, which he hates, still he unchangingly holds toward them the attitude of a true Father.[12]

> It is not worth the cost to take sides on the question whether or not the doctrine of the Fatherhood of God is taught in the Old Testament. . . Nor is it worth our time to try to analyze the New Testament doctrine of the divine Fatherhood to bring out exactly all the elements in their perfect combination. . . . The one thing essential to us in this discussion, however, stands out very clearly in the New Testament. That one essential thing is this: *God loves men as a perfect father loves his children.* The last word of revelation is not that God is a moral sovereign, but that he is a sovereign Father. Mr. Lidgett's phrase is an exceedingly happy one— God is 'the Father regnant.'[13]

Harris Franklin Rall evidenced awareness of such a designation of God as Father, and both chastised loose use of it and defended its appropriateness. He acknowledged an identifiable "easy-going, optimistic theology," which assumed that the fundamental truths of Christianity were really a matter of course, "resting on general considerations, and that they may be gained by a little study of biological evolution or comparative religion or philosophy."[14] Such an approach, in its superficial logic, cannot yield what constituted the heart of the Christian faith. Such shallowness also prevailed relevant to theology.

> There is a certain shallow and false conception much prevalent today which minimizes this relation to Christ and the abiding significance of this positive revelation. The favorite word with this conception is that of Fatherhood. Its falseness lies in this, that it assumes this conception as a matter of course. It is the new natural theology. It takes the natural relation of father and child, adds infinity, and assumes that it has God. For this reason, too, it is a shallow conception because it makes the human relation the standard for its conception of God.[15]

Rall almost appears to direct his criticism directly at Clarke and Curtis as he continues:

> A magnified human relation cannot give us the Christian God. It is not enough to analyze the contents of the relation of the human father and son. If you will look at the current conception of Fatherhood in this type of theology, you will find that the two points of emphasis are the naturalistic and the sentimental. By the former term I mean that the relation of man to God is conceived as being primarily and fundamentally a naturalistic fact, like the relation of the father to his progeny. From this quarter comes the insistent

cry, that all men are by nature sons of God, and do not first need to become sons, and the appeal is also made to the human relation in its physical aspect. Is it not time that we recognized the fact in this controversy, that we have been doing a large amount of beating of the air? Men have failed to see that this is a figurative conception of God, and that under this figure we may mean various things. I know that I am contradicting a very prevalent conception. Thus Dr. Gladden, in a recent article, insists that every other conception of God is figurative, that of Fatherhood alone represents the literal and actual reality. A little reflection should convince to the contrary. What is the fundamental relation in the fact of earthly fatherhood? It is that of procreation. What is implied in this fact of procreation? In sonship a certain natural likeness to the father, both physical and psychological, but this likeness is naturalistic, not ethical or spiritual. What is implied in fatherhood? Nothing necessarily, further than the giving of physical existence. This is the one thing that is essential in fatherhood, simple paternity; the ideal and ethical factors may be lacking. When we go beyond this, then we simply have our current ethical ideals to give the higher content to the conception.

Now wherein does our sonship with God consist? Certainly not primarily in the fact that he gave us physical life. *That* he gave to the beast of the field. Christ taught the world that sonship meant in his person as well as in his teachings of the Father. Men called themselves sons of the gods before, but it was conceived in this same naturalistic way. Christ showed us that sonship is a moral and spiritual relation. I and my Father are one, one in purpose of holy life and service, one in holy love. Not the physical relation, nor the potential possibility constitutes sonship in this truest sense. Not the physical relation, nor the term, and this we do, but it is simply using it in a further figurative sense.

A further error in this new natural theology, which assumes that the idea of God as Father is to be gained merely from the human relation and taken as a literal thing, is its sentimentalistic character. It is really a part of the naturalistic conception. What is most prominent in the attitude of the father toward his son? It is natural affection. I know it will be denied theoretically, but the modern conception of the divine Fatherhood practically makes dominant for the nature of God this idea of natural affection, and to this its weakness and sentimentality are due.

Now I have had no intention of denying here the importance of this conception of Fatherhood for our knowledge of God. I simply wish to point out that as theologians we need to recognize two facts, first, that this highest and truest word that we can use is still a figurative expression, and second that the true content and meaning of this expression must be gained from Christ. The Father God whom the Christian knows is the Father of our Lord Jesus Christ. Through him, not through any natural theology or general considerations, have we learned to call God Father, and through him must we realize what this means. And so against this new natural theology, I insist on the abiding significance for us of the revelation in Christ.[16]

The appropriateness of designating God as "Father" is discussed by Rall within the context of his thought cited earlier in this chapter. The knowledge of God comes only through a relationship with Jesus Christ, who reveals the character of God.

No mere general reasonings can yield its rich and vital content — no philosophy of nature, nor of ethics, nor of mind. When we contrast the philosophy of the ages preceding with the gospel of Christ, we too must say, 'the world by wisdom knew not God'. Here is no abstract conception, no mere Platonic transcendental idea of the beautiful and the good. It is a new life that Jesus brings. He brings it in his own person, as he lives it before men, and he mediates it through his person as the living Lord of men. In his holiness men see the holiness of God and their own sin. In that vision conscience is quickened and guilt makes its heavy burden felt. In his loving grace there appears the God of grace and love. He shows men the forgiving God and makes faith in that God possible for them. He leads them thus into the life of loving trust and obedience, with its faith in God's care, with its will to do God's will, and with the inspiration and the power to lead out the new life and character whose ideal he sets forth in word and work.

This is the reality of the Christian faith. But all this is rich and manifold and concrete as only life itself can be. No one word can express this life. No one phrase can set forth the thought of God here contained. The best word is that of Jesus, Father. But what that word is we know in this experience. The Fatherhood is not an abstract idea that we bring to this experience. It is the name for a rich and positive and living reality, the God of love and grace who comes to men in Christ and calls them into a life with him of loving trust and obedience. Christ introduces us into a new relation to God, and in this relation we know him as Father. His Fatherhood is an experience, for us, not an abstract idea that we bring to that experience. If the heart of Christianity were a general idea of Fatherhood, then we might cast loose from Christ and history when once we had this idea. But the reality of the Christian life lies in the living relation, in which the idea of Fatherhood is included. This implies the abiding significance of Christ as the revelation of that idea and the mediator of that relation.[17]

The character of God, then, must first be seen in the mission and message of Jesus Christ. As stated before, Jesus does not teach a doctrine of God as such. The Christian can only say, "God the Father of our Lord Jesus Christ." We have already seen that the originality of Jesus, for Rall, does not rest with his teaching but with the impact of his whole life upon the lives of others. If the Christian, then, wants to speak of God he must do so in the controlling light of the Christ likeness of God. For Rall, this is best exemplified by Jesus' use of the word, Father, being careful to note the misuse of it by what Rall calls "natural theologians."

> He [Jesus] sought to bring home to men what it really meant to call God Father, to believe that love really ruled in this world, that anxiety was a sin, that courage and peace and strength were the privilege of all. He turned men from the consideration of what they themselves were and what they deserved to the thought of what God was, the thought of his infinite mercy for men. From this mercy of God men were to get inspiration to pray, courage to ask forgiveness, willingness to trust.[18]

Rall goes on to say that not alone was intimacy included in this utterance, God as Father, but it meant authority as well, that type of imperative that demanded of men as answerers, the ultimate bearing of the cross.

But, it was in the person and deeds of Jesus of Nazareth that there is clearest evidence of the early disciple's sense of the presence of God. Rall, with Ritschl, always insisted upon the centrality and necessity of the historicity of Jesus Christ as the means by which to know the character of God. Ritschl categorically discounts any metaphysical "proof" or "evidence" of the Being of God. Does Rall?

The Being of God

Over the many years of writing, Rall concentrated on the "Christlikeness of God" and seldom focussed upon the arguments for the existence of God. However, in his Taylor Lectures of 1931, he not only includes a lecture on "The Grounds For Belief in God," but speaks appreciatively of the theology being advocated by Professor Henry Nelson Wieman of The University of Chicago. First he traces the background of the traditional proofs for the existence of God which, although they cannot logically demonstrate his existence, are nevertheless not to be understood as illogical or irrational or without value. In these instances, arguments attempted to relate to man's experience either with the physical world, in his moral and religious life, or in his existence as a thinking being. If one keeps in mind Rall's earlier emphasis upon religion — ergo, theology — as *necessarily* involving man's participation, then it is fairly easy to see his appreciation of Wieman who attempts to include man's experience with his concern for the ultimate. Wieman defines religion as being concerned with the achievement of the highest good. The achievent of good must evidence certain forces and conditions of the universe which generate and sustain such good, and this is what we mean by "God." As Rall interprets Wieman, the concern . . . "is not with the question of the existence of God, which is obvious, but with so relating ourselves to these forces and processes that we may achieve abundance of life."[19] Rall commends much of what he finds in Wieman:

> . . . the concern of religion with life and with the gaining of life and knowledge through right relations actively maintained, the distinction between the basic certainty of religion concerning God and specific theological formulations, the need that these latter shall be held tentatively.[20]

But Rall again reiterates his charge formerly placed against Ritschl in an earlier day: there is not provided in Wieman's thought a criterion enough "above" man to merit the possibility of God, which name always implies other-than and greater-than human life. He asks,

> Is this the dominant force in the universe? No, this is the creator and sustainer of such good as there is but not the creator and sustainer of the universe. Can we be sure of the ultimate triumph of the good? No, because this is but one force among others. Is this a unitary being? Not necessarily.... Only by a quite uncritical outrunning of his premises can Doctor Wieman use a singular personal pronoun, He, for those impersonal and undetermined and possibly plural cosmic conditions and trends and modes of behavior which together make possible the achievement of the good.[21]

What Rall is saying is that writers such as Henry Nelson Wieman, Edward LeRoy, and others can easily answer the query of the being of God, namely, that he is, by merely reducing the definition of his being to that manageable by their self-imaged, self-imposed categories. The primary question for the theologian is that of the character, namely *what* he is, of God. In answer to this substantive question, Rall indicates that his sources will include those areas that the traditional proofs centered upon, i.e., the physical universe, the moral and religious life, and man's life as a thinking being. To be sure, neither natural science nor man's aspirations can yield proof of God; nevertheless, they can and do describe the world within which God, who is above, operates and through which his revelation comes. God is God of all things and nature and man can indicate the likelihood of belief or its ridiculous nature. Science perceives a universe of dynamic order with a hierarchy of being and values attached thereto. Also, the universe we know bears intelligibility while evolution indicates a basic purposiveness. All these indices in no way "prove" the existence of God, but on the other hand, Rall urges, they do permit the theologian to hypothesize "... that the idea of an ultimate Power, unitary, intelligent, purposive, good seems best to account for these data and most reasonably to interpret them."[22]

This Power then is not sheer Power acting upon the world from without, not creating *ex-nihilo*, but one acting within the processes of nature and in tension with them. The Polarity is clear: on the one side, a process that can be scientifically described in terms

> ... of immanent forces and continuous change, with elements of spontaneity, 'freedom', and continuity, and of inertia as well as *elan vital*; and, on the other, a something more than finite, that gives unitary order and direction and works in genuinely creative fashion.[23]

Rall is arguing for the goodness of the created order and urging its acceptance as evidence of God, not saying that the world exhausts the word "God," but rather assists in locating his presence. The explanations science affords the theologian provides him rational explanations of the whole, or the unity and order of the universe of which science itself has dared to investigate, but the answers about which lie outside its province.

> We may give up the quest in confession of agnosticism, but that is to deny for the whole what science assumes for the past. And to deny unity and rationality and meaning for the whole is to make these inexplicable if not impossible for the past. Brute fact no more describes the whole than the part, and the parts which have relative meaning point to a whole of transcendent meaning and power. Thus, pressing on, we

move toward the idea of unity and rationality in God.²⁴

A second source of help toward grounds for the belief in God (might we label the first "The Ecology of Theology?") relies on value-theory as the former rested in fact. If man is portrayed as one whose being is measured by his responding to continuing moral choices, then it is possible to posit some idea of the universe and Being within this moral category. Rall cannot explain an experience of moral goodness beyond the fact of its being, but he does point out its *distinctive* meaning. A moral experience — when it is demanded of me that I declare for the highest I know — is always the objective discovered, never an insight instinctively gained. The moral experience is absolute in value, i.e., here is a good I must achieve if in my answering I wish to gain what I consider to be the fullest and highest possible for men. Thus, moral experience is that which carries a sense of the categorical "ought" and hence its object bears for me an absolute value. (Rall is too early to be placed within the current debate on situational ethics vs. principle ethics, although the nature of the debate is open to review).²⁵

If this description accurately delineates man's situation — he experiences as a human being the necessity of deciding within a value scheme how he will act — then Rall wants to raise the sticky theological question: "What is it then to which this experience points?" To follow the above logic as being descriptive of man's basic being is to put goodness (a term of character, not being), and not power, in the supreme theological category;

> ...it is to believe in God. Further, if the World Ground is moral then it must be personal. Love, truth, righteousness exist, if at all, only in personal life; that is their meaning. There is no love in the abstract; there are only personal beings who love. There is

no righteousness except in personal will that holds to what is true and just and turns from wrong and oppression.[26]

To safeguard himself against his own criticism of Wieman earlier made, Rall guardedly says he is not making God a postulate, something that must be assumed in order to validate the moral order. Rather, he is suggesting that man as man primarily lives in a moral order in which the question of the character of God's being is forced upon him. Rall pointedly states that such an apologetic approach is directed toward those outside the Christian faith who have lost any semblance of religious certainty but who in their idealism cling to the ethical. The appeal is that through action to the being of God.[27]

As his third argument or ground for belief in God, Rall contends for religion itself. He does not say that the fact of religion's prevalence in all cultures necessarily concludes there is God. He states that such a factor presents evidence of the "holy", or "sacred." In all cultures, man's choice to be "religious" indicates a possible ground for such a belief in the existence of an unseen world and a higher Power.

> Man's sense of a hunger that is not stilled with food, the appeal of the ideal that calls out aspirations, devotion, and effort, the awareness of the higher, of the numinous or holy, these point to a spiritual world whose stimulus we feel, which impinges upon us as surely as does the light upon the eye. With others, the persistent and universal phenomenon of religion is as inexplicable as would be the development of the sensitive epithelial cells into the eye without the stimulus of light. Religion is response.[28]

All these instances — the universe, as described by science, value structure as experienced by man, the historicity of religion as known by various cultures — grant evidence to the theologian of a supreme Power who must be unitary in being and moral and personal in character. Not withstanding this line of development, we need to recall clearly, however, that Rall is not abandoning the cruciality of Jesus Christ as the supreme revelation of God. As early as 1924, Rall marks out his position on the nature and method of revelation. The nature of revelation can perhaps best be understood as dealing not with information about God but with the knowing of God. "It is the difference between *kennen* and *wissen*, *Wissenschaft* which deals with things, *Bekanntschaft* which concerns persons."[29] Rall states that revelation is that knowledge in which I and my history are involved as against my being acquainted with someone else's informed history. One cannot help but recall here H. R. Niebuhr's famous, perhaps classical, illustration of this same distinction in his book, *The Meaning of Revelation*.

> The distinction between our history and events in impersonal time, or between history as lived and as contemplated from the outside may be illustrated by contrasting parallel descriptions of the same social event. Lincoln's Gettysburg Address begins with history: 'Four score and seven years ago our fathers brought forth on this continent a new nation conceived in liberty and dedicated to the proposition that all men are created equal.' The same event is described in the Cambridge Modern History in the following fashion: "On July 4, 1776, Congress passed the resolution which made the colonies independent communities, issuing at the same time the well-known Declaration of Independence." If we regard the Declaration as the assertion of an abstract political theory, criticism and condemnation are easy. It sets out with a general proposition so vague as to be practically useless. The doctrine of the equality of men, unless it be qualified

and conditioned by reference to special circumstance, is either a barren truism or a delusion.[30]

Revelation's method also comes under Rall's scrutiny. If revelation involves my conditioning as an answerer, then it also includes my activity as a receiver of that peculiar knowledge. For Rall the older concept excludes the necessary participation of man as responder to that revelation. The older, static, view of revelation promised a God of sheer power while what Rall advocates is an emphasis upon the *character* of the already acknowledged being of God.[31] Rall's point is that in Christianity man gains a clear conception of God as that Being wherein Power and Goodness are conjoined. The primary attention, however, is not to that Being, already by definition one source of religion, nor Christianity, but to the manner by which men come to receive his Being. In sum, Rall states his position.

> Revelation is not the communication of information as antecedent to religion; it is God's making himself known to men by his dealings with them as apprehended in religious experience. What comes first is the experience or the life in which man knows God. The experience through which man knows God may be of the most varied character. In its lower ranges it is apt to be nature manifestations or dream visions or ecstacy. In the higher reaches the moral and the spiritual nature is more deeply concerned. But always it is not communication apart from life but apprehension of God as discerned in life. It may be the returning shepherd who sees and sings, Jehovah is my shepherd. It may be Hosea whose vision of divine mercy is gained through his own experience. It may be a vision of the Lord high and lifted up that comes to the young prophet against the background of the death of his hopes in an earthly king. It may be through the history of the people that God speaks.

At its highest it is seen in Paul's word concerning the light of the knowledge of the glory of God in the face of Jesus Christ.[32]

Still unanswered is the question of the manner in which men participate in the revelation of God. Can man in his religious nature respond freely of his own to God's revelation? Such a conclusion might be anticipated within Rall's schema of religion as that combination of man's aspirations and the higher world Power to which man responds. However, on the contrary, Rall allows no such conclusion. He rather turns to a discussion of the second important "concept" of God as found in the New Testament: the indwelling Spirit. Rall indicates that the Holy Spirit *is* the functioning of man at his highest moral and spiritual levels. As noted above, Rall desires to reactivate the phrase *testimonium spiritus sancti internum* as symbolic not only as the ground for acceptance of revelation, but as the hermenentic as well toward understanding the Bible and establishing the contexts for evaluation of all that comes to man as revelation. It would appear that that for which Rall is pleading is a recognition that to speak of God is to speak of Jesus Christ is to speak of his controlling impression in those areas of human life dealing with man's "existential" concern, those areas where man chooses the highest as he best understands it. "God was in Christ; God gives himself to us by his Spirit."[33]

In the New Testament, especially in Paul, there is an explicit connection between the present activity of God through his Spirit and the ministry of Jesus Christ. The Holy Spirit is not a strange, unknown force, but that power that is intimately connected with Jesus Christ whose uniqueness was found in his mediation of holy love to those around him. Indeed, in Paul, the work of the spirit is intimately connected with ethical judgment in reference to the special gifts of the spirit (prophecy, healing, etc.) and the fruits of the Spirits (joy, love, peace, self-control, etc.). In the former the test of authenticity is the exclusiveness by which the gift is shared; and the latter is a series of ethical acts. Both the gifts and fruits of the spirit are evidenced by their activities in man's being in relation to another human being. Rall is attempting to "secularize" the activity of God in the present, aside from any notion of the spirit being an opposing force to man. However, he does continually qualify this immanence by stressing the holiness of the Spirit that disallows any mere psychologism within the nature of man alone. His last word on this was in his last book, *The God of Our Faith*, published in 1955.

> This is the Holy Spirit of the Christian faith. The Spirit is *holy* (trascendent), and the Spirit is the Eternal. The Spirit is *personal*, God himself dwelling in his children. Man's spirit is not dispossessed by this Spirit; rather it is fulfilled. Man is made fully and truly man. The Spirit is *ethical*. His nature is most clearly seen when we look at Christ. He is the power of a new life in man, but the power is that of love and truth and righteousness. The Spirit is not merely individually and subjectively creative; the whole self-revealing, redemptive work of God in history is the work of his Spirit. Supreme in this is the creation of the fellowship of Christ's followers, the Church of Christ. By his Spirit, God dwells in the Church and constitutes its life.[34]

The Trinity

It is of interest to the historian to note that Rall directs almost no attention to the doctrine of the trinity, even in the book published in 1925, *The Meaning of God*. In 1952, Professor Claude Welch, in his analytical book *In This Name, The Doctrine of the Trinity in Contemporary Theology*, refers to Professor Harris Franklin Rall within the chapter entitled, "The Trinity as Second-Rank Doctrine, 3. Contemporary Monarchianism," pp. 59ff. There he characterizes Rall's thoughts as the trinity of experience or manifestation; that the doctrine stems from a threefold experience:

> faith in the one living God, plus the new revelation of God in Christ, and the presence of God in the Holy Spirit. Thus faith is threefold; yet plainly in one God. Beyond this, Rall does not think it necessary to go; formal statements are not as important as the experience and faith.[35]

Since that publication Rall has written a chapter on the trinity in his book, *The God of Our Faith* (1955). Several statements need to be emphasized. 1) This is the only succinct statement on the trinity by Rall. In class lecture notes of 1936 and of 1939 Rall provides passing mention to the doctrine, with short, curt criticisms of the Athanasian Creed. These include the damnatory clauses; the apparent (to Rall) methodology of salvation by faith in a doctrine; in the assumption of omniscience, of "an ability to probe the depths of the nature of the Infinite." The summons is to belief in a metaphysical construction rather than "the God and Jesus of the Gospels, the possibility of a tri-theism.[36]

Indicating what I am uncertain, except perhaps his continuing Ritschlian anti-metaphysics pose, is Rall's concluding comment on the Creed in *The God of Our Faith*, in reference to the damnatory clauses of the Athanasian Creed:

> It should be clear how directly opposed this is to the conception of faith and salvation as found in Paul. Equally clear is the contrast with the way in which God is presented in the New Testament. Here it is a mysterious Being, described in abstract and para-

> doxical terms, asking of men the acceptance of doctrines on the authority of the Church. In the New Testament we are shown the Father, whose life and whose will are seen in Christ. To turn from sin, to trust him as Father, to receive him as spiritual presence in our hearts and lives, to walk in fellowship with him and in his way of love, this is the New Testament demand. And, wonderful as it is, this is the word about God which the least can understand.[37]

By so limiting his attention to this doctrine, Rall exhibits his noticeable lack in historical appreciation of *any* testimonies to the faith and the criterion of the moment in his ultimate criterion of theology. 2) In several different ways, Rall states his insistence on the unity of God against any possible tri-theism. 3) His "doctrine" of the trinity, then, can be seen as his attempt to speak about that unity of impact upon men of the personal presence of God, the God who is over all of Israel's doings, the God in the revelation of Jesus Christ. the God of the indwelling Spirit.

> This is the trinity which belongs to the Christian faith: the God and Father of our Lord Jesus Christ, the Christ who is Son of God and our Saviour and Lord, the Spirit who is the indwelling, life-sharing, life-giving God. This is not theory, not an abstraction of theologians. This is concrete and living fact, seen in history, known in experience, belonging to the life of every follower of Christ. This is the God of our faith, the God who comes to us in the New Testament. This is the gospel that we preach.[38]

Rall in several places devotes extended passages to the theme of God in his relation to the world and to a correlative aspect of this, namely, the problem of evil, or the thwarting of God's goal for the world. Some of our discussion on theodicy must be delayed until we speak of soteriology and the place of the Kingdom of God in Rall's theology. It may be recalled here that early in his career, Rall prophesied that the future of theological inquiry would move along the lines of a search for theories of knowledge. Following upon this, Rall developed the Ritschlian idea of practical knowledge, polarity in tension to the disavowing of any ontological dualism. He still retained and defended the categories of transcendence and "other-than-life" but reinterpreted these classical terms to mean not so much ontological separateness as moral and religious superiority. In his earlier writings, Rall wrote consistently that science could not provide answers to man's primal questions of value and moral decision but was to be welcomed for its opening the doors to wider understanding of the milieu within which man could better understand God's operations upon him. Actually, he points out that for man, there are two ways of looking at life, not at all contradictory, but complementary; that of faith looking inwardly and science looking outwardly. He alone is wrong who says there is but one side. He is rich who finds this inner presence when other men can only say nature, man, evolution, law.[39] Typical not alone of Rall, but many theologians of the 1920's was their inclusion of a poem by W. H. Carruth (*Supra,* CH. III, F.N. 22).

Later, in the 1930's, Rall shifts in his analysis of science, because of the newer shifts therein and of his opinion of the relationship between science and religion. He does assume, however, his former critique of science as having little or no bearing upon the value judgments man as man must make. He suggests that faith still lives in the realm of the unseen but theologians sometime err as they make pronouncements on the forms by which that unseen world expresses itself. In any given period theology adopts the current scientific forms which must be succeeded by yet newer forms in a later day. That is, Rall now reiterates that the function of science is not correlated with religion, but rather science helps man to understand how God works. The truth that it makes known is the truth of God, and the laws that it discloses are the ways of God.[40] Science is best described by another oft-quoted poem of the 1930's, "Watchers of the Skies" by Alfred Noyes, which Rall used frequently:

> What is all science, then,
> But pure religion, seeking everywhere
> The true commandments and through many forms
> The eternal Power that binds all worlds in one?
> It is man's age-long strugle to draw near
> His Maker, learn his thoughts, discern his law.[41]

In *Christianity*, Rall presents a very detailed account of a "world come of scientific age," recounting the vast developments that have led many to question the place of religion and God. First, Rall exhibits keen awareness as to the then current scientific scene in relation to the expanding and unified universe. With this newer picture of the world, the grounds of religion were shaken if not fissured. The dynamic, expanding universe appeared to cut away the belief in the Creator, let alone the Sustaining God. Accompanying this, Rall noted, came a loss of religious certainty on the part of many. "Only one thing seemed certain and that was that everything changed."[42]

Any discussion centering upon God and his relation to the world must include the aspects of providence and the miraculous. Providence has often been interpreted in the past as God's special brooding over an individual's destiny. Miracle has been identified as the acting by God contrary to the "law of nature," whatever might be construed under that phrase. Rall writes sparingly on both of these topics, but does conclude that the former simply raises the question as to one's basic *Weltanschauung:* What does one believe the primary ontology of the world? Can one allow for the "higher world" or "the world of the unseen?" If so, then the belief that God can direct his personal life.

> To think of the 'laws of nature' as an independent force constraining God's action is pure mythology. Science considers such law as simply summary statements of the way in which things behave as science has observed them. Religion sees them as the order which reflects the immanent reason of God.[43]

The miraculous as portrayed by "older" theologians in their use as a "proof" of God's existence had become a liability to religion. In fact, by positing God as removed from the world, the question of his action upon it, becomes an abstract philosophical problem, not an affair of religion. With belief in a living God, the question of "miracle" can pass away. As to the "signs and wonders" recorded in the New Testament, Rall contests that they must first of all be approached historically which will greatly reduce their numbers. However, Rall also contends that one cannot demythologize these gospel accounts into natural explanations. The exact interpretation of them he leaves open-ended, although asserting the worth of each to be measured by its high moral level. The newer advances in all disciplines are to be welcomed as "God-impressed" endeavors to further assist man in making these decisions. Rall's *Weltanschauung* did not presuppose a closed system whereby any advances alien to theology could cause disavowal of theology. Especially is this so if, as was the case, science exhibits growth and dynamism as its basic categories. Rall is *not* to be labeled "a naturalistic theist" at all, for in *that* position, as in Ritschl's, there is no place for a holy God whose revelation is personal disclosure, a central theme of Rall throughout his life.

But God does not achieve his goal of fulfillment for all life. What of evil? One word must be said first as to God's "not accomplishing his goal for creation." Partly, this lack of completion is due to His involvement *with* man in his creation. Also God, by definition cannot perform in certain ways; e.g., God cannot be irrational, cannot be unrighteous. Rall felt that the goal of God was freely exhibiting his humanity. "Whether you think of the kingdom of God, the Church, or the family of God, the goal of God involves an associated life, and that defines his way."[44] This deliberate choice of "togethering" (Rall's word) by God with man, implies that God cannot have sheer, irresistible power, but a limited power, conditioned by this choice of associating with man.

> Important is the consideration of how God is conditioned and limited by the goals that he has set for himself. God's goal for this earth is a humanity which can know him in his truth and love and righteousness, which will freely and understandingly choose the higher life in fellowship with him and in a fellowship of love and justice and mutual regard among men themselves. Such a life involves freedom for man; to that extent creation involves a certain self-limitation. On God's side it requires the long task of self-revelation, or the training of man, of forgiving grace and redemptive help, as well as order and judgment. In all this God limits and conditions his action, but it is a self-limitation that goes with his high purpose.[45]

Rall proves enigmatic on the problem of evil. He certainly is aware of it and at one place calls the fact of evil the greatest single obstacle of faith.[46] In addition, he acknowledges the problem of the finite God and all the historic positions relative to this claim. The enigma centers on the fact that whereas this problem has predicated a problem of God, Rall handles it easily as a problem of man. He dismisses quickly those theological positions which meet the problem head on; John Calvin, Edgar Scheffield Brightman, e.g., and speaks of the problem as a problem of the good. The criteria he uses avoid the thorny issue of the being of God and the frustration of His Being and concentrates on how one can understand and explain the conditions necessary for the greatest good:

> In a world where good is to be achieved, there must be freedom; a good world will be one of toil and struggle and resistance; a world fitted for the achievement of life must be one of order, and an order that is universal and dependable; a good world must be one of social relations and social solidarity; a world that is fitted for the achievement of life will be one of suffering and pain.[47]

By positing such a solution, it seems that Rall is obscuring the question that still begs the question: is God finite? Perhaps the strength of his position lies in his whole schema. It is right, he says that man should raise this question (of evil). All possible intellectual answers finally end begging; to deny evil is no solution, to refer to omnipotent and inscrutable will is to deny faith in the controlling character of the goodness of God; to refer to a demonic merely undercuts the question if it is couched in terms of an ethical understanding and addressed to man as a decider; to reduce God to a finite God makes the term "God" a misnomer, i.e., he is one among many. Only insofar as evil and God are linked to man making his decisions — toward what is of highest good for him — can anything adequate be said. And even then, a healthy agnosticism must prevail. "We come at last to an ultimate that is no longer inexplicable," he writes. Then all the Christian can do is hold on "70,000 fathoms deep," to trust in the God of love who has spoken ... and to give devotion to the way which this God indicates to us."[48] Maybe this is all that can ever be said.

Chapter VI

CHRISTOLOGY

To speak of God is to speak of Jesus Christ. Harris Franklin Rall criticized Albrecht Ritschl because he concluded that his theology did not in fact evidence adequate emphasis upon the activity of God in coming to man. He continues his criticism of other theologies precisely at this identical point: a lack of a convincing Christology. To put the matter another way, the "older" theologies were inadequate insofar as they "encased" the meaning of Jesus Christ into forms which substituted the Event for remembrances of that Event. He criticized the theology of Henry Nelson Wieman as failing to contain any source beyond human aspiration to either judge or promise to fulfill such hopes, let alone this source being Jesus Christ. Karl Barth is adjudged wrong, on the basis of his making of Jesus Christ an impossible feat; to be sure, Barth places Jesus Christ as the center and key of his theology, but in Rall's judgment, in such a fashion and based on such theory of religious knowledge, that makes of him an impossible figure. One would have to say that Rall clings to the centrality of the event of Jesus Christ as the sole way in which man can meet God and have his highest hopes fulfilled within the world man lives. Rall insists on the centrality of revelation in Jesus Christ, (*vis-a-vis* Ritschl and Wieman) but wants to so approach his Christology inductively (*vis-a-vis* the older theologies and Karl Barth).[1]

In his lectures at Yale University in 1900, Rall indicates his awareness of current biblical studies as he summarizes his reactions to them as they bear upon Christology.[2]

In presenting to you this position in opposition to that

outlined above, there are three or four considerations that I* wish to suggest. And first, the question as to the real Christ, who is supreme authority for Christian believers and theologians, is not merely a historical question, and cannot be settled by merely historical means. The view that I am opposing commonly runs as follows: What theology wants is the historical Jesus, not opinions of others concerning him. What the historical Jesus was, we must find out by historical criticism as applied to the tradition of his words and life. This scientific and unbiased study will show us what Jesus taught. Theology then takes as final authority what this impartial, scientific study delivers as its results.

Against this I would say, we may as well recognize once and for all that such a pure, disinterested study of Christ as is implied in this method is impossible. That results from the very nature of the object of this study. No man can thus approach Christ. To every man he puts the challenge by his very nature, "What think ye of me" and whether avowedly or not, the answer is given. The man who is best able to understand and interpret the real, historical Christ, is the man who will be furthest removed from an unbiased, purely disinterested study, for such a man will go to his work with the deep conviction that with this man Jesus there lie the secrets and issues of life. Conversely, a wholly disinterested, scientific student would be the one least fit for his task, for that very fact would show that he had no eyes to see the real meaning and nature of that which he was considering. A purely unbiased study of Jesus is for us impossible, and would be fruitless of any real result if it were possible.

No merely historical study can give us the real Jesus, because Jesus is more than a historical personage. What is meant by this scientific attempt on purely historical methods to establish the real Jesus of history? It means the as-

---

*The first person throughout this chapter, and again in chapter X, follow Rall's style of lecturing as found in the Rall manuscript and is not the person of the author.

sumption that Jesus can be understood wholly by those processes by which any historical personality is studied. These processes imply the explanation of a historical character in three ways: first by hereditary influences; second, by environing forces and factors, such as the ideas of age and nation, race peculiarities and customs, climatic and geographical conditions; third, by psychological analogy, reasoning from the universally human and applied to the known facts to interpret them and supplement them. For an application of this method, pick up some of the lives of Christ. What do we find? Under the assumption of a scientific method, the doors are opened wide to individual opinion and subjective fancy. Take Stapfer's Life of Christ[3] for example. The entire first volume is devoted to the life of Christ before his public ministry. How much do we know of that period? As much as you can write on one hand. What Stapfer gives us is an imaginative construction working on the materials of the customs and thoughts of the day on the principle of psychological analogy. This is giving us anything but the real Christ.

In this field of Jesus' boyhood it is not a matter of importance. What does it mean when applied to the real Christ of the Gospels? The strict application of the method of psychological analogy means that you assume in advance that you must judge Christ in thought and motive and character as any other man. And within your historical limits you cannot transcend this position. The whole assumption is a covert blow at the heart of the Christian faith and its conception of Christ. I repeat, because Christ is more than a historical personage, the purely historical method, as implying an assumption to the contrary, cannot give us the real Christ. You will understand, of course, that I do not mean at all that we are not to submit to historical study the life and teaching of Christ. I simply insist, that men are mistaken when they think that this study with them is purely historical, that is, absolutely disinterested and unbiased, or when they think that through the strict methods of such study they can give us the real Christ.

As a second consideration, I would suggest, that it is a mistake to suppose that in the gospels you have the simple Christ of history, while in the epistles you have the Christ of faith or creed. It is, in fact, one Christ that the whole New Testament presents to us, and that is the Christ of faith. There is not one purely historical writing in the New Testament. Not one of the evangelists was a mere historian. They were all preachers, as Paul was. For none of them was Jesus a mere historical personality. For them, as for Paul, he was Lord and Savior. Is it conceivable that their work should have been uninfluenced by this? If to hold Christ in faith as Lord is to disqualify Paul as witness, then these, too, must be cast out. Here are no mere biographies, no impartial setting forth of the events of this man's life. What they set forth is not the life, but the man. The deeds that are portrayed, the words that are recorded, the events that are depicted, all are made to serve one purpose, to set this man before men. They are at the farthest remove from that thought of tracing the development in character which is so essential to a true biography, and which the modern pseudo-scientific biographies of Jesus try to realize. Does this disqualify them as witnesses? Yes, but only for those who think that the real Christ can only be what an objective and purely scientific historical study may yield us.

And this brings me to the third consideration. The real Christ is this Christ of faith who alone is given to us in the New Testament. This is not setting up an imaginary Christ, a Christ of men's hopes or men's opinions, against the historical reality. Rather, it is a mistake to suppose that when you have summed up Christ's words and recorded his works, you have the whole Christ. The full reality of this historical personage, Jesus Christ, is only given to us in the witness and confession of faith of his disciples. I suggested above, that it is Christ as the revelation of God who is for us authority. What we have to ask now is, how is it that Christ reveals God to us? I answer that it is not primarily by the ideas concerning God contained in his teaching. It was not so much a new doctrine that he brought as a new life. His purpose was not so much to communicate new ideas, as to lead men into this life. He was not so much teacher as Savior. It is the new life that he set forth in his person, and the new life into which he leads men by his own life and death, that constitutes the work of Jesus and the heart of the Christian religion. In this redemptive purpose and work there is the fullest revelation of God to men.

But this revelation was not made merely in the words of Christ nor was it completed in the early church in the community of the first believers.[4]

Early in his career, Rall engaged in a series of books entitled "The Kingdom of God Series." He contributed three books, *The Life of Jesus, The Teaching of Jesus,* and *The Coming Kingdom.*[5] It should be noted that the intention of the series (published initially in the late Teens) was to "encourage the individual to redouble his efforts and inspire in him an unfaltering confidence in the ultimate realization and triumph of God's rule."[6] The reader could rest assured that his efforts were built upon

> . . . the Old and New Testaments and the subsequent history of the Christian centuries, to discover definite stages of advance with successive landmarks of progress in the gradual establishment of the reign of God in individual lives and in the institutions of mankind. Such a survey of progress already achieved should hearten the organized Christian forces in their forward look and their endeavor to establish still more firmly among men the principles and ideals of the Kingdom.[7]

Professor Jerry Brown has recently initiated research

into the development of biblical criticism in America in the nineteenth century. He has restricted his investigation to the years of 1800-1870 and to the region of New England and specifically to the early influence of German biblical scholarship upon the scholars at Harvard University and the Andover Seminary.[8] To my knowledge, little has been done as yet in comparable studies in the period under review. Harris Franklin Rall, however, a systematic theologian, does not begin outside his inductive approach to Christology. Thus in dealing with the New Testament, Rall follows the path of presenting the life and teachings of Jesus as they are connected with the "vitalities of life," which is another way of saying that he couched his Christology inductively. Jesus is portrayed, to borrow Erik Routley's familiar phrase, as the man for others.[9] *The Teachings of Jesus* is written from the perspective of seeing how these teachings ". . . bear on human faith and life, and with the light which they throw upon this story of the making of a new humanity."[10] Further, Rall insists, the correct definition of history is that which affects the reader personally. The history of the New Testament is invalid, for example, for the Buddhist insofar as he has excluded himself from the historic community which alone can read and interpret the eventfulness of the happening. Applying this criterion of hermeneutics to biblical study, Rall proceeds to seek out his Christology with no thought of patristic theological formulations (neither Nicea and Chalcedon nor the Reformation's categories of prophet, priest and king). He does use the then contemporary developments in the field of biblical study, historical criticism, but always from the hermeneutical *a priori* of the present experience.

> These events that are recorded, what do they mean for this movement of the Kingdom of God? These teachings, how do they witness to the growing truth and the clearer light which God is giving to men. This life of prophet and people, is it the life of God that is

to make at length the new world? . . . We want to know just what message Jesus brought to men, what he had to say about the great questions of God and our life here and our future, and what this message has meant for the growth of the Kingdom of God.[11]

Many questions integral to biblical hermeneutics and biblical theology, such as the Messianic consciousness of Jesus, form criticism, the problem of "new" hermeneutic, are not dealt with at all by Professor Rall. It is true some of these post-date his direct writings on the New Testament, but even in his lectures of 1936 and 1939, as well as his books, he does not concentrate on these issues. He was a systematic theologian and by the time of the American involvement in these issues, he was in his 60's. However, any thought of a "low Christology" in Rall must be abandoned even though he spends little effort on further creedal interpretations. He does acknowledge Jesus' self knowledge of messiaship and he acclaims Jesus' self knowledge of a unique mission in the world: he is the beginning of a new day, the founder of the Kingdom. His teachings, recognizing that the various forms of them must be accounted for their full meaning, must be understood in that light. They inaugurate a new understanding of how man is to live in society. This being so, they cannot be "conceptualized" to lose the poetic and prophetic aspects of their pronouncements. What then is here, in the teachings of Jesus?

Throughout the length of his career, Rall returned again and again to a Kantian framework for assessing the heart of the Christian message and the teachings of Jesus. Rall asked: What can I know? What must I do? What may I hope for?[12] Jesus is that one person in history for whom God was not only the supreme interest of life, but the controlling thought that decided everything in his teaching. Upon several occasions in his ministry, when asked questions about life's behavior, his answer is always referred to God: "Be ye perfect as your Father in heavens is perfect." For Jesus the answer to the first question above is know God as Father, who is infinite power and love who works through me. If for the Christian God is Father, he is in sonship with him and with others. Attitudes of humility and desire, obedience and trust, and love comprise Christian sonship. "Every man is to be God's son and is to show the spirit of the Father in his life with his brothers.[13] That for which a Christian can hope is a relief of guilt and anxiety brought about by a redeeming experience of forgiveness and fellowship. A second hope was for the life to come beyond death which was only an incident on the way to a larger life. But the great hope held out for man by Jesus (1918) was that of the coming rule of God, the Kingdom of God. This was the "good news" he preached to men. It is of lesser matter as to the manner and time of its coming when seen against the meaning of this hope, *vide.*, God's rule in the hearts of men.[14]

He believed in God so naturally that He never tried to prove His existence, but took it for granted like the air He breathed or the food He ate.

He believed in His own mission, which was to give men life abundantly.

He believed in the fact of sin, and man's redemption from it by repentance and faith.

He believed in Heaven and Hell, and taught that men make their choice between right and wrong.

He believed in the possibility of Human Brotherhood, based on the oneness of human need and dependence.

He believed in the capacity of mankind to learn and accept the greatness of the abundant life.

He believed in the fact of immortality and took it for granted, as He did the existence of God, never arguing about it.

He believed in the seriousness of life, without being gloomy or ascetic, and He taught that life should be measured, not by pleasure, but by its joy in service.

He believed that prayer is a necessity for a full-grown life and taught the need of it without arguing about its meaning.

He believed in His own teaching so much that He commanded it to be taught to every nation and laid it upon the Church as a last and binding commission.

What do you think of the creed of Jesus? Can you find a better one for yourself?[15]

As to the "miracles" attributed to Jesus, Rall is much more cautious. As far as I can discern, he wrote about the miraculous in but one article and only twice in books (one page each) published in 1941, *A Working Faith* and *New Testament History*. In each of these books, he meets the problem by avoiding the issue. Granting much of the miraculous as legendary and fragmentary, he nevertheless acknowledges that their imbeddedness in the narratives precludes any conclusion of their non-happening. Rall then summarily states:

1) If the supreme power of the world be personal, not material or natural, and if Jesus be the supreme manifestation of that Person in His purpose for the world, it is not only possible for that, but reasonable as well that such manifestation should be accompanied by the miraculous. Jesus' deeds of healing, for example, can only by unpardonable historical violence be taken out of the Gospels.[16]

2) The important thing at stake, however, here as elsewhere, is the cruciality of the question of miracles. We can note in Rall the motivation of sympathy for fellow man as of first importance.

The miracles are no support or basis for our faith, either in the actual experience of the modern man or in logical reason. What is essential to our faith is this, that the supreme reality of the world is person, that the world is neither above God nor opposed to God, but exists by his power and is here as the instrument of Him that worketh His purpose in all things. It is not the miraculous that we need to concern ourselves about, but the supernatural: that is, this divine personal as the real and supreme power of the world. 'God was in Christ,' that is our great truth. However it may have been in the past, such a living faith is not built upon a demonstration of the miracles. Rather it is because of such a living faith that such a belief in the miracles has its place with us. It is Christ who makes credible the miracles, not the miracles which bring us to the faith in Christ.[17]

Rall carries over his distinction between the natural and the spiritual worlds and, after careful notation of the records, repeats the issue in these terms.

The actual issue is whether we believe in the reality of the spiritual world. If the physical is all there is of life, then these stories are mere hallucinations. But if the real life be the personal and spiritual, then the manner of these appearances is not vital, and to attempt to decide is simply to try to answer the unanswerable. The one clear fact, without which the wonderful story of early Christianity is a mere riddle, is the fact that these disciples were following a living Lord, and not a dead and defeated leader.[18]

Rall does not estimate thereby an acquittal by resurrection but sees the foundation of the conviction of a living Lord in the personality of Jesus Christ as impressed upon the early disciples.

Here as in his doctrine of God, Rall emphasizes not the being of Christ, but his character, and this in relation to

God on the one side and man on the other. He quotes Bushnell, "'Christianity is not so much the advent of a better doctrine, as of a perfect character.'"[19] The character of Jesus can, once again, best be portrayed in the phrase, a Man For Others. Rall characterized Jesus as one completely open to other men of the type to inspire the poem, "He was a friend to man, and he lived in a house by the side of the road."[20] The holines of Jesus was not separate from his welcome of children. Rall concludes by cataloging the well-known characterizations of Jesus as compassionate, intimate, loving, loyal, etc. As to the character of Jesus in relation to God, Rall writes that he epitomizes a Christian's call to obedience. He does not couch this within terms of Israel's call to be the Chosen One as nowhere in his writings does Rall speak within covenantal terms. Rather, where Jesus ". . . thought of the will of God he saw it as the greatest good that could come to man: to do that well was man's highest calling."[21] Rall outlines his Christology from the position of ethics of the Ritschlian School. Man, and Jesus was fully man, lives as an answerer, a responder basically, and therefore measures his character inevitably by the standards of a realizable ethical norm. He can do none other. The distinctiveness of the character of Jesus lies in his whole-hearted obedience to what he understands as the will of God, within the context of his being the Messiah whose task it was, to usher in the New Humanity, or The Kingdom of God. The cause for celebration of him in prayer and praise is that his character is complete and what Rall calls "balanced." Jesus represents not one type of achievement but the highest and greatest in all human life.

> Long ago the church declared its belief in the full and complete humanity of Jesus as in his full divinity. But that is not enough. Jesus is not only a man, he is the man. In him has been shown once for all what man should be, what he might be. And so we come to the

wonderful fact of the imitableness of Jesus. It might be thought that this perfect life would by that fact be wholly removed from us and our endeavor. The saints whom the church has set up and the heroes whom men sometimes glorify are often so removed from our imitation. We cannot all flee the world, or become martyrs, or work other marvelous deeds. But the reason why we cannot imitate these men is just because they are one-sided; and the reason we can follow Jesus is just because he is so complete, we can see, every one of us, our highest life in him.

> 'O Christ! the tender, loving one,
>   In whom all deathless graces blend —
> The goal to which the cycles run
>   In spiral paths to one vast end;
> As torrents in their courses turn
>   To mingle within the mother-breast,
> All tongues and tribes and nations yearn
>   For what is found in Thee expressed.'[22]

The particular point at which Rall most clearly departs from Ritschl is the importance of historic continuity. Ritschl was concerned with history as the means by which the faith-value-judgments of the New Testament were conveyed. He assiduously avoided allowing any credence to the statements and creedal affirmations as bearing ultimate authority for the Christian believer. The Reformation represents a definite break with its preceding era as it recaptured the New Testament faith. But its Lutheran developments lost this re-presentation through abstraction. "Back to Christ By Way of the Reformation." Rall does not harbor much consideration of nor investigation into any historical period. As a systematic theologian, he established his methodology in the light of what he considered the issues of the contemporary day. This is not to say he was ignorant of the issues of historical theology, but that he did not engage them as part of his methodology.

In particular reference to his Christology, Rall takes cognizance of Nicea and Chalcedon in his lectures (mimeographed) of 1936 and 1939. Oddly enough, his 1940 book *Christianity,* which was accorded the Bross Prize for that year, does not have any discussion about the person of Christ and the trinity. One piece of correspondence in the Rall manuscripts concerning that book suggests that one chapter in the submitted manuscript be deleted because its nature and topic would disrupt the even train of thought of the over all impression. One wonders at this late date, a quarter of a century later, if these lectures of 1936 and 1939 on Christology were those deleted pages.

Nicea and Chalcedon are viewed by Rall against late New Testament writings that begin to speculate on the person of Christ, especially the writers of Hebrews, John (Prologue) and Paul. The language of Nicea and Chalcedon appears equally removed from the simplicity of the New Testament, from the interests of an ethical religion, and from the vital concern of the religious life.[23] Rall assizes these classical statements from their soteriological nexus. These creeds were not speculative statements for metaphysical discussion, but summarizations of the concern of the church fathers that

> Man could be saved, . . . only as God entered into our humanity, only as the divine and human were joined together. Only thus could our human nature, mortal and corrupt, be transformed into the divine and immortal. This was done through the incarnation, and therefore above all else the full humanity and full divinity of Christ must be conserved in the Creed.[24]

The genesis of these latter statements was due to a different language and thus necessitated a restating of the similar message of the New Testament: that God was in

Christ reconciling the world unto himself, that in Jesus, God had come to men. What makes these statements unsatisfactory is that in this new language, necessarily Greek and abstract and metaphysical, the distinctive moral context of Christianity comes off second best. God and man are spoken of not in terms of moral personality, but are discussed within the categories of non-personal nature, substance and subsistence. The actual result in theology of the "two-natures" Christ became a denial of his true humanity. Adoptionism has characterized Christian theology throughout history, concluded Rall, as he quoted an influential American Methodist theologian, Olin A. Curtis, in *The Christian Faith*:

> 'that babe was not a human babe, . . . all the personality of our Lord he brought with him into human existence. . . . The manhood is even impersonal, never anything but a lower coefficient for the abiding person of the Son of God.'[25]

Equally unsatisfactory to Rall was the Christ portrayed by Christian theology as to the manner in which the incarnation, ever essential to the faith, was held. How did God come to man? How did God in Christ come into our humanity? Traditional theology is weak at the point of picturing a *real* human being from the promise of a God "out there" coming to man "in here."

> Usually the human was thought of as incidental, as the form, not the real life of this being. How could there be a real human life if omniscience and omnipotence were ascribed? It was not only a denial of the gospel picture of the man Jesus, but it meant the inevitable sacrifice of what the Christian faith could not and should not surrender. For what we want to know is not how some divine being can assume a human *appearance,* or an *impersonal* 'humanity,' but how

we men and women, we human personalities, may have . . . the life of God in us and so live the true human life. And that has been our inspiration and help, that such a true life was once lived on earth by one who was truly human like ourselves[26]

In this 1936 lecture, Rall proceeds to outline his Christology. The first consideration is that of materials for an adequate Christology. Major attention must be given, Rall insists, to historical rather than natural or metaphysical categories. Material must include not only Jesus' life and character as recorded in the New Testament, but the impact of that total life upon the historic community that even now witnesses to him, if these can be distinguished from one another. The older theologies were especially deficient in respect to their portrayal of achievement in the life of Jesus. Their *a priori* categories of sinlessness made of him a less-than-full-human being. Rather, the New Testament seems to suggest a symmetry in his life which included all the aspects of true human character. He is not a figure peculiar and aloof; in fact, he is more human than any man. He is humanity's real self; and that is why in every age, men of every kind, of every class and condition, and of every temperament have found their ideal in him.[27] Additionally, the gospels give to men Jesus as a human being whose total allegiance was to God and who in return received a life of rich and pure fellowship with Him. The reward of this achievement was inner freedom and strength and peace.

Rall stresses that it is against *this* portrayal that the moral mastery of Jesus can best be understood and not a metaphysical argument of dual natures. Jesus was conscious of this moral leadership and that God was uniquely in him and with him as the spirit and the power of this new life. So he was not like one of the Scribes as he spoke with authority. "He is *the* man."[28] The historic community of the Church has witnessed to this claim and the claim itself bears a double significance: Jesus then is the supreme revelation of God. Even more in his spirit than through his words, we see what God is like; Christian faith is the belief in a Christ-like God. It dares to believe that we find in his spirit the revelation of the World Ground and the clue to the world's meaning. Not a theory of the person of Christ is the test, but the question of the kind of God in whom we believe. Men have debated the person of Christ as though he were an enigma. He is not an enigma, but an answer; not a dark problem but a light on life's supreme question. Our faith is expressed not so much by our saying that Christ is godlike (divine) as by holding that he is christlike. (See Archbishop Temple in *Foundations,* p. 214).[29]

The second significance is located in the claim for Jesus as Savior. Such a designation can bear two interpretations, i.e. as a theory of the forgiveness of sin or

> in it may be broadly and rightly understood to the end that he is one in whom men find God, or if you will, through whom God finds men and brings them into fellowship with himself and so to the fullest realization of life. Here is his unique meaning, and it is far more than the thought of Jesus as a moral example or enlightened teacher.[30]

Rall's Christology stresses the life of Jesus as truly and fully human, avoiding the cliche of "humanity" which portends toward a thingness or abstract concept. Jesus is also divine in terms of the ethical and spritual, and Rall avoids the cliche "divinity" which portends toward a thingness or abstract concept. He best relays his thought by lifting the moral category into priority as the distinctive way to understand God.

> God has power, but is love. 'God is God not physically but morally, not by power but by love. That is the Christian revelation. The nature of Godhead is Holy Love.

There lies the region, the nature, and the norm of its omnipotence.'³¹

That holy love is what men can appropriate and understand, for life's ways, and not power itself which he can observe in multitudinous manners. Jesus is that one whose mind and will are one with God; he had no life apart from God. We may say with Dean Inge: " 'The divinity of Christ implies — one might almost say it means — the eternal supremacy of those moral qualities which he exhibited in their perfection.' "³²

How then did the incarnation take place? How did God in the person of Jesus enter into our humanity? Discarding the traditional theological claim of two natures and its resulting less-than-real-and-human Christ, Rall states that based upon the belief that in God's being as creative and self-giving good will, the incarnation is best understood as a response to that self-giving love.

> In the fullness of time God found a complete response to himself. One life was open to him in perfect trust and obedience. And so there was a perfect unity in which Jesus and God were one. In that union of divine and human, mankind found its Christ. In him God was present with men. Through him God could speak to men, could save men. It was the divine present in this life that became for men the way and the truth and the life but the divine could come in the way only because of the perfect response of the human. And the divine is no less present because the human was there, because in this man, as the gospels reveal, there was struggle and prayer, growth in knowledge and in all of life and constant dependence upon God.³³

As noted above, Rall omits Christological considerations from his book *Christianity*. Two later writings, however, do afford us opportunity to note his position on the atonement, again, omitted in the earlier lectures as well. In *Religion As Salvation*, Rall devotes a full chapter to the work of Jesus Christ as the bearer of salvation. He carefully reconstructs the ransom theory, the incarnative view of the "Eastern" Church, the Anselmic, the penal satisfaction and the Abelardian moral influence theories. Rather than align himself to any "abstract theorizing," Rall adroitly avoids comment (except an occasional criticism of those theories which he feels demean God to less than creative love) and systematically restates the death of Christ in "religious" terms, that is, in such a way as a believer reading the gospel accounts and receiving its direct impact. Hence, he concludes Christ as the exclusive revealer of God's truth and love; his work as one of reconciling the wrong spirit and life in man (indifference, greed, unbelief, etc.) by the clear revelation of God in his holiness and love; the work of Christ to be of battle against man's selfishness and through his victory points the way to those who would have victory over sin and peace of soul. Such work is creative in that it brings as its goal a unity, man to man, to God. The death of Christ, central to the early church, symbolizes for Rall three things; it reveals: 1) what sin is and does and God's judgment upon it, 2) a final and supreme expression of the spirit of Jesus, namely, utter selfless love, 3) the way in which those who follow must tread, "not by might, nor by power, but by my Spirit." Such meanings are difficult to express, and Rall turns to the poets for his benediction:

'Wouldest thou love one who never died
For thee, or ever die for one who had not died
[for thee?
And if God dieth not for Man and giveth not
[himself
Eternally for Man, Man could not exist; for Man
[is love

And God is love: every kindness to another is a
 [little Death
In the Divine Image, nor can Man exist but by
 [Brotherhood.³⁴

CHAPTER VII

SOTERIOLOGY

Anyone who has read any book by Harris Franklin Rall has been confronted by three questions in relation to soteriology: Saved from what? Saved to what? Saved by what? We can best understand Rall's thought on soteriology by analyzing the two questions he raised in his career relative to the doctrine: "What does it mean to be saved?" and "How are men saved?"

The simplest manner to answer the first query is to say that for Rall the question demands a two-fold answer. "To be saved" can be answered according to individual satisfaction and also social action. "To sin" is to fall prey to an apathy with little or no response to the activity of God toward men through Jesus Christ. Consequences such as guilt, fear, and futility ensue because neglecting such overtures necessarily separates one from God as the source of fulfillment. From what is one saved? From fear, doubt, futility, ignorance, from one's own consequences of past actions, i.e., from guilt. Being "found" out of this past "lostness" men can then be saved to something, namely right relations toward self, nature, others, and God. While it is true that Rall did not explicitly write on individual salvation until the mid 1930's, he was asked to write the article on sanctification for the 1915 edition of the popular *International Standard Bible Encyclopedia*.[1] In his later writings, especially in *Religion as Salvation*, Rall indicates a slight shift in the structure of his discussion. He then takes into account the varying motifs of the

New Testament as part of his outline for salvation in individual life and social experience. Earlier his writings lack biblical exposition. There is no systematic plan of salvation there, he concluded, but there is the clear conviction that in Christ God reconciles men and brings them to fullness of life. Such reconciliation is expressed in a myriad of ways in the New Testament: reconciliation, justification and forgiveness, ransom and redemption, adoption, regeneration, death and resurrection. To be saved is to recover the essential matters of sonship as proffered by God through Jesus Christ. The first "step in salvation," a theme not restricted to this 1953 book, is the unmerited grace of God. Salvation is God's deed and his free gift. Rall calls this the challenge of God offered to man in hopeful anticipation of man's repentance and faith. The reward for responding to this challenge is the assurance of forgiveness and reconciliation of the individual believer.

By referrring to the encyclopedia article on sanctification and a manuscript apparently from the years spent at Iliff Seminary, one can put together Rall's views on sanctification as expressed early in this century. Initially in the Old Testament, sanctification referred to that which belonged to Yahweh. The Hebrews implied nothing necessarily moral in this usage and "holy", the English translation, can refer to any aspect of space or time. With the New Testament a similar usage continues but is overshadowed by the new referent being the moral possibility. To put it another way, the use of sanctification in the New Testament, according to Rall, is a desacralization of time and space. To be "holy" in the New Testament is not to be primarily cognizant of holy places and seasons, but to be aware of opportunities *to be holy*.[2] Rall suggests that the meaning of this word is directly connected with the writers' concept of God. As long as God was thought of as separate from or Wholly Other, "sanctify" had direct application to his "appearance" in the natural and historical environment of man. As the understanding of God grew to be non-spatial and personal, so sanctification shifted in meaning to the courage one possessed to affirm his love of God in holy living. Rall argues that one pejorative aspect of soteriology is the rather negative connotation "sanctification" carries with it, namely, elimination of evil, metaphysical beingness or a transformation of the substance of human being or nature. Rather, sanctification means for him the making holy of life by God's activity. If holiness represents the state of heart and life in conformity with God's will, then sanctification is the deed or process by which that state is wrought.[3] As to how and when this deed is wrought only the inscrutable wisdom of God knows. But, this much can be said: sanctification is an essential part of the Christian life and not an adjunct to it.

> Looked at from the religious point of view, it follows from the doctrine of regeneration. Regeneration is the implanting of a new life in man. So far as that is a new life from God it is *ipso facto* holy. The doctrine of the Holy Spirit teaches the same. There is no Christian life from the very beginning that is not the work of the Spirit.[4]

Two New Testament symbols are employed by Rall to recall this activity of God and how his spirit implants holiness: water and fire. Each of these is far from static nor is their appropriateness measured in ontic terminology. The remaining question is that of instantaneous and entire sanctification. To answer this Rall returns to Pauline thought to mark out the clear implications that even as salvation affects all of life, so sanctification must be achieved as a life work, "in fear and trembling." Ideally, wholeness of holiness can be received in a moment,

> but the real making holy is coextensive with the whole life of man. It is nothing less than the constant in-

forming of the life of the inner spirit and outer deed with the Spirit of Christ until we 'speaking truth in love, may grow up in all things into him, who is the head' (Ephesians 4.15)[5]

In 1953, Rall devoted several pages to a discussion of sanctification, noting more fully the place of the doctrine in the history of the church, but noting nothing substantially different from his 1915 articles.

It should not be surprising that Rall devoted most of his writing on salvation to its social aspect. After all, he was a Ritschlian, with modifications, through and through. One of the first evidences of this concern is Rall's involvement in the Social Creed of The Methodist Episcopal Church adopted by the General Conference in 1908.[6] In answer to a letter from Douglas Sturm, then a graduate student at the University of Chicago, Rall explains the genesis of that creed:

> The inception of the first social creed was simple. We faced a situation in which large numbers of the church thought of Christianity either as an institution (the high church group) or as essentially an individual affair. But an increasing number were realizing that religion took in all of life, alike in the demand it made upon it and in the purpose and work of the gospel — social ethics and social salvation. The Kingdom of God as a divine end which was to take in all of life. Meanwhile a small and radical group, influenced by socialist thought (I think of Harry Ward as a leader here) were inclined to leave out vital elements of the traditional Christian thought in their emphasis on the economic-political.
>
> Those interested in that first General Conference declaration wished to have the church see the social meaning and implications of the gospel in its double social reference: as indicating God's purpose in the

coming kingdom as including all the life of man, and God's saving work as being social-historical as well as individual-spiritual. At the same time they wanted to show our obligation as individual Christians and as a Christian church in relation to current social conditions and problems.[7]

As noted above, the greatest hope for the Christian, apart from that of present wholeness and future life beyond death, is the Kingdom of God, that time when *all* men shall acknowledge God as Father. This was the good news of the gospel — that such a rule was near at hand! For Jesus this Kingdom was a gift, the highest good that any man could possibly desire. It is the treasure in the field, the pearl of great price. Such a kingdom was also a challenge and test to see if man could respond to accept this gift. The conditions were obedience and love. This Kingdom of God is both inner and social, to be worked out in and among men. Two convictions seemed to be in the mind of Jesus: that the Kingdom was already here wherever God's will was being done and that its fullness would appear in the very near future. As to the time of its coming, Jesus himself begged agnosticism. That it would come, he was certain: 1) There shall be a new earth in which God's will shall prevail; 2) This kingdom will be spiritual and ethical, not a governmental structure; 3) "This rule will show itself in the way in which men live together, in all the relations and institutions of life; and its final manifestation will be a family, a community, of brothers upon the earth."[8]

It is this latter emphasis that Rall endeavors to support throughout his ministry. He does *not* advocate building the Kingdom of God; a cliché often attached to American liberal theologians of that era. It is a gift to be received. Those who have now, partially, received it are under obligation to share this rule with all others. Rall felt the best political expression of the Kingdom of God to be the social philosophy of democracy, which he links with Christianity. In connection with the social ministry of Jesus, he can say, "Democracy came with Jesus."[9] Rall insisted there were no areas of life untouched by this social salvation: from social ills to a reconstructed society.

> There is no social problem where Christianity has not gone. That problem, as men are seeing it more and more, springs from the very ideal of Jesus. There is nothing sacred in the world but manhood. Nothing in this world has absolute value or absolute rights except manhood.[10]

He certainly did not mean man alone has absolute value in terms of a philosophic pragmatism or humanistic idealism. Rather, he is saying that the heart of life is man's ethical relationships out of which nothing should demean him. He articulated his own social faith:

> 'This, then, is our social faith:
> I believe in the God of righteousness and mercy who is working in His world for the good of men.
> I believe in the Kingdom of God on earth as the goal of life, where all sin and wrong shall be overcome, where the will of God, which is the life of men, shall be done in all the earth, in court and mart, in factory and mine, in church and home, and in the soul of man.
> I believe in men: in men whom God trusts — all men, and not the few, to whom belongs government; for whom God made the earth; whose welfare is the test of business and State and Church.
> I believe in justice as the great social principle for man, as the great purpose of God. 'Righteousness and justice are the foundations of His throne.'
> I believe in the spirit of Christ as the life of men; the spirit of purity that has sworn enmity to all that

defiles and destroys; the spirit of love which reverences all man as children of God, which craves all men for fellowship, which alone can bind men together; the spirit of service in which each gives himself to his brother and spends his life for the whole. And I believe in Him who makes men new, who transforms the life of men by giving them the spirit of love and purity and service, which is Christ.'[11]

At the height of enthusiasm which marked the post-World War I era, Rall composed a Stewardship Creed which appeared in all the Christian Advocates prior to an evangelistic Conference as part of Methodism's Centenary Program. In fact, Rall penciled on an old copy, "with slight modification since will be used by the Inter-Church Movement.'

> I believe in the stewardship of the Church, that like her Lord, she is here not to be ministered unto, but to minister.
> I believe in the stewardship of the nation, that as truly as Jehovah once called Israel of old, so the God of all peoples has summoned my country to serve in the family of nations.[12]

Professor Rall also spoke out on certain specific issues, especially earlier in his ministry. In the 1920's he was adamant in his views concerning industry. He urged that a Christian moral standard be used to measure business and its impact upon human welfare, pointing out the threats by business in unemployment, inadequate wages, and autocracy in relation to the general welfare of the citizens. He advocated as the task of the church to insist "upon the proper standards in all life, including that of industry," and specifically for it to list those community actions industry should assume: security of employment, adequate wage, industry-labor cooperation through collective bargaining.¹³ Issuing a call to industry's leaders for a spirit of "cooperation instead of competition, the social principle instead of pure individualism," he happily records the words of Mr. John D. Rockefeller, Jr., to this end:

> Human life is of infinitely greater value than material wealth; the well-being of the individual, however humble, is not to be sacrificed to the selfish aggrandizement of the more fortunate or more powerful.
>
> What is the attitude of the leaders in industry as they face this critical period of reconstruction? Is it that of the standpatters who ignore the extraordinary changes which have come over the face of the civilized world, and who say: 'What has been and is, must continue to be'?
>
> Or is their attitude one, in which I myself profoundly believe, which takes cognizance of the inherent right and justice of the cooperative principle underlying the new order, which recognizes that mighty changes are inevitable, many of them desirable, and which does not wait until forced to adopt new methods, but takes the lead in calling together the parties to industry for a round-table conference to be held in the spirit of justice, fair play, and brotherhood, with a view to working out some plan of cooperation, which will insure to all those concerned adequate representation, will afford to labor a voice in the forging of industrial policy, and an opportunity to earn a fair wage under such conditions as shall leave time, not alone for food and sleep, but also for recreation and the development of the higher things of life.¹⁴

In the summer of 1921, Dr. Rall preached at the Hennepin Avenue Church, Methodist Episcopal, preaching at both the morning and evening services. The evening sessions were more in the nature of addresses on theological and social issues. Synopses of the preceding Sunday night's addresses were subsequently presented in the church bulletin for the next Sunday, with a notation that the supply of twelve hundred often failed to meet the demand. One in particular, dated August 28, 1921, dealt with international conditions following World War I. Quite explicitly, Rall speaks of the conditions necessary for world order. In this address he points out the common danger of economic ruin in the face of runaway armament costs. Even war profiteers are discouraging the pursuit of armament increases. Nations not only should recognize their common goals, but reaffirm in practice their intention to live together in a permanent association of the representatives of the people.

> We may not call it a League of Nations, but as the world each year is bound more closely together, as the common interests and tasks multiply, only some plan by which the leaders of the people can regularly meet and confer will enable us to avoid war and work out the tasks of peace.[15]

Allied with this international association will be a new view of political statehood. Absolutism must be abandoned and be replaced by a policy of a "law" of responsibility toward other nations, "... in a principle of stewardship which each nation must observe in order that it may fulfill the supreme purpose of God for His World."[16]

In 1938, Rall addressed the Institute on World Christianity meeting at the First Congregational Church, Evanston, Illinois, under a title "Christian Faith in Action: What Does It Mean?" He began,

> The heart of the Christian faith can be put into a few words. We believe in the God revealed in Jesus Christ, in creative love as the final power that rules this

world. We believe in man, not as he is, but as he may be through fellowship with God. We believe that this creative good will is the way of life that man should follow. What does this faith mean when we bring it to non-Christian lands? What are its practical implications for our day?[17]

Disowning for Christianity any political blue print, any particular economic scheme, he reiterated, nevertheless, neither is it remote, meaningless, nor vague in its principles and demands. It holds to the sovereignty of God, therefore no state or industry can claim supremacy for itself. It believes in man and that God's supreme concern is with him, not institutions nor state programs. Thus, the Church will stand

> against war that slays, against hate that destroys something more precious than the bodies of men, against greed that curses alike exploiter and exploited. Against any system that shuts off from soil and tools.... It must deny all absolute right to property, to its control and use at the sole dictate of the possessor, since there is but one absolute owner, and that is God, and one ultimate test of the right to possess, and that is the service of the highest good of men.[18]

He then admonished the Church to promote intelligent knowledge of actual conditions, without bias; to hold forth the goals of the Kingdom of God; and to raise up men who in their vocations will have the Spirit of Christ move them.

Earlier, Rall's criticism of Barthian theology was noted and now in the context of his thought about the social structures of soteriology it is appropriate to record his reaction to Reinhold Niebuhr. This he does explicitly in review of Hans Hoffman's, *The Theology of Reinhold Niebuhr*.[19] There are basic elements within Niebuhr's position that call for criticism.

What does he mean when he says that the Kingdom of God is coming but is not here? Or when he declares that the message of Jesus 'cannot be applied directly, as moral teaching, to man's relation to his environment,' that is, in the social field?[20]

The basic defect of Niebuhr is the lack of a clear and full apprehension of the Christian doctrine of salvation and God's activity in human affairs. Rall then reiterates his main thesis: religion is not credence to a theory, but living fellowship with God and the gift of the Holy Spirit as the supreme expression of this fellowship. God is not only above us, he is with us. "It is significant that the doctrine of the Spirit has little place in Niebuhr's teaching."[21]

Another defect in Niebuhr is his lack of seeing growth as a vital aspect of God's way for man. The Kingdom, to be sure, is to come, but only insofar as it grows upon its present base.

> Niebuhr has been influenced by the modern existentialist theology of Europe which stresses God's transcendence and controlling power and neglects this latter side of spiritual presence and ongoing redemptive work — the Kingdom of God which is here.[22]

In 1953, at the age of 83, Rall delivered a major address before the Department of Stewardship and Benevolence of the National Council of Churches of Christ in the U.S.A. at Buck Hills Falls, Pennsylvania. In this address many roads previously traveled are once more gone over. There are new notes of stewardship of money, of time, of the nation. Under the latter he urges freedoms for all citizens and the renewed efforts to establish a Christian democracy. He also contends for conservation of natural resources, peace and shared wealth. And this at 83!

The other manner by which to understand Rall's

soteriology is to ask, How is Man Saved? Obviously, through the action of God's creative love in Jesus Christ. Such action includes both the revelation of God *and* the response of man. (cf. *supra,* Chapter VI) Following upon this initial justifying event are the many means of grace provided by God to sustain the believer in his new experience of right relations to self, to others, world, and God. These "Ways of Help" are to be found throughout Rall's writings: the Way of Prayer and Worship; the Way of the Word, or the witness of the historic community; the Way of Common Life, the world of nature and beauty; the appreciation of the world as the bearer of God's sacrality; and friends, work, play, joy, pain.

The last item in this discussion must center on a brief treatment by Rall of the theme of *Heilsgeschichte.* In a sense it represents a further word by Rall on his earlier discussion on the relation between faith and history (cf. *supra,* Chapter II and III). Can society be saved? Rall wonders aloud if the sharp dichotomy of individual-social can at last be maintained. Is not man by nature a socialized individual? Is he not alone the one who can make use of the word "I" as he places it within the "thou" and "we" contexts? Rall quotes Buber,

> 'By We I mean a community of several independent persons who have reached a self and self-responsibility.... Only men who are truly capable of saying *thou* to one another can truly say *We* with one another! To which we may add, no man can truly say 'I' who has not learned to say 'thou' and 'we.'[23]

Such a "we" soteriology finds its adequate political structure in democracy. Democratic society *is* the explicit expression of Christian faith.

> There is a democratic faith: faith in man, in the way for freedom for social advance, and in the ulti-

mate power of ideal forces — truth and justice and good will as against physical force, even though the latter may be provisionally needed. In this confident hope for the future, this belief in spiritual forces as against physical force, in the way of truth and freedom, in this fellowship of justice and freedom which includes social obligation with individual rights, there is implied a philosophy of history as well as a moral faith. There is no direct addition of a particular religious faith, religious freedom is assured to all. And yet the reality of a higher world of values and authority is clearly involved, and the great leaders of democracy have again and again voiced their faith in God as part of their faith in the democratic way. It is clear, logically and historically, that democracy owes these basic ideas and ideals to Christianity.[24]

Transplant this basic framework some two hundred years and one can almost hear Jonathan Edwards in his last writing, albeit unfinished, *History of the Work of Redemption*.[25] To carry this analogy further, Rall also traces the evidences of this "holy history" from Israel's theology of history with its conception of the holy Yahweh, its ethical message in the prophets and in its minor apocalyptic notes, its "tracts for bad times." The Christian "holy history" begins within this latter framework but changes it to include the beginning of the promised new age. Its "holy history" consists of the goal of God for society (Kingdom of God) and for his people (*communio sanctorum*). Evidences of the former Rall sees in the democratic way of providing a basic security for all men; freedoms to shape the order under which man lives and justice in the administering of that order. The state is the servant of man, and states of each other. The goal of God for his people is a new humanity, a right relation to all their worlds. God's way will be to work *through* people toward the evolving of his goal, not over *against* humankind. His way is one of order and justice, freely creative *agape*, with periods of uncharted activity. Neither inevitable progress nor aimless change, but bursts of *Kairos* in times of *Kronos* is Rall's soteriological doctrine.

Chapter VIII

ANTHROPOLOGY

In the opening decades of the twentieth century, Harris Franklin Rall joined his "liberal" voice to those of Harry Emerson Fosdick, William Adams Brown and others in reacting to what they considered an outworn, static theology. That reaction elicited the charge that the theologians of the 1920's had produced ". . . an increasingly monistic view of the world and a humanistic emphasis in religion."[1] The thrust of this quotation is captured in Rall's secondary intention in his review of Emil Brunner's book, *Man in Revolt: A Christian Anthropology*, namely, to assess Brunner's departure from the theology of neo-orthodoxy in general and Karl Barth in particular. (*supra*, Rall's criticism of them). Imbedded within that appraisal is Rall's acknowledgement of the theological and religious milieu against which that movement arose. Although he does not say explicitly that he is to be identified with that background, implicitly he admits to leadership within twentieth century American theological liberalism. The paragraph requires quotation in full in order to lay a foundation to understand Rall's anthropology.

> Our second interest in this work concerns the matter of Brunner's relation to Barth and to the dialectical theology. Is is hardly possible to consider this aspect without raising the whole question of the meaning and value of this movement. We know how the revolt against an extreme and mechanical supernaturalism and a wooden orthodoxy, the new insights brought by

the historical and psychological study of religion, the empirical approach carrying over into other fields the prestige gained from natural science, the appreciation of the social aspect of religion that comes with the pressure of new social conditions, and the pervasive influence of a new naturalism which its proponents blandly assumed was a direct conclusion from science, all wrought together to produce an increasingly monistic view of the world and a humanistic emphasis in religion.[2]

It need not be repeated any more than this: Rall very definitely included man in his conception of religion in general and Christianity in particular. Religion must account for three aspects — God — man — world. Christ's function was that of Savior and Lord, terms in themselves meaningless without the inclusion of man. Religion is depicted as salvation of men! In 1936 he published his initial treatment on the doctrine of man, a rather late date in relation to other theological-anthropological studies. He portrays man only in the context of seeing him frail as he is, ignorant as he is want to be, seeking and aspiring after the highest he knows and living according to the highest morality possible. In 1932, Rall introduced a brief discussion of the origin and nature of man as necessary toward understanding sin and salvation. In the same year he developed the genesis of a systematic work which appeared as a second volume of a trilogy (*Christianity, Religion As Salvation, God of Our Faith*) in which he outlines his anthropology. It is from these sources we can discern the thrust of his writings along this line, keeping in mind the lateness of the publication dates and the revolutionary theological ferment abounding.

One interesting footnote must be made. Rall intended the sequence of his trilogy to be *Christianity*, then *God of Our Faith*, and then *Religion as Salvation*. As the matter worked out, the latter two were reversed in publication dates,

> chiefly by the feeling that there was urgent need for the presentation of the Christian message of salvation, a theme too much neglected by modern theology.[3]

The reason for this footnote is directly tied to Rall's discussion of current conceptions of man in *Religion as Salvation,* published in 1953. In that book he carefully and succinctly puts forth these conceptions as the "sociological," the "psychological," etc., concluding with the "social conceptions" of fascism, Nazism, communism and democracy. Here, as elsewhere, Rall draws the explicit connection between prophetic religion and political democracy. Of interest, and speculation, of course, is the possibility that Rall also felt it necessary to reverse the order of the trilogy to meet pressures being applied nationally against the freedoms inherent in the democratic society during a time that has been labeled, "The McCarthy Era."

Christian anthropology has always concerned itself with the conviction that man has his origin and destiny from God and that in his present state he is sinful and as such unlike his Creator. Older theories, Rall concluded, taught that man was perfect in his creation, complete in innocence, with moral and spiritual capacities which allowed him to share the righteousness of God. Such a view was tied directly to an image of God as separate from or over against man and best symbolized as sheer power. Tied with this view of a pristine Adam was the thought of the fallen Adam in whom the original righteousness was totally lost. "With the fall man lost the image of God; he is evil and can do nothing but evil."[4] Rall judged that such a view of total loss in man cannot be found in the Genesis account but is largely an *eisegesis* of later Augustinian-Calvinistic theology, specifically groomed by its prior belief in

...the absolute contrast between God and man, the terrible seriousness of sin, the utter hopelessness of man himself, God's grace as alone the agent of man's salvation, and God himself conceived first of all as transcendent sovereign and absolute will.[5]

What has caused a modification of this position is the recent newer interpretations of man in both science and theology; the former through the disciplines of anthropology, biology and psychology and the latter through newer theological structures which stress the kinship of God and man, their relationship in moral categories, and the revelation of God needing for completion a response by man for validation. For the theologian, the decisive element in the origin of man is the fact of God's creativity and not the method of creation. God does not act in a vacuum and just as he relates to man in redemption through nature and history so in creation he works through the natural processes. Further, when the Christian theologian is to speak of anthropology, he does not use Adam as his model (the Adamic story is mentioned only once in the Old Testament outside of the Genesis account) but Jesus Christ. "In him he can learn the sin which separates from God, how man is related to God, and what his goal is as a child of God."[6] In the light of this advice, Rall summarizes his view on the origin of man:

The individual, like the race, is a creation of God. God has created him as a body-spirit being. Like the race, the individual comes by growth. Every man is linked by heredity to the age-old past of the race, just as in his personal development he is linked with an inherited culture and a social-material environment. God is creatively at work in all these relations but most significantly in the personal life of the self as man comes into conscious relation with his Maker. For God does not create the spirit of man (man the personal being) in some pre-temporal act, nor in and with the soul of Adam nor yet as something added to the body at conception or birth. The creation of a human personality is an ongoing work, which is at once creation and salvation, which goes on through man's whole life on earth and whose completion looks to the life beyond.[7]

When discussing the nature of man, Rall acknowledges the link of man with lower animals, but stresses those differences which separate him rather than those indicating his kinship. Such differences are easily specified: man is a thinking and speaking animal, man is a social being, a being who can create and sustain a society.

If there is to be a society in the true sense, man must first learn to say "I" with an awareness of himself as a person, he must learn to say "thou" with a realization of the nature of others as persons, and he must learn to say "we" with a sense of common interests and mutual obligations.[8]

Man is also distinctive by the possession of a social-cultural heritage and a power to rule or superintend his environment. Such power has limitations but these are self-conditioned within man: the failure to curb his own destructive urges, the failure to acknowledge his dependence upon God for this freedom and power, and a failure to appropriate for himself the goal of suffering love as the way of greatest power. Rall states that man's nature, then, includes not a loss of status, but a misuse of power. Does he mean a misuse by intention, by default or by nature?

Rall's anthropology is as dependent upon his theology as was true of Augustine and Calvin in his earlier criticism of their anthropologies. Given his theology of an ever-creative, suffering-for-humanity God, Rall's understanding of man will follow similar lines: i.e., man's nature is to be a "becoming" creature, distinguished by a plasticity, "a capacity for change and growth which continues throughout his lifetime."[9] He will be self-transcending, self-conscious, self-determining, in other words a personal being.

> Man lives in a multidimensional world, and his life is unique in the relation which he may establish in these many dimensions. This is what salvation means; it is setting man right in all these relations so that he may have life.[10]

But what of man's likeness to God, the *imago dei?* Primarily such a question begs of an answer if one starts with man. The principle question of that doctrine is that of God, his nature, his character, his will. In that light, two prolegomena must be stated: 1) Man with God is a distinctive being in the personal realm. He is basically not flesh and blood, nor mind, nor intellect. Fundamentally, he is person with capacities to reason and to "know", after the manner of the Johanine use of that word. It follows that however stark sin may become in a person's life, it cannot eradicate the selfhood of that person, and hence the ground of his relationship with God. 2) Man, who is like God in being person, is to become God-like (Christ-like in Rall's theology) in spirit and character. It is the character and not the being of man that is critical for Rall. He continued what he had outlined in his lecture of 1900: to wit, the area of moral relationships is the area of primary *theological* importance. What then of man as *"imago dei?"* To be made in the image of God restates what has been just said, namely, man is a person as God is. To be a person is to be self-conscious, rational, and free to know moral values.[11]

> The essential Christian position can be briefly summarized. We are not concerned with a supposed perfection of primitive man of which we have no knowledge. Two facts stand out for us and are of deep import.

First, man is a rational, spiritual being, belonging to the world of truth and good and God, made to know this and receive this. Second, man has sinned; evil has perverted him but not destroyed his capacity to know and respond. With these facts goes our Christian conviction: the real man, the true man, is not to be found by looking back. The true humanity lies before us; it is found in the Son to whose spirit we are to be conformed. God's creative-redemptive work began when that being appeared for whom this higher life of oneness with God was possible. The creation of this man in the real likeness of God, the overcoming of evil, the molding of man by God's Spirit, this lies ahead.[12]

As to what does lay ahead for man's development by God's Spirit, such future has often been couched in terms of the goodness, or conversely, the badness, of man. Rall prefers to restate the question, and in doing so, restates the issue within the framework of soteriology. What are the possibilities in human nature? Can anything be done with man? He discounts the doctrine of total depravity and the theory of federal headship in Adam. He arrays historical, biblical, psychological and religious criticism against a position stated in the Westminster Confession:

'We are utterly indisposed, disabled, and made opposite of all good, and wholly inclined to all evil.'[13]

There is no evidence of a pristine race begetting an evil one; the doctrine rests upon a theory of verbal inspiration of the texts and a wrong focus for Christian anthropology, i.e., Adam not Christ; and, one deed cannot possibly infect an entire race. The most serious criticism of the doctrine is one Rall used in his criticism of Barth, namely, if man were in this condition, how could he possess the capacity for apprehension of the truth, for knowing God and for subsequent response to him? Otherwise, man could make no response to God, Christian nurture would be an impossible dream, and we should have to go back to ideas of sacramental magic or irresistible grace.[14]

Man, rather, is a creature in the making. Christianity shares with the romantic optimists, confidence in man as having capacities for good, cravings for "togetherness" which complete man, the hunger for beauty, goodness, truth, God. Man is a *religious* being whose capacities bear witness to the image of God, "but the real image of God, the full personality, waits to be achieved."[15] Thus, man is seen as having great possibilities but also living under a severe condemnation for failing to fulfill these possibilities. Christianity should not see man for what he is, but for what he might become.

> When, therefore, we are admonished to be realistic, and it is suggested that we move, with Reinhold Niebuhr, theologically right and economically left, we may agree, provided we include the idealism of Christianity with its realism, and take care that we do not swing so far right with traditional theology as to move beyond both Jesus and Paul.[16]

One item more: freedom. If man is to become, then how free must he be? Determinism in all its forms is ruled out by Rall: physical, psychological, religious. With determinism there can be no meaningful discussion of personal responsbility for one's act. Man, Christian man that is, recognizes his cultural and environmental limitations but is a free actor within them. The Christian doctrine of salvation is not based on the confession "I did that and I am wrong," but "I did that, and I should and could have done otherwise;" it is not merely a forgiveness for past sins, but a way of help in man's use of his freedom toward his future. Although not discussing perfection in the Wesleyan sense of that term, Rall does imply a realization in one's life of a freedom from sinning. He even goes so far as to distinguish between "formal" and "real" freedom, defining the former as that within which one struggles against lesser ideals to reach *posse non peccare, magna est libertas* — to be able not to sin. "Real" freedom is *non posse peccare, maxima est,* not to be able to sin.[17]

"The necessity of freedom brings the possibility and practical inevitability of sin, and sin seems the one point of unrelieved darkness."[18] Rall includes in this definition of sin indifference, selfishness, greed, lust for power and love of pleasure. Much earlier, in 1918, he held forth a slightly different nuance in his definition of sin: "The heart of sin is the denial of the heart of goodness."[19] There is much richness here. The sum of Jesus' teachings as to goodness is found in two words, obedience and love. Rall concurs with all Christian history in saying sin is radical disobedience which can be specifically spelled out in as many ways as there are men. What is perhaps refreshing in Rall is his insistence of talking of sin in the context of the good, as formerly he did in talking about evil. Sin is the refusal of the good, or in Christian terms, disobedience to the will of God as expressed in the total event of Jesus Christ.

What then is the "good life" against which sin can be measured. 1) Loyalty to that which man considers to be the highest and best. It is also true that loyalty itself cannot be a guarantee of goodness or sinlessness. We all know loyalty to what one might consider the highest does not necessarily correlate with the good of a particular group or community. Notwithstanding this, however, the good man is marked by the loyalty by which in effect he exhibits his integrity. 2) Unselfishness. The good man wants to relate to other men in the sharing of that which he considers the highest. 3) Faith. The good man trusts beyond himself — to another or to a higher Being, sometimes — in order to indicate his willingness to be dependent upon another. Loyalty, unselfishness and trust mark the good man. All these terms indicate man as basically a person whose life is "determined" within a moral framework.²⁰ Such a good man can also be a religious man (and he is for Rall) insofar as the basis for his loyalty, unselfishness and trust are seen within the context of a Higher Power and not society alone. It is in the light of these three aspects of goodness — and a belief in a Higher world — that Rall discusses sin.

1) Sin is disobedience, it is saying NO to the call beyond. Sin is an active vital term denoting radical NO; it does not mean "absence of God." 2) Sin is selfishness. 3) Sin is being untrustworthy and irresponsive to God the Father and irresponsible to his ethical demand upon his son. For Rall this last definition bears a dual meaning: unbelief in God or unfaith and disregard for his will. Unfaith is not disbelief in certain theological tests, but rather is "... man's refusal to respond to the God who speaks to him, the refusal of trust and obedience."²¹ The consequences of such refusal can be measured in the damage to the individual person and to society. The latter Rall discusses under the caption "social sin" where he attempts to place man as a free, moral, responsible being, accountable for his own actions, but always as a "socialized individual." The consciousness of man's sole responsibility came into history with the emergence of prophets and Jesus. This did not obviate the primitive man's social solidarity but lifted it to a higher level as a part of God's overall redemptive plan. The individual and society both then are seen as moral agents. Operating under such an assumption Rall criticizes the view of Reinhold Niebuhr that ... "only individuals are moral agents."²²

Rall posits both individual and group responsibility and sin. Under the consequences of corporate or social sin, he lists those punishments ensuing from human wrongdoing in the light of an orderly universe. There is no vindictive, no jealous God but a loving God who has set forth a morally ordered universe within which men can live together abundantly. The consequences of social sin can be seen in poverty, war, depletion of natural resources, etc. But, to return to a Rall of an earlier page, what does this say of our doctrine of God? Reflecting what H. Richard Niebuhr had earlier concluded, Rall places the notion of God's wrath within the expression of his love within a purpose to reclaim or redeem, never to chagrin or punish. Rall also notes the absence of the mention of "wrath" of God in the New Testament and where found is in Revelation and a selection of Paul in reference to the final judgment as a "day of wrath."

> Religion necessarily uses language taken from human life and relations, but Christian theology can find better terms than 'wrath' for God's attitude and then "day of wrath" to describe his judgment.[23]

The individual consequences of the "refusal to respond to the gracious act of God," is the death of the higher. For the individual this means an experience of guilt for having known the higher and having chosen the lesser and therefore he is blameworthy. Variations abound in degrees and causes of guilt but generally Rall's position seems to suggest that a child is innocent when born into this evil world and only insofar as he grows into awareness of moral decision and chooses less than the highest, can he be said to assume the personal responsibility and ensuing guilt. This in turn raises the whole question of the origin of sin and its propagation. Rall discredits what he calls the Augustinian-Calvinistic theology with its emphasis upon the Adamic Fall involving all future mankind with being a reading into an *eisegesis,* of the Genesis account. (*supra*) Genesis should be in its mythical form to present ". . . truths that will abide while scientific theories change."[24] Such truths are: faith in the one God who is Creator and Orderer of the universe; man is the crown of creation, in the likeness to respond to God, free to rule, free to disobey. The temptation story is unclear as to its meaning but it clearly excludes the ideas of total depravity and an inherited corruption for all the race. It is plain, however, that we have here a lofty moral faith: a good God, sin as man's free and responsible choice, evil as the result of man's wrongdoing.[25]

The explicit interpretation of the origin of sin for Rall will be directly dependent upon one's prior doctrine of God and his relation to the world. The origin of sin is not to explain how "'sin proceeds from a wholly inexplicable act of will in opposition to God'" but how to explain the presence of reason and love, beauty and order.[26] Man cannot be dissected to discover the conception of his soul, but he can be pictured as possessing describable factors presenting options for good or evil: the will or thrust to live, the impulses toward "togethering," the capacity of self-direction. Other and various theories can be excused: 1) Man sins because he is finite; 2) Any gnostic theory which holds creation as bad; 3) Evolution with its seeing man as physical brute of nature. With this background of placing the question of the origin of sin into an opposing question of the presence of the good, one can easily project Rall's rejection of what he viewed as the traditional doctrines of original sin and total depravity. For Rall, such metaphysical categories are talking about unrealities; sin and its "propagation" must be viewed personal-ethically. Biological transmission has nothing whatsoever to do with it. Sin is a part of the race in the same manner it is for the individual: sin is a personal matter of decision-making; one is not born a sinner, neither is he born good. Both are to be seen as organic, dynamic growth processes related to personal achievement, but always within a larger society as a "socialized individual."

Rall does not directly engage himself in writing on the doctrine of sin until after the Barthian movement came to the United States in the late 1930's. Some, then, may attempt to claim that his theology was weak in its doctrine of sin and place him within his own claim that began this chapter. I don't think this is possible in the light of *his* schema of seeing that these questions, of man and his sin, as secondary to the questions of the character of God and Jesus Christ and the presence of good in the world as being the heart of the matter. Granting this, it is hard to escape the conclusion that the doctrines of man and sin were addressed by Rall throughout his career.

Chapter IX

ECCLESIOLOGY

Professor Rall saw the church as a culmination of the activity of God in history. Holy History began with the calling of Israel, continued in Christ's coming, and now is being fulfilled in the time of the historic Christian community.[1] It is a well-known caricature of theologians in the interwar period that they ignored ecclesiology. Some historians have noted the absence of any discussion of the church in the systematic *opera* of William Newton Clarke, William Adams Brown, and others. In 1914, Professor Rall published two books, his first of major proportions. In *New Testament History,* he spent considerable space characterizing the church at the time of Pentecost, in its cultic celebrations, its mission, its organization, its origin, by commenting on the Book of the Acts of the Apostles. Simultaneously, he published *A Working Faith* in which a chapter is devoted to "The Place of the Church," preceded by selected quotations.

'The true Church is still a sort of ideal challenge to the faithful, rather than an already finished institution.'

'Every man who learns what the true goal of life is must live this twofold existence — as separate individual — yet also as member of a spiritual community which, if loyal, he loves, and in which, in so far as he is loyal, he knows that his only true life is hidden and is lived.'

Josiah Royce, *The Problem of Christianity,* I, 54, 203.

A scientist's conception of the Church: 'A place in which, week by week, services should be devoted, not to the iteration of abstract propositions in theology, but to the setting before men's minds of an ideal of pure, just, and true living; a place in which those who are weary of the burden of daily cares should find a moment's rest in the contemplation of the higher life which is possible for all, though attained by so few; a place in which the man of strife and business shall have time to think how small, after all, are the rewards he covets, compared with peace and charity.'
Thomas H. Huxley, *Life and Letters.*

'Of have I seen at some cathedral door
   A laborer, pausing in the dust and heat,
   Lay down his burden, and with reverent feet
   Enter, and cross himself, and on the floor
Kneel to repeat his paternoster o'er;
   Far off the noises of the world retreat;
   The loud vociferations of the street
   Become an indistinguishable roar.
So, as I enter here from day to day,
   And leave my burden at this minster gate,
   Kneeling in prayer, and not ashamed to pray,
The tumult of the time disconsolate
   To inarticulate murmurs dies away,
   While the eternal ages watch and wait.'

Henry Wadsworth Longfellow, *Divina Commedia.*[2]

He began his analysis of those times in words familiar to the 1960's. Renewed interest in religious concerns was reflected in drama and the novel, in the quickened social conscience for better industrial relations but there was evidenced simultaneously an accompanying *disinterest* in the group. Promising young men, alert laymen passed the church by and enrolled in social service and political careers, while engaging in extra-ecclesiastical social movements.

What is perhaps most significant in all this is the fact that the men of large vision, the men of earnest, moral spirit, are turning aside from the Church because of their very earnestness. They see the Church as an institution concerned for its own life, debating petty matters of ritual and robes, of differing doctrines and forms, and wasting its resources by its divisions.[3]

Rall sympathizes greatly with this attitude of compassion. Indeed, he would say of such that it is religion, the satisfying of man's needs. What he understands that first must be done is to clarify the meaning and mission of the Church. He notes the one rather odd fact that stands out in all this: the essential link between Christianity, the institutional church, and great social endeavors. Even though nowhere in the New Testament is there given any legal description of the church, as to its order or organization, history records that where Christianity has spread the institutional church has been present. History also exhibits the founding of hospitals and orphanages; great humanitarian efforts have been directly connected with the institutional church. Rall asks,

> Does it mean that the church is more than a matter of rule or commandment, that it is essential to the very life of Christianity and the inevitable outworking of its very spirit?[4]

The difficulty of the church is not the church, but the definition of its mission. It is not to be that of sacramentarian nature nor that institutional organization is sacred in itself. Rather, the mission of the chuch can be stated as 1) *Proclamation-Kerygma,* a truth that is believed and thus a message to be pronounced. Rall strongly insists on the basis of the church being the good news of Jesus Christ. Those abandoning the church need to be reminded that the only true salvation comes not by movements, demonstrations, revision of laws and charters, but by changed lives through the clear message of reconciliation of God through Jesus Christ. It is true, society's needs must be met, and the

> ... glory of the Church is that she brings a message for these needs. Her voice has not always been clear; her vision has sometimes paled. The Church is human as well as divine. But the great words of God and right, of justice and love, of sin and pardon, of man's need and God's help, these men could always hear. And above all else she has brought to men the Christ. Nowhere else have men found the answer to these great questions.[5]

2) *Koinonia — Fellowship.* Christianity is essentially social. The heart of the Christian spirit is love which is always a community relationship. Also, the Church is barrierless, making no distinction as to class, wealth or race. It is exemplary of the democratic way so eagerly sought in the United States. The final thought of this fellowship is its comprehensiveness. In the Church there is no East or West; no young or old; no timeboundness.

3) *Worship.* The marvel for Rall is not that so many persons absent themselves from weekly community but that so many congregate so consistently!

> The popular play boasts of its run of a hundred nights. The best seller holds its readers for a brief year. There must be some vital need that is met by an institution that can hold all kinds of men through all ages in this constant allegiance.[6]

The Church proffers to all the possibility of renewal, of commitment to God and to his Will. This spirit of reverence and awe is part of religious man who yearns to overcome his present fearfulness of his environment.

Certainly it is service to feed men and clothe them, but the highest service, after all, is to lead them into the presence of God, to show them the meaning of life, to quicken ideals and kindle aspiration, to let them bow in humble confession, and then to let God Himself send them forth to a new life.[7]

4) The Church's mission is to the world, its task is the *furtherance of the Kingdom of God.* The true church is the church at work. The Church is not the kingdom, it is the means to the Kingdom. In no other age (1914) has the church understood so clearly its task to reach out to the world — to lose its life for the sake of the world. "It is turning its ministry toward all life."[8] All this in 1914!

These themes remain central to the ecclesiology of Harris Franklin Rall throughout the next fifty years of his life. Any modifications or altered emphases are due to the peculiarities of the specific times. The Church not as an institution but as a fellowship of witnessing people is his constant theme. Some such variations of these themes can be seen in three contexts: the sacramental issues of the Church (prayer, symbols, etc.); the peculiarities of the Methodist understanding of the Church, and the impact of the Ecumenical Movement in Faith and Order.

1. Fellowship with God as constitutive of Christianity implies that both prayer and sacrament are vital elements in strengthening this bond. Rall denotes prayer as the expression of this fellowship with God and the heart of religion. Prayer is that which man holds to be his ultimate concern without which he could not subsist. And to be in the true character of fellowship, prayer must be grounded in the spirit of utter trust, and in the spirit of entire absolute surrender,

> ... so that our deepest joy will be not in the gift that may come, but in the confidence with which we leave

all our life with Him, that makes His will our final desire beyond all other wishes.⁹

Later, Rall is to return to the schema he uses in defining religion as consisting of push-pull forces. The "push" of prayer is the almost instinctive baring of oneself before God. He quotes William James' answer to the question, "Why do Men Pray?" — "Because they cannot help it."¹⁰ Prayer is the natural initiative of religious man in his appeal to that beyond him; to bare all the necessities of his life before Him. The "pull" of prayer is God's love to assist us in the fulfillment of our natural religious desires. It is a curious paradox: prayer is the greatest means of self-realization, but we fail in this if prayers keep self as the center.¹¹ We have already seen Rall's interpretation of Jesus' prayer as the Creed of Jesus (*supra*). Man's prayer should allow him to open himself to others. Its practice should be intense, persistent, regular, hopeful of realization of knowing the presence of God.

2. The Methodist Church engages Rall's energies in many different ways: preaching, teaching, writing of books, articles, pamphlets, "Dr. Rall answers," political leadership in social reform, etc. One of the earliest accounts of his activity in the life of the church centered on the Ritual Revision of the 1916 General Conference of the Methodist Episcopal Church. Rall at that time was secretary of the General Conference Commission on the Revision of the Ritual.

One issue reached the attention of the delegates of the 1916 General Conference, the first Conference at which the inner tensions of the church were revealed. This issue centered upon a proposed revision of the ritual of the church. Professor Harris Franklin Rall, Secretary of the General Conference Commission on the Revision of the Ritual, reported that the Commission had attempted to retain the traditional form as best it could while yet remaining loyal to current understandings of truth. Such minor revisions were noted and approved without debate: changes from "Holy Ghost" to "Holy Spirit," from "forgive us our trespasses as we forgive them which" to "forgive us our trespasses as we forgive those who," and the use of the American Revised version for the King James version of the Bible. The central points of contention lay in the proposed revision of the rituals of baptism and church membership. The Committee proposed to delete in the ritual of the sacrament of baptism the phrases: "forasmuch as all men are conceived and born in sin" and "except a man be born of water and the Spirit, he cannot enter the Kingdom of God." They argued that the former phrase confused the laity who may have understood it as a reflection of the Roman Catholic interpretation toward the marriage relationship. The latter, they contended, was also confusing because of the multiple meanings attached to it: if it referred to baptism, it said what the church did not say, that is, unbaptized little children will be lost; if it did not refer to baptism, the passage had no application in the ritual. It seemed better to the Commission to include the Scripture "Suffer little children to come unto me..." which set forth the belief of the church.

In the older ritual for church membership, the question for church membership read:

> Do you here, in the presence of God and this congregation, renew the solemn promise contained in the Baptism Covenant, ratifying and confirming the same and acknowledging yourselves bound faithfully to observe and keep that covenant?

Its revision was to read "Do you accept the Lord Jesus as Savior, Lord, and Master?" "Have you saving faith in Jesus Christ?" became "Do you receive and accept the Christian faith in the New Testament?"; "Do you believe in the doctrines of Holy Scripture as set forth in the Articles of Religion of The Methodist Episcopal Church?" was omitted altogether. The entire report was referred to the Board of Bishops for final action. The two contested phrases in the baptism ritual were deleted. Ruling upon the ritual for church membership, the Bishops retained the older question relating to baptismal vows and the affirmation to the doctrine of Holy Scriptures as set forth in the Articles of Religion, and disallowed the question of saving faith in Jesus Christ and its alternate.[12]

The center of the attack upon this revised ritual came from Bishop Thomas B. Neeley of the Philadelphia area. He charged that those who revised the ritual had eliminated selections of the Old Testament as though it had little or no authority in the Christian Church, had greatly modified the old doctrinal statements from no apparent need, blotted out declarations as to natural depravity, had destroyed or beclouded the doctrine of salvation from sin, through repentance, prayer, faith in atonement of Jesus Christ (such as represented in "Have you saving faith in Jesus Christ?"), and had diminished within the ministry, particularly the episcopacy, the power to attack and destroy doctrinal errors, as though inviting latitudinarianism.[13]

Rall in the April 15 and April 22, 1920, issues of the *Christian Advocate* replied to the critics of the revised ritual by citing the importance of the revision which had been largely unnoticed and at the same time expressing his fears of possible revisions of the revision at the forthcoming General Conference of 1920. Although not a ritualistic church, he wrote, Methodism had a ritual which when used with sincerity and earnestness, assists in worship and religious education. In fact, the ritual often expresses for the congregation its beliefs more adequately than any doctrinal standards. Ritual revision must be carefully developed taking into account the historic forms of the Church universal, the specific Church understandings and what Rall calls "the word and spirit of Christ." These articles attempt to elucidate the theological basis for changes in the baptismal, marriage, burial services and the conditions for church membership. The new form of the baptismal ritual makes clear the Methodist position:

We do not believe that baptism is the washing away of original sin, whether this be connected with procreation and birth or not, or that it works a regeneration. We give the Scripture basis for infant baptism, therefore, in the broad fact of God's covenant relation with man, wherein children are included, and in our Lord's gracious invitation to children.[14]

The most extensive form of liturgical revision was the proposed change of the burial service. The former ritual depended too much on the Old Testament with only scantiest reference to Christian hope. Thus the shift to a New Testament basis with that future hope associated with the teachings of Jesus Christ.

In defense of the revision of questions for those seeking church membership, Rall cited Wesley's criterion for such membership as "a desire to save their souls." He argued this simple query to be in the spirit of Jesus and Paul that the greater part of American Methodism held to this, insisting upon credal acceptance only after 1864. Of this falling away, Rall said:

> Above all it contradicted the fundamental spirit of Methodism. Early Methodism was never attained with the heresy of intellectualism, the idea that the holding of correct doctrine was the essence of religion. It never conceived of faith in the Roman Catholic manner as the acceptance upon authority of doctrines which the believer did not understand. Faith was a personal and trustful surrender to the God who came to men in Jesus Christ. Religion was a personal fellowship with this God, a vital experience in the power of God's Spirit. The reality of religion was life. The Church had its doctrinal standards indicative of its beliefs, whose acceptance was required of its preachers. For its membership it relied upon spiritual life to conserve purity of doctrine, and did not trust in doctrinal standards to

assure spiritual life. It had not forgotten Wesley's words: 'I will not quarrel with you about any opinions. Give me solid and substantial religion; give me a humble, gentle lover of God and man.'

One other point should be noted. Methodism is not a society within the Church, nor a sect that has broken off from the Church. It is a branch of the Church Universal. It is not Methodist baptism that we offer to people, but Christian baptism. We invite them to join not simply the company of Methodists, but the Church of Jesus Christ. But if we stand as representatives of Jesus Christ and His Church it is plain that we have no right to limit fellowship or refuse baptism by conditions that are of our own making. Our demand must be as searching as that of Jesus, but we have no right to block the door with that which is not included in His demand.[15]

As far as I can find, Rall does not write on matters of ritual or sacraments again until 1953 with the publication of *Religion as Salvation*, in a chapter entitled, "Symbol and Sacrament." This discussion follows immediately his chapter on the various means of grace by which God sustains man in his personal fellowship with Him. Rall categorized symbols and sacraments as additional means to assist man in his apprehension of a Higher World, unseen but real. Parenthetically, he criticized that theology of the "Wholly Other" as being bereft of possible use of symbol and analogy in the use of its conception of God, for symbol and sacrament imply a certain likeness and kinship. Consistent with his personal-ethical definition of Christianity, Rall contends for an understanding of the sacraments as

> ... no more and no less than a setting forth of the gospel itself, of God's love and the summons to man to respond in faith and obedience. And they bring the same gift that is promised when men receive the gospel.

God's gift of himself in love and fellowship and as the power of a new life.[16]

Sacraments, in other words, are of soteriological and not ontological assistance. This prophetic view is neither subjective, nor atomistic as Rall holds that such sacramental grace is God acting within the historic community of the Church. He followed with a brief description of baptism as a church right setting forth God's forgiving mercy and cleansing from sin by his spirit and not washing away of original sin. Infant baptism is justified as a total act of The Church, a declaration "... that the God of grace has saving access to the child and that he can use home and church as means of grace for the child."[17] The Lord's Supper is described as commemoration, Thanksgiving fellowship with the spiritual presence of Jesus Christ. The only sacrifice evident is Jesus Christ's giving of himself for all and the celebrants doing likewise in the acceptance of his way.

At about this same period, Rall became involved as well with recruitment and training of ministers within The Methodist Episcopal Church. In 1924, the Commission on Life Service of that church engaged Miss Margaret Bennet to conduct a sociological survey of "The Ministry of The Methodist Episcopal Church, Educational Status and Numerical Strength." An 80 per cent return from effective Conference members and 67 per cent of the supply pastors provided the data. What of the education in the ministerial ranks? The assumed standard of that year included college and seminary training. Miss Bennett reported this base to be a pious wish as the actual standard proved a high school education. In addition, by a two-thirds majority vote of the Annual Conference a man who had been preaching three years might be accepted into the Church's effective ministry. The report also indicated 25 per cent of the pulpits were occupied by men with no formal education, 45 per cent were college graduates, and 20 per cent had seminary training. The supply pastors accounted for 66 per cent of those attaining high school education and 33 per cent with grade school. The overall picture, according to Rall, indicated two things: 1) 15 per cent of the men had college and seminary training;

> The report offers us two carefully worked out comparisons. It takes first the reports of the men admitted during three five-year periods: 1886-1890, 1901-1905, 1916-1920. In the first period 30 per cent of the men admitted into full membership had only a high school education or less, in the second period this dropped to 21 per cent, in the third period it rose to 27 per cent. The percentage of college graduates, with and without seminary training, was 41, 50, and 46 for the same three periods. Apparently there was a period of advance in the last years of the last century, with a period of decline in the first twenty years of this century.[18]

2) A decline in this percentage over the preceding years.

Rall's concern for an educated ministry centers upon his conviction that the more adequately trained man can better meet the perplexities of the new era. His proposed solution is not immediate establishment of higher standards for admission but a more positive attitude toward training on the part of Bishops and district superintendents.

> Our second need is a revived interest in education as vital to the church, and particularly the education of our leaders. A hundred and fifty years ago Methodism faced the peculiar conditions of a new world beginning to flow westward from the Atlantic coast into a wilderness of forest and prairie. The summons was to an itinerant ministry, to men who were willing to leave school and give up the thought, in many cases, of home and settled pastorate. The day has changed. The test of devotion now is whether a man will make the denial necessary to get his training, as the would-be physician

is required to make it. In this case, the responsibility rests, not with the state, but with the men already in the ministry. That responsibility we have shirked. We need to repent.

Let us tell our young men what we want and what they must have; the men will come up to it if they know we are in earnest. If they do not, then we must face the serious question whether they are of the kind that the church wants in her ministry. Where will this road lead us that we are following, this way of lowering standards in order to make it easy for our candidates, in order that enough of them may offer themselves for admission? We have today a very simple course for local preachers, quite too brief and simple. Yet in a certain Conference where large numbers of local preachers are used as supplies, it was stoutly asserted but recently that if we insist that these supplies must study this course they will give up their work, while from a second Conference there came at almost the same time a like statement as to the many supplies employed there. How much is the kingdom of God advanced by the work of men like this? Are we losing confidence in our own religion as to the preachers themselves?[19]

3. As the 1920's, 1930's and 1940's progressed, the fact of Professor Rall's involvement in Faith and Order Conversations led him to write of Methodism's self-understanding as a Church, and of the Ecumenical Movement as well.[20] In the 1940's he prepared a substantial report on "The Methodist Conception of the Church" for the study booklet *The Nature of the Church,* A Report of the American Theological Committee of Continuation Committee of the World Council of Churches, Faith and Order Commission. The framework of the address was two-fold: to outline the distinctiveness of the denomination's ecclesiology and to answer ten guide questions proposed by the Faith and Order Commission. Rall noted Methodism's beginning was not as a Church,

but a movement within the Anglican Church. Thus, he concluded, the primary or distinctive claims of Methodism were not doctrinal but evangelical and ethical. It selected what befitted its movement from the doctrines of the Church as a whole.

> The insistent Methodist emphasis has been on Christianity as a gospel and a way of life.... This emphasis on Christianity as gospel and way of life helps to explain the position of Methodism in matters of doctrine, with its combination of liberalism in principle and conservatism in conclusion.[21]

Methodism sees Christ as the founder of the Church in the sense that he created a fellowship by his impact upon men's lives. There is no New Testament prescriptive in matters of church organization including Orders, specifically the episcopacy, Methodism does not believe that the Church is set against the world — it "... no more believes in total social depravity than in total individual depravity."[22] Emphasizing the functional over the institutional, Methodism holds forth no one polity and structure as sacrosanct, but has made constant adaptation of its structures to changing conditions. So far as any specific contribution Methodism may make to Faith and Order discussions, Rall (by the bye, he had sought counsel from ten unidentified Methodist leaders) projects that this is to be found in the way it unites "elements of the Christian heritage which other movements tend to oppose one to the other in exclusion."[23] Methodism's inclusiveness has come by seeking to set forth the full meaning of the Christian faith.

> Thus it has stressed personal faith but keeps it free, and has held to the historic faith of the Church but has not identified it with any one statement or given any statement legal authority. It has placed high value upon the Church and the corporate nature of the

Christian life, but refused to make the institution an end in itself. It has renewed in its life the Christian fellowship as intimate and actual group relation, but without the separatist tendency of the sects or pietistic groups. It has united the ethical and the religious, man's freedom and responsibility with his dependence upon God. It has regarded the gift of God as a demand, and has seen the demand as possible only through the gift, opposing equally moralism and quietism. With its emphasis on evangelism, and on conversion and sanctification as works of God's grace to be consciously experienced, there has gone a due regard for religious culture and the work of education. In its preaching it has been insistent upon the transcendent holiness of God, the sovereignty of God, man's sinfulness and his total dependence; but its primary emphasis has been personal-ethical, upon the moral character of God rather than upon sovereignty and irresistible power. Recognizing man's sinfulness and affirming that what he is and has all comes from God, it has insisted on man's nature as personal-ethical being linking him to God, upon his capacity for response, his freedom and responsibility, and upon the gospel as involving not only forgiveness but a transforming power. Stressing individual experience, it has rejected religious atomism. It has seen that the personal-ethical emphasis involved the social-historical. So it has thought of the world as the subject of redemption and of history as the sphere of God's work. Holding to the hope of a final consummation, it has prayed for the coming of the kingdom of God upon earth. In this realm, too, while recognizing that all is of God, it has affirmed God's grace in working through man and man's opportunity and obligation as worker together with God, rejecting both activism and quietism.

Without assuming to call Methodism a 'bridge church,' we may see its service as a unitive force alike in its life and in its conception of Christianity. Not only has it united these and other elements that tend to become disparate, but it has served historically to bring together what Troeltsch indicates as the Church and the sect conceptions of the Christian religion.[24]

Two remaining papers are in the Rall Manuscripts which deal specifically with Methodist worship and "The Ethical Element in Methodist Preaching as Related to the Concept of the Church," the latter being a paper prepared for the Chicago Discussion Group of the World Council of Churches. The paper on worship repeats many points noted earlier: the necessity of worship, the aspect of worship as an expression of the church's faith and life, and the framework within Methodist worship in particular. A major portion of the paper is devoted to Rall's judgments on the "typical" Methodist services of worship in the 1940's; mention is made of the sermon, the Scripture Lesson, congregational singing, the sacrament of the Lord's Supper and its meaning, frequency of celebration, prayer, etc.

The latter paper traces Wesley's preaching and his view on the Church (*supra*). Following Wesley's death, Methodism lapsed more into individualistic pietism (Rall's words). Then Rall concludes, and in effect traces his own leadership within The Methodist Episcopal Church:

> The last generation was marked by definite developments. The Methodist church actively participated in the rise of the so-called social gospel. It was first in organizing a group within the church committed to the new ideals of social service, and the so-called social creed of the churches, as set forth in 1908 by the Federal Council, was in substance that previously adopted by the Methodist General Conference. It was saved, however, from those faults which are now rather indiscriminately charged against liberal-minded and social-minded thinking. It was not romanticist, for it

faced the facts of man's sinful nature. It was not moralistic, for it stressed the need of divine grace and the fact of divine salvation. Its confidence in God and in the power of spiritual forces set it off equally from apocalypticism and evolutionary optimism. It was the legitimate result in a new situation of elements that had been present from the beginning: the church as a fellowship of those who are committed seriously to the Christian way of living; the worth of the individual man not because he is innately good but because he is potentially and in God's purpose a child of God; the Christian gospel as involving not merely forgiving mercy but saving and transforming help through God's Spirit; finally, with all the recognition of man's sinfulness and indeed the emphasis upon it, the belief in man's moral freedom and responsibility and in what man through God can become and do.[25]

Harris Franklin Rall was sixty-seven years of age when he attended the Second World Conference on Faith and Order at Edinburgh in 1937. Yet he not only entered fully into that Conference but extended his energies in the following two years in criticism of its results and suggestions for further Faith and Order discussions. His report of the Conference in the *Sunday School Journal* of December, 1937, mixed homey appreciation for the city of Edinburgh and the many individual and personal contacts made there with some constructive comment on the progress toward the reunion of Christendom.

Granted that for all delegates, Christianity was a divine religion, something given by God, not simply evolved by man, with source and center in Jesus Christ, the differences arise as to just exactly what is given, an 'institutional' Church or a Church of 'fellowship?'[26]

In two further articles Rall develops this theme of recurring division among member churches of the World Council of Churches. The position of the Church as "given" is asknowledged as having the weight of tradition behind it.

> Christianity is a divine creation; not an historical growth or a human achievement, but the deed of God, the gift of God to man. Elsewhere we have man's search for God, here we have God's revelation to man; elsewhere human efforts at amelioration, here a divinely wrought redemption; elsewhere socially developed institutions, here a divinely established church. What God has thus done has not been dependent upon man or conditioned or limited by man. As a divine deed it is absolute, perfect, unchanging. As such it is authoritative, asking simply for acceptance. And it is definite and objective, not an idea or an influence, but something which God in strict sense has instituted and to which men may be summoned. When we have this, we have Christianity.[27]

Among the adherents of this position are variations on the particular focus of each denomination: the sacraments, the ministry, or the Scriptures. The other conception, a newer one, is described by Rall as the "gathered" Church, the emphasis being upon "personal-spiritual." Elements of this type of Christianity are the view of God as personal, ethical being, righteous in character, a living God. "Christianity, stressing the personal and ethical in its conception of God and religion and salvation, is still a prophetic religion."[28] Rall in defense of the latter definition, is at pains to point out that the distinction between the two is one of emphasis and not mutual exclusion. The institutional church does not rule out the personal and ethical and spiritual. The prophetic church does not rule out the necessity of corporate nature of Christianity, the testimonies of significance in history, nor the sovereignty of God and his grace. The fundamental area of disagreement is that the former insists on a giveness and completion of the activity of God in the

Church while the latter insists upon the emphasis of a "becomingness" as integral to the nature of the church.

Rall's point in all this is that the question as to the nature of the church was premature at Edinburgh. The basic questions left untouched there needed to be explored fully, even at the risk of clogging the progress of Faith and Order. Nevertheless, progress was indeed made at Edinburgh. It was natural that the background of both Lausanne in 1927, The First World Conference of Faith and Order and Edinburgh focused upon the institutional image of the church. The 1937 conference was noted for the common affirmation of unity in the worship of one Lord, "...who claimed our common allegiance and in whom God had spoken to us, one Spirit of the living God who had wrought in us this faith and fellowship."[29] The core questions of Edinburgh remained:

> the nature of authority, the conception of God and his relation to the world, and the bearing of historical-critical studies upon our traditonal conceptions. Above all, we must consider constructively what is this Christian faith of ours, what it is that divides us from the paganisms of our day, and what the message is that we have to bring to our world.[30]

Rall was hopeful that with these new questions, a new phase would be reached in ecumenical discussions. He remained persuaded that the gulf between the two views of the church need not remain impassible. His concluding remarks can only bear fruit with complete quotation.

> What may be expected from such a continued and thorough-going study as has been here proposed? I believe that our free churches of the West have much to learn from those who follow the Catholic tradition: the corporate nature of religion, the meaning and method of worship, the place of tradition in relation

to faith and authority, and the meaning of ecumenicity are instances in point. I believe that the prophetic conception also has much to offer, and not simply as to the nature of personal religion but as to the way to unity. The institutionalist viewpoint from its very nature must insist upon particular formulations of faith and order. Rome is the extreme but logical expression of this position. The prophetic view recognizes these differences, but asks us to consider whether the heart of our faith and the ground of our unity may not lie elsewhere. Laying the emphasis upon the personal, it points to Christ as determinative for the nature of Christianity, Christ as the revelation of God, as the Word that speaks God's will for our life and God's grace for our salvation. Here is that which unites us, and here is the line, distinct and deep-running, that separates Christianity from the secularisms and paganisms and unbelief of our day. Of course, this is a difference in viewpoint, and the prophetic group has no right simply to say: Accept our position and give up your own. What it can say is: Explore these matters with us. See if this be not the basic difference. Consider with us which way it is that God has taken to come to men, to express His will, to give men life.

One point needs special emphasis. Under the influence of the Lausanne-Edinburgh method of piecemeal consideration there is a good deal of discussion about the particular differences which remain to be removed, or the tensions that await resolution. What we need to see just now is that differences and even tensions will remain, and that there is a Christian unity which has place for them. As regards the differences, they were present in the Apostolic Church, and in Christian history the method of enforced uniformity has tended to create schism rather than secure unity. Our immediate need may be a larger view as to the possible place of such differences in the one Church of Christ.

The question of 'tensions' is a somewhat different matter. Specific tensions may become divisive in church life and destructive in the life of the individual, but they may also root in something ultimate and enduring and belong to life itself. The basic principle of polarity must be reckoned with here. Many tensions have their source in this, and thus have a legitimate and permanent place in life. The prophetic conception of Christianity, emphasizing the living process and not the static form, gives place to these. Basic is the tension which appears in the contrasted emphasis, now on the divine in its absoluteness, its all-sufficiency, its all-determining action, and now on the human with its freedom and responsibility. Even when the extremes are avoided, the tension remains. Independence and dependence, moral freedom and determinism, Calvinism and Arminianism, activism and quietism, social gospel and apocalypticism, these are variants of a general theme. So we have the emphasis on tradition and authority over against the spirit of experimentation and exploration, the stress on the individual and that on the corporate, to name but a few. They rest back upon a polarity that belongs to life itself and are not to be resolved by eliminating one side or the other, or by moving on to a Hegelian synthesis, or by the rather mechanical device of "both and." Our problem does not lie in these tensions, nor is any idea of church unity acceptable which does not leave room for them. In tensions like these, challenging us now this way, now that, denying easy rest, whether in thought or life, there are found the spring of life and the richness of the Christian truth and way.[31]

Chapter X

ESCHATOLOGY

If theology in all its separate doctrines is first of all dependent upon the understanding of God in his relation to the world, then the last question to be raised is that of that relation at the end of the times. One might suppose that Professor Rall in his continued emphasis on the personal-ethical might neglect eschatology. On the contrary, much of his activity in the 1920's is caught up with those proposing a pre-millenial theology. Mention has been made of the necessity of the theologian's apologetic task to establish a ground for his theology and then to measure other variant themes against that ground. Ritschl did so by way of the Reformation and subsequently found Roman Catholic theology as his "opponent." For Rall, a similar authoritarian theology is found noticeably in the Roman Catholic Church, and thus that church is used illustratively by him as that against which he is developing his theology. But primarily in the nineteen Teens and 1920's Rall's opponents are the fundamentalist and conservative churchmen both within and without Methodism. The major point over which the controversy rages is that of eschatology.

At this time he found it incumbent to rescue John Wesley from the ranks of "those modern chiliasts" who claim him. Of all the churches in the country, none has given as little place to premillenialism as the Methodist Church, Rall notes the most recent (1914) listing of premillenialists, only 8 of 269 are Methodist, and of these, none is a bishop, general officer, District Superintendent, or a teacher from any Methodist college or seminary. He points out that nowhere does Wesley discuss a single aspect distinctive of premillenialism. As a matter of fact, largely based on his collected sermons, Wesley refutes that position by stressing many aspects of the religious life in opposition to premillenial theology.[1]

As defined by Rall, the essence of premillenial theology is:

> It is not the idea of a future period of blessedness nor even that of the visible appearing of our Lord preceding this. It is the idea that the world must grow increasingly evil, that no work of preaching or power of the Spirit is to save it, that it is to be saved by visible and external forces at the coming of Christ, and that the resultant kingdom is to be a visible and political realm upon earth presided over by Christ and his saints.[2]

The professed outline of premillenialism consisted of a three-fold belief: 1) There is no hope for the world in this age. 2) The world will be saved when Jesus appears in visible form and at the head of armed forces, destroying some of his enemies, and assuming lordship of the earth, and, 3) For one thousand years he is to reign at Jerusalem as head of the Jewish world empire, and suppress all evil. Premillenialism is no mere matter of words, but an entire system of theology.[3]

Wesley certainly concerned himself with the coming of the Kingdom of God, but did not subscribe to a picture of the world growing worse. The present is the best yet because of the increase of the work of God in renewing men's inner spirits through the active power of the Holy Spirit. Against the appeal to a miraculous intervention, the second coming of Christ, as man's only hope, Wesley again and again persisted in the confidence in his work of bringing this hope to England's down-trodden. Against the appeal to outer force is Wesley's doctrine of the Spirit which, when proffered, awaits response of the individual. Rall alludes to several misquotations from Wesley as used by premillenial writers to "claim" him. He then concludes that the differences between Wesleyanism and premillenialism run far deeper than details in present research. It is the opposition between Methodist and Calvinist conceptions of God and his relation to the world. Rall is not saying Calvin and Augustine were premillenialists. He is saying there are Calvinist emphases present in premillenialism, especially the distinctive emphasis on God's separateness and hence his power. Methodism claims distinctive emphasis on God's nearness and hence his character. Premillenialists accepted man's passivity and enlarged it to apply to world history and the coming of the kingdom. Satan rules now, man must await God's direct, overpowering intervention. Mr. Wesley's view, on the other hand,

> ... emphasized as strongly as any man the thought of salvation by grace alone. He had as high a conception as any of the power of God and his sovereignty, but he saw that the sovereignty that God desired was a moral sovereignty, resting upon the free love and loyalty of his children. He magnified the power of God, but it was the power of God's Spirit exercised through the truth and in the realm of freedom, not as a coercive force. Religion thus became for him a personal relation moving in the realm of moral forces. And against the rigid determinism of the Calvinistic system, he proclaimed God's will for the salvation of all men, a will whose defeat could have only one source, the refusal of man. But enough has been said to make clear Mr. Wesley's fundamental difference of standpoint from modern premillenialism, and why this has found so little entrance among Methodists.[4]

Rall directed major attention to premillenialism in two books of the 1920's, *The Coming Kingdom* (in the Kingdom of God Series) and primarily in *Modern Premillenialism and the Christian Hope*. His schema in the latter book is divided into three parts: a tracing of the hope of the Kingdom of God in history, an analysis of premillenialism historically and in its present theology, and an apologetic for the Christian Hope of the Kingdom of God. In the first part, Rall traced themes we have already considered, carefully distinguishing two tendencies of hope in the Old Testament, that of the spiritual, ethical and universal as opposed to the nationalistic and external. In each of these, premillenial notes are noticeably absent and only arise in late Judaism in what Rall labels "Tracts for Bad Times", or, the apocalyptic literature. This literature is the chief source of premillenialism and as such in its time served a necessary function to preserve faith in troubled times.

The question naturally arises for Rall as to the thought and teaching of Jesus within this apocalyptic framework. Was he an apocalyptic? Is his entire message eschatological? He acknowledged this conclusion of Albert Schweitzer, but suggested that he had selected individual texts to support his conclusions, a dangerous hermeneutic.[5] The center of Jesus' teaching was his thought of God and his relation to the world and the fellowship proffered to man. To be sure, Jesus used the language forms of the day including the apocalyptic, but fashioned such views according to his central teaching of the character of God. As such, in opposition to the apocalyptic characterization of God as sheer power, this teaching on the character of God places Jesus totally outside the premillenial context. In his emphasis upon the rule of God's love over men, is no interim ethic. It is the present experience of God that is stressed and the rigid opposition of the future kingdom of love and the present kingdom of Satan breaks down. It is true that Jesus' great emphasis is on consummation in the future, but he saw the beginning of this rule in his own unique ministry. As to how the consummation is to occur, the sources indicate much silence by Jesus, although he apparently expected in the near future some great manifestation of the power of God which would bring in the kingdom, and somehow he himself would return to consummate the work he had begun and that this return would make clear to all his Messiahship.[6]

The sum of the gospels indicates little detail as to the future but does provide a conception of God now present in Jesus Christ who calls men to faith and service. Paul and John together reflect the modifying of the apocalyptic hope, translating the literal return of Jesus into a present spiritual presence. The contrast is not there between two moments in time, but between two worlds of life and death, light and darkness. In Paul there are two conceptions: the apocalyptic, is viewed by Rall as valuable in its day of realization of salvation as a present experience within the Christian fellowship. The Apocalypse of John, to be sure apocalyptic, is viewd by Rall as valuable in its day of turmoil as were those of the Old Testament in their day. "Its apocalypticism no longer commends it to thoughtful men, and the hope of the Christian Church looks forward to a different moment of salvation."[7]

Rall then traces in rapid survey the history of premillenialism as evidenced throughout the history of the church. He points out that chiliasm has always been rejected by the mainstream of Christian theologians and its sole support has come in smaller groups. That is to say, those Christian theologians whose thought has shaped Christian theology have been opposed to this doctrine or have left it aside. Also, the major creeds of the Church exclude premillenialism as symbolic of the Church's faith: the Apostles' Creed, the Nicene Creed, and the Athanasian Creed. The source of modern premillenialism is biblical literalism. It differs from the unreflected hopes of the early church in at least two respects: its environment is not hostile to the world but impregnated with a culture amenable to Christian influences and modern premillenialism has developed into a system of theology.

Following his discussion of the basic tenets of this system,

Rall criticizes the practical results of such a theology. It holds that democracy is vain and its ideals are false (recall Rall's judgment that the democratic state is the historical evidence of faith in God and Jesus Christ). Chiliasm stands for individualistic salvation and repudiates social hopes. It denies the possibility of a Christian state, a Christian civilization, a Christian social order. It views the Christian Church not as an agent to foster the Christianization of the world, as the world itself will be destroyed. In particular, such a movement within Methodism was at direct variance with what Methodists were engaging in during the Twenties. In its Centenary Program Methodism has adopted as its creed, the following:

> We believe in a living God, mightier than selfishness and oppression and greed and war and every power of sin; a God who is present and working in his world today.
> We believe in the Kingdom of God, the Kingdom that is already here wherever men love and believe and serve, the Kingdom that shall come in fullness when all men shall know God, and all the life of men, industry, and state, shall be lived in love and righteousness.
> We believe that this new world is to come through the preaching of the gospel and the power of the spirit of God in the hearts of men.
> We believe in the God who works with men and through men, and that fellowship in the world's service is the highest glory of human life.[8]

Rall could keep silent no longer against the growing strength of premillenialism within Methodism and in the *Zion's Herald* specifically details the dangers and changes required if The Methodist Episcopal Church should embrace the doctrines of modern premillenialism and "follow out their logic in its work." He makes quite clear the theological basis of present programming of Methodism.

What is this that is inspiring the church to action and guiding her program? This working faith of the church may be stated briefly as follows:

We believe in the God and Father of our Lord Jesus Christ; not the God of a distant past alone, or of some far-off hope, but a living God, dwelling in His world and working with men today.

We believe in Jesus Christ. It is in Him that we see this God in whom we trust; it is in Him that God reveals His will for us, and gives Himself to us in forgiveness and fellowship; it is in Him that we see not only the Saviour of souls but the Lord and Saviour of all life, the rule of whose spirit will be the salvation of the world.

We believe that this new world of our hopes, this kingdom of God, is to come through the gospel of Jesus Christ, and the power of the Spirit of God in the world.

We believe in an all-inclusive gospel: that it is God's will that all men should be saved, and that all the life of man should be redeemed in home and state and industry.

We believe in the kingdom of God present now and coming in its fullness on earth. For us the kingdom of God is the rule of that spirit of Christ which is the Spirit of God, the rule that shall win the hearts of men and control all human life.

We believe in a God who dwells in men and works through men, and in the church as the fellowship of His people, in whom His Spirit dwells and through whom He purposes to win the world for Christ.

What if the church should once get hold of this great truth, the vision of a God working in His world, loving and redeeming and self-giving; the vision of a world that is being made; the vision of the sure triumph of the kingdom of God upon earth; the glory of the life of man and of the vocation of the church as the dwelling-place of God's Spirit and the instrument of His great purpose. These are the convictions with which we are working in the church today. They are molding the plans of our great societies and setting the goal for our faith and prayers and toil.[9]

In the light of these doctrines, he sets forth his proposals: First, our hopes would need revision; the kingdom of God is not here and we have no right to expect it until Jesus returns bodily. Also, only a limited number will be saved. Secondly, our ideas of the Church must change. The true saints will be the Elect, and, in fact, the present churches must be denounced. Third, we must redefine the mission of the Church. "The business of the Church is not to Christianize the world, but simply to evangelize it. And evangelizing means simply to proclaim the message of the gospel."[10] Fourth, we must relinquish all our social ideals and aims. "A Christian China, for example, cannot be our goal any more than a Christian America."[11] Fifth, we should have to give up our old-time Methodist confidence in the power of the gospel and of the Holy Spirit. "God does not intend to save the world by such spiritual means, but by force, by supernatural, irresistible power .... Not the Christ of the golpel and of Calvary, not the indwelling Christ working by the Spirit of God, is to save the world, but a Monarch at the head of His armies, crushing revolt and setting up a literal throne, just as the Jews expected of old."[12] Finally, we would have to give up our message of stewardship.

Premillenialism fervor was tied with other conservative movements following World War I but by the end of the decade such movements had slipped into eclipse. Rall does not write more on this until the latter days of World War II when he noted no such revival of the teaching of the Second

Coming of Christ, but a certain definable growth of what he calls the new apocalypticism. Whereas premillenialism resided mainly among lay people, the new apocalypticism was to be found primarily in scholarly circles. The new apocalypticism, however, carried over those other dominant notes of the 'Twenties, ...

> a sense of hopelessness as to the achievement of good in history or by human effort, the belief in the existence of powerful forces of evil and their dominance over humanity and the course of events, and the conviction that human hope must rest upon a final, decisive and irresistible act of God in the overthrow of evil and the establishment of righteousness.[13]

The new apocalypticism is pictured by Rall as an attempt to deal with the problem of evil in mass society. He then raises the question as to the relation of the biblical view of eschatalogy — the new age is at hand, and the central event was the visible and personal return of Jesus to do his messianic work — and the times of the Second World War? The modern premillenialists had added nothing new to older ways of thinking, he concluded. The new apocalypticism, on the other hand, is very different from the older chiliasm. It did not feel bound to adhere to strict New Testament forms. It did see the world in terms of "demonic control,... though it is hard to tell what it means by its favorite term, 'demonic'..."[14] It appears as an attempt to regain the New Testament faith buy putting its hope for the future in a final act of God, not in his activity through chronological time. Rall assizes elements of strength here, such as the "otherness of God," alike in emphasis of the Neo-Orthodox Theology, although the other polarity, the kinship of God, he feels is also necessary. The difficulty with the neo-apocalypticism is its neglect of a social-historical as the proper field of God's redemptive purpose.

When Rall discounts premillenial theology he by no means

is discounting the final Consummation nor is he discounting life beyond death. Religious man, *homo religiosus*, has as part of his essential nature an urge to live beyond death. History reveals in various religions attempts to meet this need. The theological issue at hand is one of time relationship and eternity. For some theologians the answer is bifurcation of time as present and eternity as something "out beyond," when time shall be no more. Rall rather sees Christianity as saying these two worlds interact in the present, that eternity is present in time through the historical activity of God in Jesus Christ. In modern parlance, we live in a realizing eschatology. He returns to a familiar theme, that the question of life beyond death resolves into a question of the character of God and his relation to the world.

What are the grounds of the Christian belief in what Rall calls "immortality?" A few preliminary definitions are in order: by "immortality" he did not mean continued existence after death.

> Eternal life rather than immortality expresses the Christian faith. It is not a matter, first of all, of life after death. Man's life is eternal when he enters into a living relation with the eternal world, that is, with God; and this life may be here and now.[15]

Nor did he mean that of a life of a disembodied spirit. He argued against bodily resurrection, but for the Pauline idea of a "spiritual body." The "resurrection of the body" can only mean that there man will not lack for means of contact, for effective action, for fellowship with others.[16]

The grounds for eternal life, interestingly, have little directly to do with Jesus Christ. In his book, *The Coming Kingdom*, Rall mentioned that the resurrection of Jesus assists the believer's faith in immortality, although it is not a proof of man's immortality.

What it did mean to the early church was this — that God had set his seal upon his servant, that he was indeed, 'declared *to be* the Son of God with power,... by the resurrection from the dead.'[17]

To my knowledge this is Rall's only direct mention of the resurrection of Jesus and eternal life. Rather, he established his grounds for eternal life in the character of God and the order of the universe. Christian faith holds that the ultimate ground of being is spiritual and if there is an ultimate Power sustaining justice, truth and love, creative good will, a God whose gracious purpose was to proffer to man the fulfillment of his most basic needs, surely man can have this presence here in time and mere death cannot destroy. Also, the world of rational order and creative purpose supports the idea of eternal life. It would indeed be odd if a universe with such characteristics would bring to nought the "highest product of this age-long movement."

But, how is man to believe in what lies beyond death? Streets of gold? Pits of fire? Rall does not avoid the doctrine of eschatology as early in his ministry — New Haven, Connecticut, 1903, he preached on "The Fact of Hell." In the summer of 1921, he concluded an address at Hennepin Avenue Methodist Episcopal Church with these words:

> The teachings of Jesus and the facts of life as we see it alike point forward to a dividing of ways between men, to a final separation. We see men there from without, but even we can see how the boys that started with us in the old home place have moved apart. And the one division that counts, growing deeper with the years, is the division of character. The saint and the sinner may dwell in the same man, but in the end the one or the other wins the mastery — there is no neutrality here, Judgment is not a reading of books, not a sentence imposed from without. Some time we shall become what we really want to be: that is character. Some time

we shall be made manifest for what we really are: that is judgment. Some time, by the inevitable law of gravitation, we shall go to our own place; that is destiny, and that will be heaven, or hell.[18]

The views of Life Beyond will be in relation to the present experience of the presence of God in one's life. "Life with God, life in the presence of God, life fulfilled, that is the meaning of heaven."[19] Such life will be a conscious personal life, fulfilled in active creative fellowship, release for pain and sorrow, and the threat of death and continuing growth. What of judgment and hell? Rall again reverts to the questions of the character of God and the order of the universe. A God who seeks ever the lost will do all in his power to redeem all men through proffering himself for man to respond. The moral order of the universe seems to demand certain essentials: man becomes what he chooses and such choices increasingly fix or establish his character. There is also a law of gravitation and a law of separation equally present in a given community. In the life beyond men will separate and gravitate according to the fixity of their earthly habits. This is hell, that evil desire shall be fulfilled in evil character and that men of evil shall find themselves with those of like kind.[20]

All remaining questions of infant damnation, irrevocable distinguishing and separation at death, the destiny of those beyond the hearing of the gospel, Rall, realizing his own human limitation, can only surmise that the God he knows in Jesus Christ will provide the greatest possibility of growth to those who seek him in sincere repentance.

Chapter XI

HARRIS FRANKLIN RALL'S IMAGE, IMPACT, IMMERSION INTO "AMERICAN" THEOLOGY

By definition every period demands shifting perspectives.[1] Such new interpretations of reality expose both the period under review and, perhaps more importantly, the newly-agreed upon criteria for the assessment. Every historian knows the tenuousness of judging the "thought" of any era, especially if the factor of impact on that period is employed as a measure of that time. Let me illustrate by the use of popular music.

During a recent table conversation I asked who had been adjudged as the music man of 1970.[2] Those at the dinner quickly answered by naming their favorite vocalists: Tom Jones, Steppenwolf, etc., without realizing that the person in question was a composer, Burt Bacharach. What is significant here are the variants employed: age and sex of respondents, their capabilities as to the purchase of records, which might be considered important when ranking popularity, and the criteria of judgment relative to selecting the music man of 1970. Why Burt Bacharach and not Bob Dylan? Why Burt Bacharach and not Aaron Copland? Additionl conflicting factors must also be considered, e.g., the production management of the record companies who program certain singers and styles and who, in effect, determine the music styles and subsequently the music popularity of the society. Disc jockeys must also be accounted for in their selections as to frequency of playing record X, and the time slot in which it is offered. Of course, public relations agents also determine public taste.

Similar approaches might be used to delineate and decipher any medium in any age relative to its importance to its time. Dwight MacDonald has for years brought to battle his antipathy against what he calls mid-cult and mass-cult literature. He asserts that for two centuries Western culture has in fact been two cultures: the traditional kind (he labels it High Culture) that is chronicled in the textbooks, and a novel kind that is manufactured for the market. He labels the latter Mass Culture or "... better yet Masscult, since it really isn't culture at all."

> In the novel, the line stretches from the eighteenth century 'servant-girl romances' to Edna Ferber, Fannie Hurst and such current ephemera as Burdick, Drury, Michener, Ruark and Uris; in music, from Hearts and Flowers to Rock 'n Roll; in art, from the chromo to Norman Rockwell; in architecture, from Victorian Gothic to ranch-house modern; in thought, from Martin Tupper's *Proverbial Philosophy* ('Marry not without means, for so shouldst thou tempt Providence: But wait not for more than enough, for marriage is the DUTY of most men.') to Norman Vincent Peale. Thinkers like H. G. Wells, Stuart Chase, and Max Lerner come under the head of Midcult rather than Masscult.)[3]

MacDonald judges Masscult as not even having the theoretical possibility of being good; it is anti-art, without standards, obfuscating commnication between individuals which allows for the total subjection to the spectator. He is even more caustic against Midcult which uses the Masscult formula, "but it decently covers them with a cultural fig-leaf .. it pretends to respect the standards of High Culture while in fact it waters them down and vulgarizes them."[4]

The importance of MacDonald's essay in this instance is to signal the strata or units within a culture and so differentiating them, assess their relative values. According to MacDonald's *literary* criteria, most of the literary genré are boorish. But, and here is my point, in gaining a perspective of an era, who is to say John Barth is more to be read than James Michener, or Reinhold Niebuhr than Norman Vincent Peale? It is well to keep in mind the problems of intellectual history as set forth by Franklin Baumer as they bear upon gaining a perspective of an era: (1) discovering the climate of opinion or *Zeit geist* of a particular era of history; (2) the problem of causation of intellectual change; (3) to what and precisely how do ideas effect the majority of non-intellectual people; (4) the uses of intellectual history.[5]

What has this apparent excursus to do with Harris Franklin Rall? Much, if Baumer's points above are kept in mind, particularly (1) and (3). Temptations upon intellectual historians are great to assess any period by the accepted norm of sophisticated writing. Another way to say this same opinion would be to cite the importance of Wolfhart Pannenberg, Johannes Metz and Jürgen Moltmann for contemporary American professors of Christian theology, and hence perhaps conclude that they represent the current thought of American theology. I would suggest that in America Billy Graham, Oswald Hoffman and Norman Vincent Peale provide a more adequate index and gauge to the current theological understanding. The impact of Pannenberg, Metz and Moltmann will be slight outside the circle of the theological intelligentsia.

An additional temptation upon the historian is to assess a previous era according to criteria that informed his own era and perhaps are more appropriate to the investigator's time than that of the era under review. The New Left historians are presently making this argument with effective force. I can cite a personal example: my dissertation centered upon the American Methodist theological responses to the theology of Karl Barth during the Interwar Period 1919-1940. In establishing the general theological milieu in America during that time, I paid particular attention to the "Chicago School" of theology (Gerald Birney Smith, Henry Nelson Wieman, et al). I, at that time, caricatured them as having relinquished all semblance of the Christian theological heritage in the face of the apostate desire to be relevant to those times. Only several years hence did a review of Kenneth Cauthen's book on the period, *The Impact of American Religious Liberalism,* by Professor Bernard Loomer of the Divinity School of the University of Chicago cause my eyes to be opened to the actual parameters of the intellectual climate of The University of Chicago during the 1920's, within which the "Chicago Theology" developed.

I am not arguing the indefensible *vox populi, vox dei,* but I am stating that in research of any given era, perhaps more attention should be given to non-intelligentsia in order to ascertain the mood as well as the thought patterns of a given time. It may well be that Professor Ray Browne and the Popular Culture Association, of which he is the guiding genius, will provide a better gauge of America's moods and thought patterns today than all the learned journals on reserve library shelves.

The periods of the late 19th and early-to-mid 20th centuries are just begining to be investigated for their theological motifs.[6] Hopefully, studies will emerge focussing upon midcult and masscult theologians. The Lynd studies of Muncie, Indiana, might well be followed as indices of a major mood and theological thought pattern of the two decades 1910-1940.[7] More importantly, denominational leaders and theologians identified specifically with major parochial seminaries will need to be studied in the same depth as has been Harris Franklin Rall among the Methodists. Religious journals, many, if not most, now defunct, will need careful assessment relative to their themes and their audiences. The impact of revivals upon major urban centers and subsequent social reform will need an investigation similar to that of a former era by Timothy L. Smith.[8] In particular, weight will have to be given the traumatic instance of World War II, and all its socializing ramifications and the emergence of major theologians not necessarily identified with parochial and denominational seminaries

(A similar argument will have to be made on the cruciality of Vatican II and the breakdown of a Roman Catholic ghetto theology in the 1960's and 1970's.)

Harris Franklin Rall's importance to American theology lay in his leadership of the Mid cult and Mass cult kind. To understand the Interwar Period Christian theology within its American context, and to measure the men who best articulated that theology in that particular society, the historian and scholar should examine Harris Franklin Rall. To put the matter yet another way, until the fifth decade of this century, *denominational theologians,* rather than what I call "movement theologians" (Tillich, the Niebuhrs) made the greatest impact upon America. Christian theology was borne in greatest manner through single denominational leaders. The impact of Harris Franklin Rall upon The Methodist Episcopal Church can be duplicated by other denominational leaders.[9] That influence was experienced among the mass culture as it only could be, given the peculiar nature of the church in America.[10] Textbook authors have distorted the accurate theological understanding of the past because of their concentration upon "movement theologians" at a time when labyrinthian if not parochial denominationalism proved the common mode of communication.

Harris Franklin Rall rightly deserves attention as one of America's most important midcult and masscult theologians. His impact upon the public can best be measured through his leadership in The Methodist Episcopal Church, the largest single denomination in America during the Interwar Period. As noted above, (chapter I, pp. 18ff, chapter IV, pp. 6-14), he preached in its outstanding churches, participated on various committees of several General Conferences, served as secretary, treasurer and vice-president of the Methodist Federation of Social Service during its most active years, lectured at and wrote many studies for the very influential Annual Supply Pastors' Institutes, wrote not only many books on various theological themes, some as texts, but also penned an important column appearing weekly in the official magazine of the Church. In 1937, members of the Church elected him a delegate to the World Conference on Faith and Order. The listing of key Methodist leaders who acknowledge their indebtedness to him would be too long to list. They included numerous bishops, board executives, editors, professors and preachers. Professor Murray H. Leiffer has touched upon that influence, when he eulogized:

> Few men exerted so great an influence on the thinking of ministers in the first half of the twentieth century as did Harris Franklin Rall. Through his teaching, his preaching, his writing, and his participation in organizations of the church — from the Commission on the Course of Study to the Methodist Federation of Social Service — he touched the lives of literally tens of thousands of Methodist ministers and laymen, and not a few beyond the bounds of Methodism.[11]

Such an acclamation points toward Harris Franklin Rall's role as theologian *to* The Methodist Episcopal Church: training its ministers through his teaching at Garrett, advising its supply pastors through the Conference Course of Study, and leading its leaders in the Methodist Federation of Social Service. Words remain to be written of these two latter emphases.

As early as 1820 a course of study was established by The Methodist Church for ministerial candidates, to be directed by the bishops. Almost a century later, in 1916, the General Conference, at the instigation of several leaders of whom Professor Rall was one, adopted new procedures in ministerial training to supplant what appeared to the Conference as not requisite enough. A Commission on the Course of Study consisting of bishops, educators, and pastors became born. Professor Rall was elected its executive secretary and in that capacity executed controlling influence over the recommended books in the new four-year program, including two of his own.[12] Each Annual Conference was instructed to conduct a summer school to direct its candidates for admission and once a year in Evanston, at Garrett, a national conference was held for Annual Conference leaders, entitled, A College of Preachers. Professor Rall lectured extensively at these schools.

Rall's connection with the Course of Study provided the single instance of his direct involvement in the Modernist Fundamentalist Controversy of the 1920's. Harold Paul Sloan, prominent pastor of the New Jersey Conference, spearheaded a drive which led to partial revision of the mechanics of the Course of Study in the General Conference of 1920. During this Conference, he criticized as examples of the liberal content of the Course, the works of Harris Franklin Rall and George Albert Coe, which he claimed were at variance with Methodist doctrines. In the absence of Professor Rall, Garrett Biblical Institute's President Charles M. Stuart rose to defend his colleague against this assault. He stated that an obligatory promise is made by all Garrett professors to teach doctrines conformable with the Methodist heritage. Stuart countered that he considered Sloan's charge against Rall a reflection against Rall's doctrinal integrity and his moral obtuseness to a sacred contract.

The Course of Study grew in magnitude and serviceability and in 1926 could report an enrollment of 2500 ministers in its correspondence school. Sloan, as president of the Methodist League for Faith and Life, blacklisted thirteen of the Course of Study books as impregnated by naturalistic theology, and specifically charged Rall with having no place for the Virgin Birth, the bodily resurrection, and propitiatory atonement. He urged the 1928 General Conference to refute this theology found in the Course of Study, repeating his earlier prophecy that "we do not believe that Professor Rall can persuade the church to substitute his opinions for the positive declarations of the Lord Jesus Christ."[13] His appeal fell on deafened ears. Professor Rall's books remained in the Course of Study reading lists into the 1950's supplemented by *A Faith For Today, According to Paul, The Christian Faith and Way, Christianity,* and, *Religion as Salvation* at various times.

Although many social pronouncements were issued through the various conferences, and agencies of the Methodist Episcopal Church, the Methodist Federation of Social Service indexed the penetration of the Social Gospel Movement into American Methodism. The Methodist Federation of Social Service originated on December 3, 1907, in Washington, D. C., with the intention to "deepen within the church the sense of social obligation and opportunity, to study social problems from the Christian point of view, and to promote social service in the spirit of Jesus Christ."[14] The Federation was intended, according to one of its presidents, Bishop Francis J. McConnell, to be in the forefront of the church on all social issues.

> So often the church is criticized because it fails to lead in the fight against social injustice. This can never be said of the Methodist Federation of Social Service. For twenty-nine years it has set the pace for the Protestant Churches of America. We take just pride in this. Can you, can I, sit calmly by and fail to take an active, aggressive part in helping to fight the evils of our economic system?[15]

The unofficial status of the Federation granted it the freedom necessary to pursue unfettered a prophetic role. Through it and due to it several social issues were met to the degree that a historian of this time could say, "The Methodist Federation for Social Service quickly became the most influential organization of its type within American Protestantism."[16] Joining Rall in the leadership of the Federation, and again, representing the degree of his influence in the Methodist Church were such leaders as Bishops Herbert Welch, Edgard Blake, and Francis J.

McConnell; Editors Dan Brummitt and Halford Luccock of the *Christian Advocates*, L. O. Hartmann of *Zion's Herald*, and George Elliott of the *Methodist Review;* and various national leaders of the Church: Frank Mason North, Georgia Harkness, Edgar Brightman, Harry F. Ward, Ernest Fremont Tittle, and G. Bromley Oxnam. Each of these persons wielded extraordinary impact upon the religious situation during the 1920's and 1930's through preaching, charimanships of sundry Boards of the Church and through professorial influence (e.g., Brightman at Boston University School of Theology and Harry F. Ward at Union Theological Seminary in New York).

Two more crucial items must now be enjoined before concluding the place of Harris Franklin Rall in 20th century American Christian theology. What is the "American Experience" and theology's relation to that experience? Secondly, have the portrayals of American Christian theological indebtedness to Friedrich Schleiermacher been accurate?

Professor Joseph Haroutunian provides an interesting structural analysis pertinent to the first question.[17] In distinction to the European experience, he cites several unique aspects that separate the American Experience from an errand into the wilderness.

> (1) Americans have been in the main peoples of European extraction who have found themselves in 'a land of opportunity.' ... The Americans... have been a practical rather than a theoretical and speculative people.... In the process they have cultivated a technical rather than a contemplative reason. They have kept thinking toward the improvement of their goods rather than toward a vision of the ultimate Good...
> (2) These esrtwhile Europeans have had palpable success in their pursuits of happiness.... It appeared that the Adamic curse under which mankind had been laboring was removed, and that a new age had dawned

in a new world where men of good will and industry might live in contentment and hope.... (3) European social life was realized by way of systems of laws and offices and stations.... (a) *In American experience* human individuality was radically modified. The dependence of the individual has been not so much upon fixed institutions as upon the cooperation of his fellow men in his pursuit of the good things of life . . . he [the American] has developed a new sense of his fellow-humanity through his steady dependence upon those around him without whose cooperation he would have failed in his pursuit of happiness ... this shift in American experience, from dependence upon permanent institutions to dependence upon cooperating people, has had profound effects upon American Character and religion.... One is hardly surprised to find that people of 'the new world' have come to think of themselves as 'the new Adam,' a new species of humanity, that has given the lie to 'old world' views of man and human life... (b) *The American feeling* for freedom which is in a sense the American soul or life, must be understood as an expression of American experience.... In short, the sheer opposition of lust for freedom to prudent behavior in an established and sovereign social order is replaced in an American experience with an exercise of freedom which is inseparable from the use of intelligence in trans-action.... (c) *There is in American experience a* new aspect of the use of reason.... Hence [for the European] the highest use of reason has been conceived in terms of insight into the actual ties, coherence, harmonies, and laws of reality, together with a knowledge of the kind of attitude and conduct demanded by given and universal Being.... Such traditional rationality was greatly altered by American experience.... Truth was not so much the given as the accomplished; reality was not so much out there as at the end of hard work;

wisdom was acquired more by intelligence than by contemplation; things were made to cohere rather than found coherent; and the Good gave way to good things which although mutable were solid as well as available.[18]

Haroutunian then lists seven elements in the American experience necessary for a separate, viable American theology: (1) Nature is without power to man but the crux of man is located in his cooperating with other men. "In a land where human beings have worked together to build a City of Man, natural religion survives by the presence of traditional sentiments." (p. 8) (2) Theology must be particularistic. "Insofar as in the theology of the churches God is the philosophical poets' Great Being, the American cannot take even God seriously. He takes God least seriously of all." (p. 9). (3) Theology must note the great affinity between biblical language and American experience. "Their [the Americans] God has worked and rested, He has set Himself to particular ends and produced particular effects toward peace." (pp. 9-10). (4) The Great Being is a myth of European Establishment; the Living God is the Creator of a community of persons working toward better things. American experience knows no God apart from the mutual communion of fellowmen trans-acting for their several goods." (p. 10). (5) As men work together, so they speak together; so as Americans know God together, they work together and do His work. (6) Men know God as they work together. "In American experience the place of God's self-revelation is properly the people's work together, in the temptation which besests them to use one another rather than to help one another, which is the sign among them of their breaking the covenant of life." (p. 11). (7) No one vision of truth is adequate, but communion of ideas bears validity. "American experience, working together as against working under an Establishment, requires its own discipline under the conditions of cooperation." (p. 11).[19]

219

The second preliminary matter is of equal importance to understanding the importance of Harris Franklin Rall relative to American theology in the 1920's and 1930's. What European theological context was prevalent in America during that time? Was Walter Lowrie correct following his depiction of twentieth century evangelical liberalism, when he said, "... with regard to the value of religious experience (and the 'Christian experience' most of all) we are as yet troubled with no doubts. We have all become Methodists, i.e., — without our knowing it we have all become disciples of Schleiermacher, 'the father of modern theology.' "[20]

It need not be reiterated here that Albrecht Ritschl differentiated his theological attempts from Friedrich Schleiermacher, who he nevertheless acknowledged as his theological mentor (cf. *supra.*) Of greater instance is a cataloguing of coalescence between Ritschlian Theology and the "American experience", or on the other hand, the theology of Schleiermacher with that same experience. Earlier (Chapter One) I have quoted the interesting parallel between Ritschl and Horace Bushnell, who is often suggested as the father of Liberalism in America, an analysis sympathetically accomplished by Professor George B. Stevens of Yale and one of Harris Franklin Rall's theological professors. Both William Hutchinson and Robert Handy make mention of the relation between Ritschl and Ritschlians and important American theologians of The Liberal Era:

> Most liberals were equally ready to acknowledge their more recent members, both European and American. . . . By the end of the nineteenth century, this way of arranging theological discourse had achieved its archetypal expression in the work of Albrecht Ritschl of Göttingen and the work of his pupil Adolf von Harnack at Berlin.
>
> American liberalism enjoyed direct intensive contact with these European sources. Among the thirty most prominent liberals of the period between 1875 and 1915,

over half had studied at German universities, and had incurred intellectual debts to a long list of scholars headed by Ritschl, Harnack, and R. H. Lotze of Göttingen.[21]

In the development of their theological thought, American Christocentric liberals were greatly stimulated by such great German scholars as Schleiermacher and Ritschl, and their successors. During this period numerous younger Americans went to Germany for advanced theological study, including Henry B. Smith, Lewis French Stearns, Egbert C. Smyth, Borden Parker Bowne, Arthur C. McGiffert, Henry Churchill King, Walter Rauschenbusch, and William Adams Brown. Inevitably their minds were deeply affected by this stimulating experience. Through them, Ritschlianism became very influential in this country.[22]

I wish here to categorize the four areas of the "American experience" in particular which tie directly to the theological schemata of Albrecht Ristchl and which by so doing lay claim that he and not Friedrich Schleiermacher should receive acclaim as the father of modern *American* theology. (1) Ritschl and History. Professor Philip Hefner has delineated with care current negative criticisms of Ritschl, as found in the standard commentaries of Barth, Dillenberger and Welch, H. R. Mackintosh, and H. Richard Niebuhr.[23] Fundamentally, these critics see in Ritschl's thought a basic antagonism between man and the natural world in which man sees himself as a helpless fragment caught in an inexorable causality of nature vs. his understanding of himself as a child of God, a free, spiritual being with worth far surpassing nature. Christianity, alone, represents the successful attempt to provide a solution out of this dilemma. In Christianity, man discovers his goals of self-assertion and self-fulfillment also as God's goals and the work of Jesus Christ was aimed at precisely this fulfillment ". . . which man sees over nature."[24] Christianity then, for Ritschl, according to his critics, is a moral enterprise and its God portends to be the authenticator of man's struggle for superiority over nature. God calls and binds men together in their moral striving into His Kingdom, which is therefore equivalent to their moral ideals.

Against such an interpretation, Hefner argues that in Ritschl the description of the human predicament is not exhausted at all in the discussion of man's antagonism against nature. Rather, Ritschl's focus is on the vitalities of man's existence, on his innate drives toward wholeness, in which his whole life takes its place in an ordered system. Man is discomfited, antagonized, by the notion of his being only *part of* the natural causal choice because such offers him an inadequate sort of wholeness, i.e., according to nature, and not his unique humanity. Hefner develops the thesis that beginning at this understanding, a completely different set of implications follow: the concern of interpreting Christianity as it speaks to the unique human situation, the chief aim of man subsists not in *overcoming nature*, but in integrating his existence into a whole, that human meaning become commensurate with his essential self-hood. "This entails *freedom from nature*, independence from natural causality *as the chief determinant of action or as the primary motive for existence.*"[25] Albrecht Ritschl was attempting to deny nature the power or claims given it, that its processes are self-explanatory and thus capable of intimidating man. Nature, too, must be viewed under a larger perspective, as with man. So, Christianity and its God, for Ritschl, is not the authenticator, but is ". . . the comprehensive system or whole within which man can find his fulfillment and his self-hood and within which nature is accorded its true meaning as well.[26]

The heart of Ritschl's theology, then, pulses with the vitalities of nature and history. Man is related to both and the wholeness he seeks, manifests itself as a system of cohesive completeness, a system of values which to him merit his allegiance in his moral striving. Whatever impact religious faith has on man must be in his relationship to the world, and, furthermore, if religious faith bears any relevance to man, it must relate to the terms of a value system around which man can orient his moral activity. Such religious faith is informed by a power beyond man's moral world, however. It shapes the moral while ". . . the moral constitutes the form in which man gains knowledge of God. The moral is the subjective correlate of God's objective action upon man."[27] Christianity acts as a stimulus to moral activity as well as provides the system of value to which man must commit himself if he is to attain his ultimate wholeness.

This extensive restating of Hefner's "rediscovery of Albrecht Ritschl," for that is what it is, has been necessary to suggest the parallels and correlation between the Ritschlian belief in history and its value-development and the "American experience" as delineated above by Haroutunian. Americans are a people whose cultural bent is toward completion and accomplishments, who view their time as fulfillment time. Especially was such a concentration upon the vitalities of history evident in the period of the late nineteenth century (The Manifest Destiny) and the first three decades of the twentieth century (The War to End All Wars). Several commentators have noted the resurgence of the former in the 1890's, in particular, and the continuing themes of evangelization and Christianization of the world of the latter.[28] Several decades earlier Philip Schaff delivered perhaps the best *apologia* of the American religious experience in its manifest historical thrust.

> For these Americans have not the least desire to rest on the laurels of the past and comfortably enjoy the present; they are full of ambition and national pride, and firmly resolved to soar above the Old World. They are a people of the boldest enterprise and untiring progress — Restlessness and Agitation personified. Even

when seated, they push themselves to and fro on their rockingchairs; they live in a state of perpetual excitement in their business, their politics and their religion....

The grandest destiny is evidently reserved for such a people. We can and must, it is true, find fault with many things in them and their institutions — slavery, the lust of conquest, the worship of Mammon, the rage of speculation, political and religious fanaticism and party-spirit, boundless temerity, boasting, quackery, and — to use the American word for it — humbug.... But we must not overlook the healthy, vital energies that continually react against these diseases: the moral, yea Puritanical earnestness of the American character, its patriotism and love of liberty in connection with deep-rooted reverence for the law of God and authority, its clear, practical understanding, its talent for organization, its inclination for improvement in every sphere, its fresh enthusiasm for great plans and schemes of moral reform, and its willingness to make sacrifices for the promotion of God's kingdom and every good work.[29]

(2) Albrecht Ritschl and pragmatism. Michael Novak has recently written of the need for an American philosophy for the Future. But, he asks, to whom better might we turn than to those men of the "Golden Age" of American philosophy, Royce, Pierce, Mead, Dewey, James, Santayana, and Whitehead?[30] It is of interest in this manuscript to note that Ritschlian thought buttressed the thoughts of these American philosophers, if they so would choose to have read theology. The point is that Ritschlians shared a basic neo-Kantian epistemology with them. Kenneth Hamilton has noted that in German theological academic circles at the turn of the century a basic shift had occurred in the intense debate of the Christ of faith vs. the Christ of history. This focus of interest, he claims.

...was no doubt the result of a growing tendency to move from transcendentalism to empiricism (and from 'universal history' to concrete historical studies). This shift of interest eventually led to the dethronement of Hegel in philosophy. But the theological influence here was, above all, that of Albrecht Ritschl. Liberal Protestantism, most particularly in its Anglo-Saxon form, stems from his influence.[31]

With this particularizing stress on the historical events and away from "universal history", the Ritschlian tradition clearly separates itself from both psychic feeling and general human nature by locating the nexus of life in historical individuals and their trans-actions with other individuals. In so doing, it agrees with a, if not the, dominant philosophy of America's "Golden Age." A. C. McGiffert, a student of Ritschl, credits Ritschl with an interesting combination "...of what may be called the pragmatic method — though he did not call it so — and the historical."[32] We belong to two worlds of things and ideals. Faith in God is due to the need of winning the victory for our ideals.

(3) Albrecht Ritschl and the Social Gospel. Until recently, social and intellectual historians believed in and furthered the myth of Horatio Alger.[33] With the dawning realization that the latter decades of the nineteenth and early decades of the twentieth centuries reflect not "rags to riches" but "elite to elite riches" has come the full force of the significance of the Social Gospel Movement within the American Christian Churches.[34] Of particular notice here is a focus upon the theology of Walter Rauschenbusch, often regarded as the personification of the Social Gospel in America. Sydney Ahlstrom harmonizes such a title with the fact of Rauschenbusch's rise from relative obscurity to national prominence precisely during the years under review, a time when a pervasive social awakening occurred in American Protestant Churches. "The significance of

Rauschenbusch, therefore, is very great. He was an exceptionally forceful expositor of the Ritschlian theology, which during his lifetime was at the height of its influence throughout the Protestant world. He is thus a major example of religious liberalism."[35] In these distinctive ways he reflects Ritschlian influence. (1) He remained in touch with the Church's evangelical tradition and tried to express his demands in doctrinal terms; (2) He prophetically reminded his fellow-Christians of their inextricable involvement with the neighbor and in that insisted on the reality of the power "out there" preventing and denying man's wholeness, evil was to be fought not subdued as an inner demon; (3) He catalogued his social theories in isolation from doctrines of personal sin and salvation, even disparaging them for their sedative effect on men's social consciousness. In this latter emphasis, he acknowledges but rejects the Ritschlian intention.[36]

(4) Albrecht Ritschl and evolutionary natural science. C. M. Mead had attempted to secure Ritschl's place in the history of Christian doctrine as early as 1894. His rise and the rise of "the Ritschl type of theology," he concluded, could be attributed to two problems with which Christianity was confronted in the late nineteenth century: the discordant schools of theology diverging from Schleiermacher, and the threatened conflict between Christianity and natural science.[37] Genesis vs. geology had been reconciled; now the question of the miraculous origins of the species threatened, and researches in the disciplines of biology and psychology tended to blur if not eradicate the distinctions between the natural and the supernatural. Belief in a personal God, and the manifestation of that God in the life, death, and resurrection of Jesus Christ were questioned to the point of denial. Ritschlian theology attempted to focus man's religious faith, by ignoring metaphysical problems, on spiritual interactions between man and God and man to man. "The Ritschl theology, while it gives (as it should) a free rein to all scientific investigation, whether in the

realm of physics, history, or literary criticism, holds that religion and theology belong to such a different and higher region that no attack upon them from this lower region can possibly disturb them."[38]

The record of American religious and theological response to science, contrary to the above areas of delineation, has yet to be adequately explored. Several preliminary works have been published, but specific responses to, let us say, Darwin, Freud, and Marx, have yet to appear.[39] Generally, the pattern of theology toward particular scientific discovery and theorem is one of ignorance, hostility and rejection and finally accomodation. That Darwin in the nineteenth and Freud and Marx in the twentieth centuries provided grist for the theological mill is beyond doubt. Against the scientific demand for creditability, distinct patterns ranging from adoption through rejection to being unable to understand the demand, emerge. Particularly is this the case in the second and third decades of the twentieth century.

Albrecht Ritschl and history, philosophical pragmatism, the Social Gospel Movement, science. If the latter are accepted as largely defining or at least symbolizing "the American experience" of the period under review, and they are so generally accepted among contemporary historians of the period, then it is Ritschl and not Schleiermacher whose theological thought best supports and informs that experience. Little attention is given to inner psychic feelings, absolute or contingent, but to the manifestations of a Power in historical instances. Nor is a Hegelian metaphysical umbrella found helpful to the measurement of trans-actions among men and institutions. No, it is Ritschlian value-judgement and involvement with the vitalities of history that is most congenial to the American experience and those theologians noted by Handy and Hutchinson who studied in that theology were the men who best convey and coalesce Ritschl to the peculiar development of the American experience at that time. Harris Franklin Rall is to be counted among such men.

I can best emphasize the importance of Rall in restating themes of Albrecht Ritschl, and specifically within the unique American experience, by quoting directly what I have written above in the analysis of the theological methodology of Rall:

> American scholars have long credited Friedrich Schleiermacher as the most significant influence upon the emerging American theological scene of the early twentieth century. The evidence seems to be mounting that it was Albrecht Ritschl who claims that place. If such a reevaluation becomes commonplace, Harris Franklin Rall must stand as one of his initial interpreters to Americans. Ritschl's theological themes as expressed by Phillip Hefner resound in Rall's theological methodology: The centrality of the question of reconciliation for theology, the fundamental category of theology as personal and religious; . . . the central theological schema of soteriology, Christocentrism and eclessiology; . . . the testing of reconciliation by faith interpreted as trust; . . . the Church as a fellowship, matched by commitment and faith rather than by doctrine; the task of theology as that of describing the action of God in the life of the Christian believer as he lives in the Holy Spirit, or, to say it differently, the material of systematic theology is the consciousness of the Church; the criterion for judging phenomena from Schleiermacher's *meaningfulness* to the category of *adequacy*; the necessity of placing Christian faith and theology within the 'vitalities of life,' to use Hefner's catching phrase, and thus insisting in theology on turning away from abstraction and using life as its primary datum.[40]

Rall somewhat disparages the label, "Ritschlian", but owns to the fact that he did receive clarifying assistance in his theology from the Ritschlians:

Yet, while I at no time accounted myself a Ritschlian, I must acknowledge the help that it then gave me. It set before me the problems that I had to study. Ritschl, like Schleiermacher, called men to consider first of all what religion was as a distinctive interest of man. He anticipated Hoffding in pointing out its concern with the values of life. He was a pragmatist before the pragmatists. His followers corrected much that was one-sided or lacking in him. They showed that a concern for values did not exclude metaphysical reality, but that through the realm of values one makes the surest approach to the realm of the real. Standing alike against the speculative and the dogmatic, they made plain the place of faith as personal trust and ethical venture and its centrality in religion. In Max Reischle, too little known and dying all too early, I found a discriminating discussion of these matters. In Martin Kahler of Halle I came to know not only a rare combination of saint and scholar, but an interesting fusion of modern outlook with an appreciation of the old evangelical spirit. Himself not a Ritschlian, he had not a little kinship with right wing Ritschlians like his colleagues, Loofs and Reischle. I came to see more clearly the dependence of theology upon religion and the nature of theology, not as master of religion but as its minister, not as drawing from independent sources of knowledge, whether in Scripture or dogma or speculation, but as setting forth that which is implicit in religious experience and faith.[41]

Harris Franklin Rall must continually be seen as a major interpreter and purveyor of Ritschlian theology to America. He must also be adjudged as working with the American experience as outlined above by Joseph Haroutunian. His constant theme of religion as salvation, with personal and religious as primary theological categories, coincide in remarkable fashion with the seven elements listed above (pp. 7-8). Furthermore, in his role as denominational theologian to the Methodist Church, Rall identified with a social and religious institution Professor Jaroslav Pelikan of Yale University has labelled, "The Most American of Churches."[42]

It is generally believed that the three major religious groups owing their origins to American soil are the Church of Christ, Scientist, the Disciples of Christ, and the Church of Jesus Christ of Latter-day Saints. But only in a technical sense may The Methodist Church be excluded from such a list. As Schaff correctly pointed out, 'Methodism . . . may almost as well be called an American product, as an English. ... In fact Methodism established itself independently in America, even before it did in England.' The history of American Methodism actually spans the history of the republic. Despite the difficulties encountered in the years of the American Revolution, the church soon lost the stigma of Torysm and became so closely identified with the new nation that it was, and still is, thought of as the most American of churches, embodying many of the characteristics associated by both natives and foreigners with the typical American.[43]

Pelikan develops the themes of the religious and cultured vocabulary of America being impregnated with Methodist phraseology, the adoption of Methodist "new measures," including revivals, by other churches whose origins lay on the European continent, the majority representation of Methodist members of Congress since the Civil War, the realization of the free church as the American Establishment, the division of that church according to political boundaries related to the slavery issue and the dual establishment of two strong branches of the Methodist tradition — each is used to substantiate the claim of correspondence between Methodism and "the American experience." Of particular moment here is Pelikan's commentary on that peculiar Methodist theological thought of free grace and free will.[44] Pelikan designates this distinctive theme as a "theology of freedom," and argues that this is the feature of Methodism that unites it with the American spirit. In the polarity between destiny (a Calvinist theme) and freedom (a Pelagian theme), Methodism leaned toward the latter while insisting upon the freedom of God to act. Such a position has led some interpreters to misread American theologians either as amateurs or at best improvisers of borrowed theology. Colin Williams has presented, however, a reasonable case that the Wesleyan stress on the intrinsic holiness of the individual (upon his free choosing) joins to the unstated assumption in John Wesley's thought of the visible Christian community as evidence of Christ's presence (upon God's free choosing). Following the split from Anglicanism, the latter became pronounced and may have been the reason for the latter day "moralism" of American Methodism.[45] Notwithstanding, the theme of salvation, fellowship, freedom, and divine free grace, mark both American Methodism and the American experience.

Bishop F. Gerald Ensley of The Methodist Church designates his church as "An Experiment in Secular Christianity."[46] By this phrase he intends a church which measures its success by the transformation of that society. A critic might wish to plead parochial pride in this designation, but the bishop does outline the impact of his church with the historical facts of United States history: frontier development, urban beginnings, social service organizations. As Harris Franklin Rall has said, "The insistent Methodist emphasis has been on Christianity as a gospel and a way of life."[47]

It comes, then, as no surprise that Professor Rall can reflect in his autobiographical contribution to an important series on American theologians in the interwar period, 1919-1939, that theology must be empirical[48]. His statement bore the title, "Theology, Empirical and Christian." Two strong interests shaped his thinking about religion:

> First there was the concern with religion as a personal matter. My interest in theology sprang first from the meaning that religion had for me in my own life. That had its mystical side; religion meant God, and in my boyhood home and in my own life God was something very real. And it had its practical side: it was through religion that I sought the deepest satisfactions of life. I conceived the goal of life through religion, and in the fellowship with God I sought the help for living my life. This personal religious interest and the experiences that have gone with it have furnished my point of departure for theological thinking to this day. My theology has not been a philosophical system which left incidental room for religious needs. Its concepts have gained alike warmth and substance from this ongoing life in which God has meant fellowship and help, and in which He has given life its supreme meaning and worth.
> My second interest in religion lay in my research for a rational world-view and philosophy of life. The impulse to philosophize was not independent of religion, a matter of curiosity or of separate intellectual concern. Religion itself meant to me seeing life whole, knowing that the object of trust was real and was the ultimate reality, and finding some meaning and purpose for the world order and human life. The rational had for me a religious meaning. I agreed with Plato: 'The unexamined life is not worthy of a man.' Religion was the summons to think as well as to live — or rather, to think was itself an essential part of life at its highest. Faith in God meant for me faith in a world that had unity and order and meaning. I found a genuine religion note in Browning's word:

> This world's no blot for us nor blank;
> It means intensely and it means good.
> To find that meaning is our meat and drink.[49]

Allied with these twin concerns of religions as personal and the search for a rational world view, Rall insisted upon empirical verification within the structures of society.

> From the first this social concern furnished me material for my religious thinking. This was for me religion, though I did not cast overboard my concern with religion in other forms. Nor could I go with those newly found social interest, even while they remained within the Church, led to an easy neglect of basic problems of thought or a general contempt for theology. It may be, as some have told us, that the concern with theology as with ritual and architecture means for some men simply a flight from the challenge of social problems. But it is equally possible that men may flee from intellectual difficulties to the eager discussion of social problems or a devotion to social service. The remedy for an adequate theology is not the disavowal of all theology.[50]

These contexts for Rall's theology originated with the Methodist tradition as delineated by Pelikan and Ensley. His pursuit of the rational world view overlay his concern that social ethics be allied with new twentieth century cultural motifs of unity on the one hand and freedom on other. (cf. *supra*, "the American experience"). Any timely theology for Rall must include a new interpretation of God and his relation to the world, the focus upon the moral personality of Jesus, and must instruct Christians as to what they might give to society. Rall again and again stressed the absolute necessity of the new social-ethical influence in theology. Basic to its new social faith were certain convictions:

The supreme worth of human personality, personal freedom alike as a good and as a way of achievement, faith in human nature and in the forces of truth and justice and good will as compared with physical compulsion, justice as the concern of all in securing the fullest opportunity for each, human solidarity, and the obligation of cooperation in service.[51]

Rall picks up the theme noted earlier in Stevens' comparison of Bushnell and Ritschl, that theology needs to divest its indebtedness to Greek philosophical thought structures and realign to the Hebraic ones (cf. *supra.*, "the American experience.") Such a theology will be empirical in its required method, it will be of faith in that it will be experientially value-religion originated, and for Rall, Christian, in that he envisages ". . . that the power that is back of all is creative and redemptive Good Will as seem most clearly in the Spirit of Jesus, and that this Spirit points out to men the way of life and life's highest good."[52]

I have attempted throughout this book to illustrate both the importance of Ritschl upon Rall in various theological themes and methodology as well as Rall's early pronouncement on Ritschl in his lectures at Yale. Seen within the context of American theology during the Inter-War Period, a context wherein denominational theology was most crucial for understanding the temper of the times, and, seen as a major theologian of the largest church in America then, and seen as well as a theologian cognizant of the major intellectual themes of the Inter-War Period (historical progress, pragmatism, the Social Gospel, and evolutionary science), Harris Franklin Rall emerges as a dominant theological figure.

Ours would not be the first such time to acknowledge such acclaim. Rall received three doctor of divinity degrees: from Denver University in 1914, Ohio Wesley University in 1915, and Garrett Biblical Institute in 1940. Ohio

Wesleyan also granted him a doctor of laws degree in 1934. He gave the Nathaniel W. Taylor Lectures at Yale in 1913, entitled *Some Studies in Religion*. He delivered the Quillian Lectures at Emory University, published in 1925, *The Meaning of God*. In 1924 he gave the Ayer Lectures of Colgate-Rochester Divinity School under the title, *Paul and the Faith of Today*. At Garrett Theological Seminary an annual lectureship has been named in his honor. Finally, his book *Christianity: An Inquiry into Its Nature and Truth* was adjudged best in the Fiftieth Anniversary Bross Competition, and received a cash prize of fifteen thousand dollars, then the largest cash award ever made in America for a religious book.

Bibliography of the Writings of Harris Franklin Rall
I. BOOKS

DER LEIBNIZSCHE SUBSTANZBEGRIFF. Halle: Erhardt Karras, 1899.

THE SOCIAL MINISTRY OF JESUS. In *The Social Ministry*, edited by Harry F. Ward (New York: Eaton & Mains); Cincinnati: Jennings & Graham, 1910), pp. 27-55.

A NEW TESTAMENT HISTORY. New York: Abingdon Press, 1914. Second half translated into Burmese.

A WORKING FAITH. New York: Abingdon Press, 1914.

SANCTIFICATION: In *The International Standard Bible Encyclopedia* (Chicago: Howard-Severance Co., 1915), pp. 2681-85.

THE LIFE OF JESUS. New York: Abingdon Press, 1917. Translated into Korean.

TEACHER'S MANUAL FOR THE LIFE OF JESUS. New York: Abingdon Press, 1918.

THE TEACHING OF JESUS. New York: Abingdon Press, 1918. Also published in Spanish, Korean and Hindustani translations.

TEACHER'S MANUAL FOR THE TEACHING OF JESUS. New York: Abingdon Press, 1918.

MODERN PREMILLENNIALISM AND THE CHRISTIAN HOPE. New York: Abingdon Press, 1920. Reprinted as pamphlet from the above: Was John Wesley a Premillennialist? Toronto: Methodist Book and Publishing House, 1921.

THE COMING KINGDOM. New York: Abingdon Press, 1924.

THE NATURE OF REVELATION. Fourth Biennial Meeting of the Conference of Theological Seminaries and Colleges in the United States and Canada (Evanston, Ill., 1924), pp. 24-30.

THE MEANING OF GOD. Nashville, Tenn.: Cokesbury Press, 1925. Emory University, Quillian Lectures. Reprinted in part as a chapter in *God in Christian Thought*, compiled by H. J. Harwood. Rangoon, Burma, 1939.

THE PATH TO GOD. In *Week-Day Sermons in King's Chapel*, edited by Harold E. B. Speight (New York: Macmillan Co., 1925).

THE STORY OF THE FAMILY OF OTTO AND ANNA STEINER RALL. Privately printed. Chicago, 1925.

MODERN PHILOSOPHY: ORIGINS OF ITS METHOD; THE SERVICE OF FOUR FAMOUS THINKERS TO THE CHRISTIAN FAITH. In *An Outline of Christianity; The Story of Our Civilization*, Vol. 4, edited by Francis J. McConnell (New York: Bethlehem Publishers, Inc., 1926), pp. 131-50.

CHRISTIANITY AND JUDAISM COMPARE NOTES. By Harris Franklin Rall and Samuel S. Cohon. New York: Macmillan Co., 1927.

CHRISTIANITY TODAY (editor and joint author). Nashville, Tenn.: Cokesbury Press, 1928.

THE TEACHING OF JESUS. In *The Abingdon Bible Commentary*, edited by Frederick Carl Eiselen, Edwin Lewis, David G. Downey (New York: Abingdon Press, 1929), pp. 904-13.

WHAT DOES BEHAVIORISM MEAN FOR RELIGION? In *Behaviorism: A Battle Line*, edited by William P. King (Nashville, Tenn.: Cokesbury Press, 1930), pp. 288-304.

THE JESUS OF THE NEW TESTAMENT AND THE JESUS OF TODAY. In *The Minister and His Bible*, Annual College of Preachers (New York: General Conference Commission on Courses of Study of the Methodist Episcopal Church, 1930-31), pp. 23-29.

THE SIGNIFICANCE OF THE DOCTRINE OF THE SPIRIT FOR PRESENT-DAY LIFE. Seventh Biennial Meeting of the Conference of Theological Seminaries and Colleges in the United States and Canada (Chicago, 1931), pp. 71-80.

THE PREACHER MUST BRING GOD. In *"They Went Forth, and Preached Everywhere, the Lord Working With Them,"* Annual College of Preachers (New York: General Conference Commission on Courses of Study of the Methodist Episcopal Church, 1931-32), pp. 47-50.

THEOLOGY, EMPIRICAL AND CHRISTIAN. In *Contemporary American Theology,* edited by Vergilius Ferm (New York: Round Table Press, Inc., 1933), pp. 243-73.

THE QUEST FOR GOD THROUGH JOY; THE QUEST FOR GOD THROUGH SUFFERING; THE QUEST FOR GOD THROUGH SERVICE. In *The Quest for God through Worship,* edited by Philip Henry Lotz (St. Louis: Bethany Press, 1934), pp. 58-59, 134-35, 226-27.

THE EXPERIENCE OF GOD IN THE SOCIAL ORDER. In *Experience,* Annual College of Preachers (New York: General Conference Commission on Courses of Study of the Methodist Episcopal Church, 1935), pp. 57-61.

A FAITH FOR TODAY. New York: Abingdon Press, 1936.

WHAT FAITH MEANS. In *Faith,* Annual College of Preachers (New York: General Conference Commission on Courses of Study of the Methodist Episcopal Church, 1936), pp. 18-23.

THE MEANING OF GOD FOR OUR PREACHING. In *Preaching,* Annual College of Preachers (New York: Conference Commission on Courses of Study of the Methodist Episcopal Church, 1937), pp. 24-28.

THE CERTAINTY OF GOD. In *God,* Annual College of Preachers (New York: General Conference Commission on Courses of Study of the Methodist Episcopal Church, 1937), pp. 16-19.

RELIGION AND PUBLIC AFFAIRS (editor and joint author). In Honor of Bishop Francis John McConnell. New York: Macmillan Co., 1937.

SOME CURRENT CONCEPTIONS OF MAN. In *Man,* Annual College of Preachers (New York: General Conference

Commission on Courses of Study of the Methodist Episcopal Church, 1938), pp. 47-52.

JESUS AND THE FAMILY OF GOD. In *The Family of God,* Annual College of Preachers (New York: General Conference Commission on Courses of Study of the Methodist Church, 1939).

DIRECTIONS AND HELPS. Conference Course of Study, ed., 5 vols. New York: The Methodist Book Concern, 1917, 1921, 1925, 1930, 1932, 1937.

CHRISTIANITY. New York: Charles Scribner's Sons, 1940. The 50th Anniversary Bross Prize.

ACCORDING TO PAUL. New York: Charles Scribner's Sons, 1944. The Ayer Lectures, Colgate-Rochester Divinity School 1942.

THE CHRISTIAN FAITH AND WAY. New York: Abingdon-Cokesbury Press, 1947.

RELIGION AS SALVATION. Nashville: Abingdon-Cokesbury Press, 1953.

THE GOD OF OUR FAITH. New York: Abingdon Press, 1955.

II. PAMPHLETS

THE OBLIGATION OF METHODISM TO TOMORROW. Baltimore, 1910.

WHAT TO READ. Privately printed. Baltimore, 1910. Also in many printings by the American Bible Society under the title, How to Use the Bible.

STUDIES IN PAUL. Outline of addresses at Epworth League Institutes. Chicago, 1911.

A CHRISTIAN'S FINANCIAL CREED. First published in 1914 by the Colorado Conference of the Methodist Episcopal Church, then in successive editions and printings by the Commission on Finance, and by other churches.

THE MASTER TEACHER. Denver: Iliff School of Theology, 1914.

THE CONFERENCE COURSE OF STUDY. New York: General Conference Commission on Courses of Study, 1918.

A TEACHING MISSION. Philadelphia: Board of Home Missions and Church Extension of the Methodist Episcopal Church (1918?)

THE BROTHERHOOD AND SOCIAL SERVICE. New York: Methodist Brotherhood (1920?)

DOCTRINAL PREACHING AND THE NEW DAY. Philadelphia: Board of Home Missions and Church Extension of the Methodist Episcopal Church, 1921.

A STATEMENT OF THE METHODIST FAITH. Prepared for the Board of Home Missions and Church Extension and contained in the pamphlet, *Facts Concerning the Methodist Episcopal Church*. New York: Methodist Book Concern, 1921, 1922. Printed in Czech, Lithuanian, Polish, Russian, Slovak, Italian, Portuguese, Spanish, Arabic, Finnish, Hungarian.

WHAT CAN I BELIEVE? Minneapolis, 1922. Last edition, Chicago: Board of Education of the Methodist Episcopal Church, 1933.

WHAT CAN WE BELIEVE? Seattle, Wash.: Plymouth Congregational Church, 1922.

I BELIEVE. Chicago: American Institute of Sacred Literature; 1924, and in later reprintings.

THE RELIGION OF THE BIBLE IN THE WORLD TODAY. Chicago: American Institute of Sacred Literature, 1925.

WHAT IS SPIRITUALITY? Chicago: Board of Sunday Schools of the Methodist Episcopal Church (1930?)

THE CHRISTIAN CONCEPTION OF GOD. One of fourteen pamphlets on *The Significance of Christ in the Modern World*. New York: Board of Foreign Missions of the Methodist Episcopal Church, 1931.

THE GARRETT OF TOMORROW. Evanston, Ill.: Garrett Biblical Institure, 1937.

PLANNING THE COLLEGE COURSE FOR MINISTERIAL STUDENTS. Nashville, Tenn.: General Board of Christian Education, 1937.

WHAT HAVE CHRISTIANS TO SHARE WITH NON-CHRISTIANS? Chicago: Movement for World Christianity, 1937.
WHICH WAY THEOLOGY? Evanston, Ill.: Garrett Biblical Institute (1937?)

III. ARTICLES

DO WE NEED A METHODIST CREED? *Methodist Review*, March-April 1907, LXXXIX, 221-30.
THEOLOGY AND THE HISTORICAL METHOD. *Methodist Review*, March-April 1910, XCII, 194-210.
THE LIFE AND TEACHINGS OF JESUS, a special course of lessons for adult classes prepared under the auspices of the Committee on Curriculum of the Board of Sunday Schools of the Methodist Episcopal Church. *Adult Bible Class Monthly*, Jan. to Dec., 1916, IX.
PREMILLENNIALISM AND THE SCRIPTURES. *Sunday School Journal*, Feb. 1916, XLVIII, 96-98.
PREMILLENNIALISM AND JUDAISM. *Sunday School Journal*, March 1916, XLVIII, 177-79.
PREMILLENNIALISM AND THE WORK OF THE KINGDOM. *Sunday School Journal*, April 1916, XLVIII, 271-73.
THE CHRISTIAN HOPE. *Sunday School Journal*, May 1916, XLVIII, 365-67.
WHY I DO NOT ACCEPT PREMILLENNIALISM, in a symposium on premillennialism. *Sunday School Journal*, March 1917, XLIX, 149-51.
PREMILLENNIALISM. I. The Issue. *Biblical World*, July 1919, LIII, 339-47.
PREMILLENNIALISM. II. Premillennialism and the Bible. *Biblical World*, Sept. 1919, LIII, 459-69.
PREMILLENNIALISM. III. Where Premillennialism Leads. *Biblical World*, Nov. 1919, LIII, 617-27.
A STEWARDSHIP CREED. *Christian Advocate*, Jan. 22, 1920, XCV, 119.

METHODISM AND PREMILLENNIALISM. *Methodist Review*, March-April 1920, CIII, 209-19.

METHODISM TODAY. *American Journal of Theology*, Oct. 1920, XXIV, 481-501.

WIIL YOU? *Epworth Herald*, April 23, 1921, XXXII, 410-11.

THE NATION TOMORROW — A STORY IN DEMOCRACY. *Epworth Herald*, Oct. 29, 1921, XXXII, 1062-63.

THE NATIONS TOMORROW — A WORLD SURVEY. *Epworth Herald*, Nov. 5, 1921, XXXII, 1084-85.

INDUSTRY TOMORROW; A TEST FOR CHRISTIANITY. *Epworth Herald*, Nov. 26, 1921, XXXII, 1167-69.

WHAT WILL BE THE RELIGION OF TOMORROW? *Epworth Herald*, Dec. 10, 1921, XXXII, 1220-21.

ARE LAYMEN INTERESTED IN THEOLOGY? *Zion's Herald*, Sept. 27, 1922, C, 1226.

A CHRISTIAN'S FINANCIAL CREED. *Christian Advocate*, March 13, 1924, XCIX, 313.

NOT INTELLECTUAL CREDENCE BUT PERSONAL TRUST, in a symposium on "The Faith Once Delivered to the Saints." *Methodist Review*, March-April 1924, CVII, 253-57.

WHAT ABOUT OUR MINISTRY? *Methodist Review*, May-June 1924, CVII, 401-12.

MAKING A METHODIST THEOLOGY. *Methodist Quarterly Review*, Oct. 1925, LXXIV, 579-96.

THE HISTORIC MEANINGS OF RELIGIOUS EXPERIENCE. *Religious Education*, Oct. 1925, XX, 330-36.

EXPLANATORY NOTES AND LESSON EXPOSITION, on the Improved Uniform Lessons. *Church School Journal*, Jan. to April, 1926, LVIII.

THE GOSPEL OF JOHN; ITS DISTINCTIVE PURPOSE, CONTENT, AND AUTHORSHIP. *Church School Journal*, Feb. 1926, LVIII, 86-87.

EXPLANATORY NOTES AND LESSON EXPOSITION, on the International Uniform Lessons. *Church School Journal*, Jan. to June, 1927, LIX.

MAKING YOUR OWN BIBLE. *Senior Quarterly,* Jan.-March 1927, XLV, 2-4.

THE CREED OF JESUS. *Christian Advocate,* Jan. 13, 1927, CII, 40-41.

JESUS IN THE THOUGHT OF TODAY; A GLIMPSE OF SOME RECENT BOOKS ON JESUS. *Christian Advocate,* May 12, 1927, CII, 584-86.

THE POPE AND THE PROFESSOR. *Religious Education,* March 1928, XXIII, 178-79.

LECTURE FOUNDATIONS AND RELIGIOUS BOOKS. *Christian Advocate* (Nashville, Tenn.), May 18, 1928 LXXXIX, 617-19.

WHAT IS THE MATTER WITH RELIGION AND WHAT IS TO BE DONE ABOUT IT? In a symposium. *Religious Education,* June 1928, XXIII, 509-11.

LUTHER B. WILSON; THE CHURCH OF A LIVING FAITH; BEHIND THE EDITOR'S BACK; THE DUTY OF HATRED; GREAT DEEDS AT KANSAS CITY; ABOUT WAR AND PEACE; UNFINISHED BUSINESS. Editorials in the *Northwestern Christian Advocate,* June 1928, LXXVI.

BELIEF AND FAITH AND EDUCATION; GOD AND MR. BARNES; THE MEN THAT STOOD BY; "A PREFACE TO MORALS;" ADVENTURES IN FRIENDSHIP; WHO IS THE EDUCATED MAN? WHO WAS THE MURDERER? WE THANK GOD AND TAKE COURAGE. Editorials in the *Northwestern Christian Advocate,* May and June, 1929, LXXVII.

JESUS AS TEACHER TODAY. *Adult Bible Class Monthly,* Jan. 1930, XXIII, 29-30.

HOW MEN ARE THINKING ABOUT GOD. *Methodist Review,* May-June 1931, CXIV, 309-17.

A DISCUSSION GROUP AND WHAT IT ACCOMPLISHED. *Church School Journal,* July 1913, LXIII, 374-75.

WHICH WAY RELIGION? *Christian Advocate, Northwestern Edition,* Aug. 13, 1913, LXXIX, 806.

PUTTING OVER THE CHRISTIAN MESSAGE. *Christian Advocate, Central Edition* (and other editions), Sept. 17 and 24, 1931, LXXIX, 923-33, 949.

THE IDEA OF GOD IN RECENT LITERATURE. *Religion in Life,* Winter 1932, I, 55-69.

THE CLIMATE OF RELIGION. *Religion in Life,* Spring 1934, III, 245-56.

A FAITH FOR TODAY. A series of articles appearing in the *Church School Journal,* Jan. to Dec., 1935, LXVII, under the following titles: A FIFTH FOR TODAY; WHAT IS CHRISTIANITY? WHAT IS THE BIBLE AND HOW SHALL WE USE IT? HOW SHALL WE THINK ABOUT GOD? KNOWING GOD; GOD AND THE WORLD; GOD AND THE WORLD OF EVIL; CONCERNING PRAYER; WHAT DOES IT MEAN TO BE SAVED? CONCERNING SOCIAL SALVATION; I BELIEVE IN THE CHURCH; THE LIFE TO COME.

EDINBURGH 1937; THE SECOND WORLD CONFERENCE ON FAITH AND ORDER. *Church School Journal,* Dec. 1937, LXIX, 620-21.

AFTER EDINBURGH. *Religion in Life,* Winter 1938, VII, 22-35.

THOU SHALT LOVE THYSELF. *Epworth Herald,* Aug. 20, 1938, XLIX, 484-85.

THE STORY OF CREATION. *Christian Advocate, Northwestern Edition* (and other editions), Sept. 8, 1938, LXXXVI, 926.

THE CHURCH GIVEN OR GATHERED? *Christendom,* Spring 1939, IV, 164-73.

HOW FAR SHOULD OUR CHRISTIANITY BE EXPERIMENTAL, EXPLANATIONAL, SOCIAL? *World Christianity,* Fourth Quarter, 1939, III, 29-33.

THE AUTHORITY OF OUR FAITH. *International Review of Missions,* Jan. 1940, XXIX, 130-39.

"DR. RALL ANSWERS," *Christian Advocate,* 1941-1956, *Together,* 1956-1957. "Dr. Rall had reached the age of 87 and

wished to be relieved of the responsibility of this column."
James Wail editor *Christian Advocate*.

WAR AND THE SECOND COMING. *The Christian Century*, Volume 60, August 18, 1943, pp. 941-42.

SIN AND SALVATION. *Religion in Life*, Volume XXI, Number 2, Spring, 1952. pp. 185-94.

IV. BOOK REVIEWS*

A NEW DICTIONARY OF RELIGION AND ETHICS. *Journal of Religion*, March 1922, II, 210-12. Review of Shailer Mathews and G. B. Smith: A DICTIONARY OF RELIGION AND ETHICS.

SOME MODERN INTERPRETATIONS OF CHRISTIANITY. *JR*, March 1925, V, 196-202.
Review of Harry Emerson Fosdick: The MODERN USE OF THE BIBLE;
E. G. A. Holmes: DYING LIGHTS AND DAWNING;
Albert C. Knudson: PRESENT TENDENCIES IN RELIGIOUS THOUGHT;
Shailer Mathews: THE FAITH OF MODERNISM;
Carl S. Patton: RELIGION IN THE THOUGHT OF TODAY;
Gerald Birney Smith: PRINCIPLES OF CHRISTIAN LIVING;

*Editor's Note. Since Professor Rall has, unfortunately, never kept track of the book reviews he has written, and since he has written many hundreds of them and in innumerable magazines and journals, it has been found impracticable to make the listing of his reviews anywhere near complete. We list here merely those which have appeared in two magazines, the *Journal of Religion* and the *Christian Century* and *Religion in Life*. These magazines will be abbreviated (after the first citation of each *JR* and *CC* and *RIL* respectively.

Herbert A. Youtz: THE SUPREMACY OF THE SPIRITUAL.

INTERPRETING MODERN CHRISTIANITY. *JR* July 1926, VI, 432-35. Review of Benjamin W. Bacon: THE APOSTOLIC MESSAGE; William P. Merrill: LIBERAL CHRISTIANITY.

THE HERESY OF THE ORTHODOX. *Christian Century*, Nov. 6, 1929, XLVI, 1376. Review of William Peter King: FAITH IN THE DIVINE FATHERHOOD.

THE ENDLESS QUEST. *CC*, March 4, 1931, XLVIII, 308-9. Review of W. R. Matthews: GOD IN CHRISTIAN EXPERIENCE.

REALISTS OF MANY KINDS. *CC*, Feb. 3, 1932, XLIX, 156-57. Review of D. C. Macintosh: RELIGIOUS REALISM.

THE GROUNDS OF HOPE. *CC*, Jan. 3, 1934, LI, 20. Review of John Baillie: AND THE LIFE EVERLASTING.

A GERMAN RELIGIOUS PSYCHOLOGIST. *CC*, March 7, 1934, LI, 330. Review of George Wobbermin: THE NATURE OF RELIGION.

PARADISE REGAINED. *CC*, July 4, 1934, LI, 900. Review of Shailer Mathews: IMMORTALITY AND THE COSMIC PROCESS; William Pepperell Montague: THE CHANCES OF SURVIVING DEATH.

A RECALL TO ORTHODOXY. *CC*, Nov. 7, 1934, LI, 1415-16. Review of Edwin Lewis: A CHRISTIAN MANIFESTO.

SELF-CRITICAL LIBERALISM. *CC*, Jan. 2, 1935, LII, 21-33. Review of Walter M. Horton: REALISTIC THEOLOGY.

WHAT DOES CHRISTIANITY OFFER? *CC*, Jan. 16, 1935, LII, 82. Review of Oscar Macmillan Buck: CHRISTIANITY TESTED.

RELIGION FOR UNDERGRADUATES. *CC*, Oct. 2, 1935, LII, 1248. Review of Horace T. Houf: WHAT RELIGION IS AND DOES.

WHAT THE THINKERS THINK. *CC*, May 13, 1936, LIII, 706-7. Review of Henry Nelson Wieman and Bernard Eugene Meland: AMERICAN PHILOSOPHIES OF RELIGION.

CATHOLICISM OF THE WORLD. *CC*, July 7, 1937, LIV, 871-72. Review of Nathaniel Micklem: WHAT IS THE FAITH?

GOD'S OTHERNESS. *CC*, Sept. 8, 1937, LIV, 1104. Review of Emil Brunner: GOD AND MAN: FOUR ESSAYS ON THE NATURE OF PERSONALITY.

THE MYSTERY OF MAN. *CC*, Dec. 8, 1937, LIV, 1528-29. Review of Nicolas Berdyaev: THE DESTINY OF MAN.

Review of *The Validity of Religious Experience*, by Albert C. Knudson. "Critical Reviews," *JR*, July 1938, XVIII, 323-25.

GOD'S PART AND MAN'S. *CC*, Nov. 2, 1938, LV, 1332-33. Review of Edgar P. Dickie: REVELATION AND RESPONSE.

AN ANGLICAN THEOLOGY. *CC*, Nov. 2, 1938, LV, 1332-33. Review of Oliver Chase Quick: DOCTRINES OF THE CREED.

WAYS TO A KNOWLEDGE OF GOD. *CC*, Oct. 4, 1939, LVI, 1203. Review of Norman MacLeish: THE NATURE OF RELIGIOUS KNOWLEDGE.

BRUNNER IN REVOLT. *CC*, Jan. 3, 1940, LVII, 17-19. Review of Emil Brunner: MAN IN REVOLT.

THE CHRISTIAN PERSPECTIVE. *RIL*, Autumn 1950, 633-34. Review of Edward T. Ranesdell: THE CHRISTIAN PERSPECTIVE.

THE GARRETT TOWER, a quarterly publication which has appeared since 1925 and which was initiated by Dr. Rall, has contained reviews of current theological literature from his pen in each issue since its founding. Totaling some hundreds, the list is too long for printing here. Occasional reviews in other periodicals are likewise omitted.

APPENDICES

A. Lecture Notes, 1919 - 1950

A. B. C. March 15, 1925

HOW FAR DOES GOD CARE FOR EACH MAN PERSONALLY?

Can we believe in a personal providence today? We think of God as Father and ourselves as children. Can we carry that through and believe that God cares for us as a father thinks of his children individually and plans and cares for them individually? And what does such care mean?

I am assuming that we all believe in a God and a God who is just and good as well as wise and powerful. Otherwise we have to believe in the world as a great machine, a set of blind forces which have somehow brought into existence this humanity of ours and flung us up on the shores of time as the sea may sometimes fling up on the beach shells from its depths or drift wood. To such blind forces it is as useless to pray as to the waves of a sea in a storm, and it is useless to look forward to anything in the future. We and our dreams, our ideals and hopes, are like clouds lit for a few moments by the dying sun and glorious in its light, only to fade away and be lost forever. The Christian view is opposite. We believe that this world with its beauty and order is the product of a great and wise being, that we with our high ideals of love and truth and with the noble lives which humanity has produced in its best examples, in its saints and heroes, have come from such a Being who is not only wise and strong but who is good, that the highest which has appeared in man of love and mercy and righteousness is not higher than what is in God himself.

The thought of such a God would point to such a loving and personal care as our subject suggests. Why cannot we believe in it? What makes it hard? Yes, it is sometimes hard and there are reasons for it. Note them.

(Marginal notes: paragraph I. B. Russell)

(1) There is the thought of the *great and the little*. What a world this seems to us. The long generations before even the light (cf. swift as the light!) can come from one of these. Miles, even millions of miles, are too small a unit by which to measure. Light travels 186,000 miles a second, over a million miles a minute, but we measure their distance not by minutes of light nor even days of light, but by light years. And size: Mira 250,000,000 miles in diameter. The psalmist said long ago, What is an that thou art mindful of him, or the son of man that thou considerest him. But cf. the world of which he thought then with our world as we know it. How can the infinite God who made and upholds this universe care for these little creatures that crawl on the surface of this tiny speck of matter which we call the earth.

The answer. The difference between *big and great*, between *size and value*. The effort to terrorize the imagination. What would we think of the man who spent all his thought on the miles of land which he owned and none upon his little daughter because she was so much smaller. Are we to think of God as less wise, less god? The lesser as means to the higher, the great house has its meaning just for those few that live in it. The shame of a nation is to worship things and make them an end, to care more for territory and trade than for folk. A great universe, but the stars are unthinking, and man can comprehend. Pascal: "the reed that thinks." The way in which the physical universe is being mastered and used. Of the great sun Mira, that man can tell its constituents and measure its size. (This itself as gas!) But not simply greatness of reason, of skill. Moral greatness, meaning of personality. Man as the creature like God, the one with whom God can have fellowship. "Thou hast made us unto thyself." Crusoe finds Friday, what it means. Human beings count above things, above all things. The greatest, the most significant, is not to be measured, it is to be understood and valued. What kind of God who simply looked at bigness and offenders of world which he had made. What God cares for. Does not include other personal beings in universe.

(2) The many and the one. The objection: Why value the individual so. It is the race that counts, the race that God is developing. Does not evolution suggest that? Do not the facts point that way, the way in which generations of individuals are sacrificed in order that the race may go on and up? The impossible assumption that God could know and could care for each.

The Answer. Take again human analogy. What do we think, for example, of a Rousseau who sentimentalized out humanity in general and left his own child on some one else's doorstep to be cared for? What counts is not love for humanity in general, that is a mere empty sentimentality; it is love for men. What is the human race? Not a thing apart, it is men. If Jesus be the revelation of God, then it is clear. Jesus had a wide vision that took in the multitude, but he cared for individuals, for men and women and children. God cannot be less good than that. Jesus' great word as to the sacredness of human life, human beings never as means, always as ends, always to be reverenced and served. So he lived, so he demanded we should live. Can we think of God as less than that? As regards the God who cannot care for all, think of all, are we not simply putting our finite limitations in the way of God? We cannot conceive just how God can do that. But then we cannot conceive how God can sustain a universe of a million million suns.

(Marginal notes: paragraph 2. To assume val. of society apt. for individuals, or indiv. as merely means to this end, is to deny sacredness of personality).
Develop Jim's idea of God.
    Influences leading to changes in the conception of God (Note varied points of view in references given)
Smith, G. E., Social Idealism and the Changing Theology
Ames, The New Orthodoxy
King, H. C., Reconstruction in Theology
Rall: A Working Faith, ch. I; Meaning of God, III
Streeter, B. H., Reality
Rauschenbusch, W., A Theology for the Social Gospel
Dyman, E., The Experience of God in Modern Life
Youtz, The Enlarging Conception of God
Eeckwith, Idea of God, I.
Moore, E. C., Christian Thought Since Kant
Gwatkin, H. W., The Knowledge of God and Its Historical
    Development

    How can we speak of a growing knowledge and especially of a changing conception of God, if we believe in revelation as a true source of such knowledge? The answer is in a right conception of revelation, not as external, as intellectual, but as involving common activity on the part of God and man, and mutual relations in that activity. Human experience is always the correlate of divine revelation. Only in the experience of man can God make himself known, as man observes, reflects, weighs, questions, trusts, acts. We should therefore expect that the idea of God would be a growing, changing affair, and that is would be related to all the life of man. That does not exclude the reality of a revealing God.
    What is the experience which will affect man's conception of God? Nothing less than the total of human exper-

ience and thinking. More especially: his religious experience, his experience and thought in the moral and social realm, and his knowledge of or experience with nature.

As to the physical world and natural science: note outstanding advances changes:

The world as a world of *order,* an order that reaches throught the universe.

The pushing back of the barriers in *time* (evolution of life, of universe of man), in *space* toward the infinitely *distant* (astronomy) and in relation to the infinitely *small* (physics and the atom, biology and the microbes).

The idea of *development:* cosmological, biological, historical.

The *dynamic* conception of the universe — away from the static, but away from the purely mechanical also.

All this bears upon our conception of God as revealed in his world and upon our idea as to how God works in his world.

I. The Nature of God

1. The Sources of the Christian Idea of God.
2. Modern Influences Bearing Upon the Idea of God.
3. The Transcendence of God — God as Other.
4. God as Limited or Conditioned
    Pluralism and theism, the problem of the one and the many.
5. The Concept of God in Nontheistic Humanism.
6. The Immanence of God.
7. God as Indwelling Spirit.
    Primitive ideas of the Spirit; O.T.; N.T.; in recent theology; value.
8. God as Personal.
    Meaning, objections, the problem of anthropomorphism, validity, value.
9. The Moral Character of God.

       Holiness and goodness in historical development; significance of the ethical ideal for religion.
10. The Significance of Jesus for the Christian Concept of God.

II. The Meaning of God

11. God in the Natural Order and in History.
       Creation (and evolution), control (and the natural order); providence; the indwelling Spirit as creative and redemptive.
12. God and the Moral Order.
       The meaning of God for a moral faith, for the moral life; religion and ethics.
13. God and the Social Order.
       Christianity and humanism; the democracy of God.
14. God in Personal Religion.
       Prayer, worship, the mystical experience, religion as fellowship with the divine and experience of the divine, the path of God.
15. God and the World of Evil.

III. Some Final Questions

16. The Grounds for the Belief in God.
17. How Can a Man Know God?
       Revelation and discovery, the nature of the knowledge of God and the ways of knowing God.
18. How Shall We Think of God? — A Summary.
19. The Christian Doctrine of the Trinity.

THEOLOGY CI
Outlined by H. F. Rall

PART II. *THE DOCTRINE OF GOD*
A. HISTORICAL

I. The Idea of God in Hebrew-Jewish Thought

The N. T. has the O. T. for its background and assumes the O. T. faith. What concept of God did Christianity take the O.T.?

1. *The transcendent God.* (1) The God of majesty and power, evoking awe, reverence, fear. This is the primary and dominant meaning of holiness. (Ex. 15:11-18; I Sam. 6:20; Ezek. 20:41; 28:25; 36:23; 38:16; 44:19). (2) This came to mean transcendence not simply in power but in righteousness and love and purity. (Isa. 55; Hos. 11:9).

2. *Monotheism.* One God, creator and ruler of all. (Gen. 1; Ps. 19; 104; Isa. 40). Universalism follows from this and especially from the ethical conception of God. (Amos 9:7; Isa. 19).

3. *The supreme prophetic achievement in the O. T. was the ethical idea of God.* (1) The God of righteousness. (Amos 5; Isa. 1; Micah 6; etc.). Not mere distributive justice, but justice as positive, creative, motivated by good will. (2) The God of grace and mercy, of undeserved and unearned love. (Isa. 1:2; 55; 63:8, 16; 64:8; Hosea; Jer. 3:14, 19; 31:9, 20; Ps. 103).

4. *The "living God".* The God of creative and redemptive activity, of purposive and gracious will. This seen in the creation of the world, control of nature, direction of history. So a philosophy of history. See especially Second Isaiah.

5. *A personal God.* One with whom man may have fellowship. (Psa. 23; 27).

6. *Judaism showed some deterioration.* (1) A tendency to extreme transcendence in apocalypticism; also in Pharisaism with its emphasis on a legalistic holiness conceived as separation from evil. (2) A renewed emphasis on a particularistic and nationalistic God as against universalism. (3) Legalism's emphasis on God as lawgiver, ruler, and judge.

II. *The New Testament Conception of God*

1. *The God of Jesus is the God of the O.T. at its highest prophetic level.*

(1) He emphasizes especially the universal, gracious, and unconquerable good will of God (Matt. 5:43-48). God not only forgives the penitent (so in O.T. and Judaism) but goes out to seek and win the sinner.

(2) But this mercy is *ethical* in the highest sense, is searching and absolute in its demand (Matt. 5:48). He is a righteous God and a God of judgment.

(3) God is *near* in loving purpose, in active deed, and in personal relation and care.

(4) He is the *far* God, transcendent, holy.

(5) He is the living God, who will bring in his kingdom.

2. *The conception of God in the primitive church*

(1) God is the *Christlike God*. Determinative is not so much the teaching of Jesus as his spirit, and his life and death as God's deed. Rom. 8.1:11 (significant interchangeable use of God, Spirit, Christ); Rom. 15:6; II Cor. 4:6; 5:19. 4:6; 5:19.

(2) *The indwelling God:* consider the significant idea of an ethical, life-giving presence of God as *Holy Spirit*.

(3) The *redeeming God*, the God of active, redemptive good will: seen in the cross of Christ and in the coming deliverance.

III. *The Idea of God in the Theology of the Church*

Theology expresses the meaning of faith in the thought forms of the day. These forms necessarily limit it, as does the level of the religious life of its time.
1. The Eastern Church was influenced by the very philosophy it rejected. The Hebrew-Christian concept of God is personal, ethical, historical. The Eastern Church thinks of God in terms of substance or essence. God is eternal, incorruptible, spiritual; man is mortal, corruptible, earthly. There is extreme transcendence, a dualistic opposition of divine and human, yet mystical relation, and a gospel of Incarnation and Sacramental change.
2. The Western Church retained the ancient creeds but thought of God especially as Ruler, with the emphasis on sovereign will and absolute authority.
3. Modern thought shows conflicting tendencies: (1) The emphasis on immanence continues. (2) The Barthians have renewed the emphasis on transcendence and sovereignty — God as wholly other, as absolute will and power, as unknowable. (3) A realistic (empirical) tendency insists that we consider the concrete world of nature and history, seeks to use the results of science, and inclines sometimes to a finite God, sometimes to a nonpersonal God (God as order, or urge, or integrating principle).

B. THE CHRISTIAN CONCEPTION OF GOD

Philosophy is interested in God as the world ground, the ultimate reality, the principle of unity. For *religion* God has certain definite and special meanings: (1) He is the God who is far, the holy transcendent one, the power on whom all depends. (2) He is the God who is near, near as immanent energy and life, near as love and saving help. (3) He is the personal God with whom we may have fellowship, whom we may worship. (4) He is the good God, the goodness that we trust, to which we aspire, which demands loyalty. We will study, therefore, the concept of God as personal, as good, as transcendent, as immanent.

I. *God as Personal*

1. *The meaning of personality in man:* (1) Man is not only conscious (aware of his world), but self-conscious (aware of self); there is a central point of reference, a *unitary subject* of all conscious life and this is known, despite growth and change, as involving *identity* with the past. (2) he has capacity for rational reflection, (3) for self-direction and control of his world, (4) appreciation and choice of goods and ideals, (5) for apprehension of God and fellowship with him.

2. *The objections raised to thinking of God as personal:* (1) We are making God in our own image (anthropomorphism): he is just the projection of man's self. (2) We are limiting God by ascribing these characteristics to him.

3. *What we mean by a personal God:* (1) Not the limited personal life that is in man. Personality in man is finite and partial with regard to unity (integration), rationality, self-determination, and control of his world. God is the source of this personal life of man, as of all life. Personality is limited in man, complete in God. (2) Not an individual being at some one place in the universe. (3) It is the affirmation, not of limitation, but of the richest, most positive life in God. God is not mere blind force or impersonal order but is conscious, rational, purposive, good. It would limit him to say less.

4. *As to anthropomorphic projection:* (1) We are not asserting that God is like man but that man is like God (made in his "image"). (2) Only so can man know God. All knowledge is by analogy, including that of the physical. We know God the same way. (3) Only, we take the analogy of the highest to know God; not mechanism or abstract idea or impersonal order, but conscious, rational, purposive, good life. (4) God must include the highest to be adequate to

his world. (5) We do not limit God to personality as we know it. He may include far more. We may call him suprapersonal, though for us that is just a word. But, though more, he cannot be less: irrational instead of rational, blind force instead of conscious purpose, non-moral instead of moral and good. The world which is orderly, which has produced beauty and truth and goodness and the vision of a high end, indicates such a God as its adequate ground and meaning. (6) All thinking is interpretation and projection of our ideas. The question is: Does the projection "hit something"? Does it fit with other knowledge? Does it put us into effective working relations with our world?
5. *The significance of the idea of divine personality:* (1) Religiously it means that we may have a fellowship with God, a relation of trust and worship on our side, of knowledge and gracious purpose on his. (2) Ethically, it means that the good is grounded in the universe, is more than our subjective idea, has authority over our life. (3) Socially, it gives a basis for a humanistic and democratic conception of the world, a world where personality is sacred and truth and justice the supreme forces, as against a world where brute power is supreme and selfishness the highest rule. Man can be really at home in the universe with such a God.

II. *God as Good — The Moral Character of God*

1. *The supreme conviction of religion is that power and goodness are one.* In the *Christian* religion it is the conviction that God is like Jesus Christ. The moral goodness of God has a five-fold significance for us:

(1) The good God is the object of *trust* and ground of hope. The universe has meaning and end. Man can feel at home. The values of life are secure.

(2) He is the rightful object of supreme *loyalty*. Ethics has a basis. The good and right are man's gradual discovery, but not his invention. They are inherent in the ground of all things. Right is not constituted by the arbitrary will of

God; its ground and eternal reality are in his nature as good.

(3) As good, is the object of highest *aspirations*.

(4) It is a *creative* goodness, the source of all good.

(5) As good, God is always and actively *opposed to evil*. (Cf. ideas of wrath and judgment).

2. *Love, or good will, is central in Jesus' concept of God.*

(1) Love is the will that seeks the highest good of its object; it is *self-giving*, undeserved, unlimited, unconquerable.

(2) It is through and through ethical, since it seeks to give the highest life, not pleasure and ease. Hence it will not shrink from ways of conflict, struggle, pain; hence it demands an ethical response.

(3) Such love, joined with truth and righteousness, is the supreme reconciling, redeeming, creative power in individual life and social relations.

3. *Fatherhood* expresses this idea of creative and redeeming love. It must be conceived ethically, not sentimentally, and must include moral authority. Is God Father of all? Yes, in so far as his attitude of good will is concerned; but the Father-son relation is mutual and ethical, and demands a response from the son for its full meaning. Are all men his children? Yes, as objects of his love, and as those intended for the highest relation and with capacity for it. In the full sense, no, since they do not meet Jesus' test of moral kinship (Matt. 5:45).

4. *Righteousness*

(1) An inner quality of character expressed in attitude and conduct. It involves the hatred of the evil, unjust, harmful; devotion to the just and good.

(2) It is not negative but positive, creative, redemptive. Its goal is a new order, the Kingdom of God. It is not apposed to love. As the will to the highest good its motive is love. It is joined with mercy in the O.T. Isa. 45:21; Ps. 85:10. Righteousness and love are completed each in the other.

(3) Retributive justice is not excluded, if we mean by

this differing results which evil and good bring. A universe that made no distinction here would be non-moral, or immoral, and intolerable. "If the rulers of the universe do not prefer the just man to the unjust, it is better to die than to live," said Socrates. Cf. Gal. 6:7, 8. This is no mere matter of impersonal order but of the positive attitude of a righteous God in relation to good and evil. It is not, however, legalism and not vengance.

5. *Holiness* primarily denotes transcendence, power, majesty. Later it came to mean moral transcendence. (Isa. 6:56; 5:16; Hosea 11:8, 9). It represents not merely the purity of God, but the absoluteness of his righteousness and the majesty and authority of the ethical.

6. *Wisdom* is a quality of character, and as such is more than knowledge or intelligence. It is seen in the choice of worthy ends and right means.

III. *The God that is Far-Transcendence, Power, Sovereignty, Holiness, Perfection*

1. There is a certain paradox in our concept of God. Only as he is the far God, more than we, do we turn to him with reverence and hope. Only as he is the near God and touches our life, is related to us, can he be of help. So we know God as the one that is far, transcendent, holy, power, the creator.

2. *Transcendence* is not spatial; it means not a God separate from his world, but more than his world. He is transcendent:

(1) As power, creative, the continuous source of all life;
(2) As purpose and providence, directing all to his ends;
(3) Morally, as absolute goodness and righteousness;
(4) As personal;
(5) As the unknown; revealed, yet never fully known;
(6) And though akin to us, yet also other than we. The world is always dependent on him; he is always more than his world.

3. Traditional theology has tended to set forth God as transcendent and absolute in an extreme manner. This has appeared in two forms:

(1) Under the influence especially of neo-platonic philosophy, it has tended to assert the extreme otherness of God, wholly different from the human and finite: heavenly against earthly, spiritual against fleshly, eternal against temporal and corruptible. God is conceived as *totaliter aliter*. With this dualism it is hard to see how religion as a real relation with God is possible, or revelation as a real knowledge of God in experience.

(2) He is a God conditioned or limited through that the emphasis was upon God as will, as arbitrary sovereign with absolute power. The will of God determines what is right. What is right becomes such by "the mere fact of his willing it". (Calvin) God is an arbitrary monarch. From this follows foreordination, predestination, irresistible grace, "the horrible decree". God thus becomes responsible directly for all evil.

4. A finite or limited or conditioned God has been proposed by some. Arguments: the presence of evil and imperfection in the world, the slow advance of the good, suggests a God, who, if he is good, is not absolute in power; and absolute God would rule out the reality of the many, of freedom, change, growth, which the world shows. The general position takes two forms:

(1) The pluralistic theory with a God who is one among many cosmic forces, it may be one who came into being in time, who is growing and struggling for power: (Wm. James, H. G. Wells, cf. J. S. Mill, S. Alexander).

(2) He is a God conditioned or limited through that which he finds in himself or in the universe, and which is not there because of his will (W. P. Montague, E. S. Brightman).

5. The world of experience reveals two aspects or tendencies: It shows unity, order, rationality; it shows diversity, individuality, freedom, change, conflict. This is the

problem of the One and the many. We must have place for both.

6. Christian faith implies the conviction that ultimate Power is good, that goodness and power in some ultimate sense are one. It does not rule out the fact of evil or the need of conflict and pain. It has faith that God will ultimately overcome evil and achieve the good. It believes not in the omnipotence of force but of love, and of a love that will use its own ways to conquer.

7. In what sense may we conceive God as absolute?

(1) He is absolute being in that he is dependent on nothing and all else is dependent on him.

(2) He is absolute goodness in character and in the purpose to give good to his creatures.

(3) He is absolute wisdom in his choice of those means which will reach his ends.

(4) He is not absolute power in the sense of irresistible force but as being equal to the achievement of his ends. His ends, being concerned with the values of life, beauty, truth, goodness, must be attained by congruous forces and ways.

8. In what sense is God conditioned or limited? Not by some hostile power outside himself or some imperfection in himself, but by the ends that he sets and by the very nature of the rational and good, which is his nature.

(1) God's goodness is such that he seeks to create beings who shall share life with himself. This life at its highest is rational and ethical, the life of moral and intelligent beings, as in man.

(2) This end of God can only be achieved by means suited to it; not by sheer force, not by direct action, but by the power of truth, love, and good will.

(3) So far as we can see, such higher life can come, not as a direct creation, but only as achievement, by growth and slow progress, in a world where there is both order and freedom. In such a world and for such ends God himself is under the law of struggle and even of suffering to

achieve his ends, as is the whole creation. The world is still in the making and God himself is creatively at work.

(4) In a real sense, these limiting conditions represent not hindrance but opportunity — conditions under which God can create and man achieve.

9. The perfection of God. A limited or conditioned God is not an imperfect God.

(1) The perfection of God has sometimes been conceived as something negative, abstract, static, lifeless. The result is a God utterly contrasted with his world, separated from its life. At other times as the perfection of sheer and irresistible authority and power.

(2) God's perfection rather is that of life, active, creative, purposive, good, self-giving. It is found, not apart from this world of suffering and struggle, but in it — in it (a) as the unity and order and power that sustains it, (b) as the purpose and love that are working to create and redeem.

IV. *The God That Is Near — the Divine Immanence*

Immanence and transcendence, rightly understood, *do not exclude but require each the other*. A transcendent God is of significance to us only because he draws near, because he is immanent in the world's life. And God's immanence is significant only because we believe him to be more than his world, because he is transcendent person and power and goodness. Christianity shows here, as elsewhere, a double polarity in unity.

1. *The meaning of immanence*

(1) It is not spatial, not God being *in* things. Nor does it mean identifying God with his world, so that God *is* all things (or all energy,) and all things are God. (Pantheism)

(2) Immanence defines not so much the nature of God as his *relation* to the world and the way he *works* in the world: an intimate and vital relation as against the external and mechanical. The mode of God's immanent activity

differs on different levels: in the inanimate, the animate, the personal-spiritual, in history, in redemption.

(3) Immanence means *in nature* creative activity, and sustaining energy as the ground of all being.

(4) It means in the world of *life* "an indwelling spiritual presence, a creative, organizing, and perfecting power," bringing forth the ascending levels of being: sensitive, rational, moral, and spiritual.

(5) The *higher immanence* of God is seen (a) in the love of God as he comes near to men, to give himself in forgiveness, in fellowship, in saving help (Jesus the supreme expression); (b) in the idea of an indwelling Spirit of God giving life to men.

2. *Considerations supporting the immanentistic concept*

(1) The conception of nature in terms of energy, activity, development. God is present as immanent energy and life, or he has no place.

(2) Religion, alike in history and individual experience, suggests an intimate, inner, and ethical relation.

(3) The conviction that nature, history, moral experience, social hopes and efforts, all have a divine meaning, that God is related to all these.

3. *The significance and value of this conception*

(1) It gives a richer meaning to the common life.

(2) It has changed the conception of human nature.

(3) It has overcome the nature-supernatural dualism.

(4) It has influenced all doctrines that deal with God's activity in the world: creation, revelation, providence, incarnation, salvation; it is against the externalistic, mechanistic, magical (as in sacramentarianism).

4. *The dangers in the emphasis on immanence*

(1) It may mean the loss of God. The effort to bring him near may simply remove him altogether. When God becomes everything, he becomes nothing.

(2) Danger, too, of blurring distinctions between God and man, of overoptimism as to man and human effort, of failing to see need of God, of underestimating the forces of evil.

(3) If we still call God which is left, then he has lost the real meaning that God has for religion. There are lost for us moral distinction or character in God (all is God equally — the imperfect, perfect, evil); moral standards and authority; a personal God and religion as personal fellowship; salvation, a meaning for nature and history, a goal and the assurance of its achievement.

(4) Such dangers disappear when we think of God as *personal* and *ethical*. So long as this is held fast, immanence may be strongly stressed.

PART III. GOD AND THE WORLD

A. AS TO CREATION AND CONCEPT OF THE WORLD

I. Historical

1. Hebrew conceptions of the cosmos

(1) The form of Hebrew cosmology does not concern us; it was common in that day: a geocentric universe, flat earth, solid firmament. Note that there are various pictures of creation: Gen 2:4-24 (beginning of 8th century); 1:1-2, 3 (about 536); Isa. 40; Pss. 104;139; Job 10:8-12; 38: 4-39, 30. Cf. Job 26:11; 37:18; Pss. 24:2; 78:23; 93:1; 104:5; 136:6; 148:4; Isa. 14:9-11; Amos 9:6.

(2) The interest of the writers is not in scientific ideas, but in religious content: God as creator, power, wisdom, purpose, order. Sin is recognized, men's responsibility indicated, but, so too, God's control and ultimate triumph. No theoretical solution of problem of evil. Note sublimity of narratives, poetical-picture form as against prosaic-scientific.

2. Influence of Greek thought

(1) Seen in Stoicism: pantheistic; the logos as immanent principle of life and reason.

(2) Seen in Platonism and neo-Platonism: dualistic, opposition of spirit and matter; its conception of evil naturalistic and intellectualistic, rather than ethical.

II. *The Doctrine of Creation*

1. The doctrine of creation in traditional theology was influenced by two factors: (1) a theory of the Bible which took Genesis statements literally; (2) a conception of God which so emphasized his transcendence as to make him external to the world, working by irresistible power. Hence the doctrine of creation *ex nihilo*, in six days, of a completed world. (But Origen held to the eternal existence of the universe, and Augustine had a doctrine of development).
2. The change in the form of the Christian doctrine is due to both science and religious thought: in part to the idea of evolution; even more to fundamental changes in conception of religion, Bible, God, and God's relation to the world.
3. What is evolution? The term is used loosely, often undiscriminatingly, in three ways: (1) for certain facts, namely, an observed mode of change in the world; (2) for scientific theories of these changes; (3) for a philosophical world view built on those facts and theories.

(1) *The facts:* What is has come to be by a process marked by continuity and change (the appearance of what is new, but always in relation to what went before). This applies to the whole realm of existence, not only to biology, to the atom, chemical elements, the astro-physical world, human life and history. (There may be devolution, *Abbau*, as well as evolution, *Aufbau*).

(2) *Science:* Science observes these facts, describes the process, points out the significant elements, seeks to set forth in simplest possible manner the observed regular modes of behavior, i.e., natural laws, and propounds theories as to how the changes take place. It does not consider ultimate causes of final explanations.

a. *Darwinism* is one theory of evolution. Its main features are (a) fortuitous variation, (b) the struggle for existence due to excess reproduction, (c) natural selection through the survival of the fittest, (d) fixation (or preservation, conservation) of variation by heredity. Variation by chance and mechanical selection suggest a mechanistic theory, ruling out intelligence and purpose, bringing mere addition, mere increase of complexity.

b. *Emergent evolution* stresses the significance of wholes; the appearance of something new and different (a higher level) as compared with the constituent elements; the fact of new laws, or modes of behavior, that come with the new level.

(3) An evolutionary *philosophy* is an attempt, using evolutionary facts and theories, to arrive at some final explanation of the world. (Herbert Spencer). Such philosophies are commonly pure naturalism, ruling out the ideal, the personal, and God, limiting the real to the data of natural science. Of late, the idea of emergent evolution has been used as the basis of a philosophy. This may take several forms:

a. Evolutionary naturalism, with no place for God — the principle of emergence is supposed to explain the development of the universe.

b. A doctrine less than theism which yet holds to some organizing, integrating, or creating Principle or Nisus, or which may think of God as himself the highest level to be gradually achieved.

c. A theistic theory, a God who is the environment and the necessary condition for calling worth that which is higher.

4. *The objections to evolution from the religious standpoint*

(1) These have commonly been three: (a) It contradicts the Bible, (b) It eliminates the supernatural, ruling out God as creator. (c) It denies man's spiritual nature and reduces him to the brute.

(2) In reply it may be said:

(a) The authority of the Bible is in religion, not in science and history.

(b) Evolution as a science has nothing to say for or against belief in the supernatural, that is, in God as the ultimate reality and explanation of the universe.

(c) Not what man came from nor the road by which he came is decisive, but what he is and where he has arrived. (So with the development of the individual from the microscopic germ). Evolutionary thought today (emergent evolution) emphasizes a creative aspect, the emergence of the new. On this general subject, read *Christianity*, chs. 6 and 16.

5. *The Christian doctrine of creation*

(1) The essential elements in the Christian idea of creation remain unchanged. It is not a matter of when or how. It does not involve creation out of nothing or at one point in time. It is the conviction that the world now, as always, is dependent for its being upon God, and that God works as a creative Power.

(2) Our conception of creation today will take its form in the light of the best knowledge of our day.

a. Creation is by evolution. The method of God in his world is that of growth, or development, alike in the making of stellar systems, the evolution of life, the creation of character, and the coming of the Kingdom of God.

b. Evolution is creative. It is the appearance of that which is new, in ascending levels, the higher related to the lower, conditioned by it, but going beyond it. It is a continuous self-giving of God, an ever fuller realization of himself in his world.

c. Such a process is supernatural in the true sense. We see at once the immanent and the transcendent God. It is the orderly and natural process of immanent energy; it is the work of a God who transcends his world. The supernatural is here, not in one or a few special creative acts, but in the reality of God as continuous source, sustaining energy, and guiding purpose.

d. Creation so conceived involves a certain spontaneity or freedom. "Beings are not turned out like ready-made articles, but are given an opportunity of making themselves." Hence the cost of creation, the need of long ages, of pain and struggle and countless blind alleys, the slow upward movement of human life. Such a conception gives help in relation to the problem of evil, and a far loftier idea of the love and patience of God.

B. THE CONTROL AND DIRECTION OF THE WORLD

I. *Introductory*

Religion is concerned vitally with the questions: Is this world under the control of blind forces and a mechanistic order? Or is there an eternal Spirit of Good Will which is moving in it, directing it, carrying out his ends? Does God make a difference in the world? Questions involved: (1) *Providence* in individual life and in history; (2) the relation of the *supernatural and the natural;* (3) how God works in his world; (4) "answers to prayer"; (5) *the problem of evil;* (6) the spiritual value and meaning of the *natural world.* The question of providence is inseparable from the questions. Creation, revelation, salvation, providence are all one work of God seen in different aspects. (On the following sections, cf. *Christianity,* chs. 6 and 16).

II. *The Method of God in His World*

1. *The method of God in Nature*

(1) An orderly method. We learn this by observation. It is assumed by science. It is set forth in "natural laws", which are not forces ruling over nature but simply the nature of things as manifested in their orderly behavior. Such order is the expression of the rational and dependable nature of the World Ground, God.

(2) An element of spontaneity, self-activity, freedom, contingency in nature.

(3) The method of immanent power, not extraneous force; this does not exclude a transcendent intelligence and gracious purpose.

(4) The method of growth (evolution).

2. *The method of God with men*

(1) Physical man is under the laws of nature. But other and higher laws are also operative. God's method with man is related to his higher nature as rational and free moral being. The principles noted above apply, but on a higher level.

(2) Evolution with man enters upon a new stage, that of conscious and purposive self-direction. Man becomes co-creator with God. Reason and freedom enter in.

(3) Man is a social being. The lower world shows not only organization but association. With man this gains a rational and ethical basis, and becomes far more extensive, complicated, and significant.

(4) The method of God with humanity is seen in all this. It is not that of external power which compels, or of sheer autocracy which commends. It is the method of truth which appeals to understanding, of righteousness which speaks to conviction, of love which summons to free return. At all points it is the method of freedom, asking free response. It asks surrender, yet imposes responsibility. On God's side it involves a higher immanence, or nearness, that of a patient, waiting, suffering, toiling, self-giving personal Spirit.

III. *Concerning the Supernatural*

1. The term supernatural is used in various ways and with considerable confusion. It is necessary to distinguish and define. For religion it means the spiritual world which un-

derlies all reality and gives it meaning and worth. This spiritual world has its being in God; to the supernatural means ultimately God himself.

2. *Naturalism* is a philosophy which asserts that the only world is that evident to the senses. This rules out God. It tends to limit knowledge to what is quantitatively measurable, to make of the world a mechanism, to exclude not only God but moral ideals and values, moral freedom, and human personality itself. The new naturalism (M. Otto, R. W. Sellars) rules out God and a self-existent reality of spirit, but seeks room in the sensible universe for ideals and higher values. It recognizes the higher but makes it incidental, not ultimate.

3. Traditional supernaturalism emphasized God's transcendence, and thought of him too often as arbitrary will and external power. It tended to find the super-natural in special acts of God, in events not explained "naturally", in the intervention of special force. It emphasized creation as against evolution, miracles as against natural law. Traditionalism and naturalism both make the same mistake: they suppose that the natural excludes the supernatural, the human the divine.

4. The relation of natural and supernatural. By the world of *nature* we mean the physical universe as perceptible by our senses. By *supernatural* we mean the world of the spirit, of the personal, of meaning and value. The supernatural is more than the world of nature but it is not separated from it; it is indeed the final reality and meaning of nature. It has its own order, but it does not conflict with the order of nature. The order of nature is the expression of divine reason and the servant or divine ends. Nature, in the final analysis, is thus supernatural. Yet, though God (the supernatural) is present in all, there are lower and higher levels of value and order, and these reflect in different degrees the active presence of God and the meaning of the world. And God himself is transcendent, not only immanent in nature.

IV. Concerning Miracles

1. *Traditional theology* defines a miracle as a special deed of God, contrary to natural law or beyond the possibility of "natural" agencies. Its conception of miracle is determined by its idea of God and his relation to the world. For this theology, miracle plays an important role. By it God proves his existence to man, does special works, gives special messages, or affords credentials. The miracle has here supreme evidential value.

2. A *miracle* is an event in which the presence of God is especially manifest. This definition is religious. (H. H. Farner, *The World and God,* p. 110, says, "It is an event or complex of events through which man becomes aware of God as active towards himself in and through his own personal situation." It is God speaking to man through events. Farner assimilates the idea of miracle to those of revelation and salvation.) Its emphasis is *not on the method* (contrary to law, beyond natural forces.) It welcomes rather than opposes a "natural" explanation. It does, however, emphatically hold to a living God, working in his world, manifesting himself to men. The world of *nature* is an instrument, a *means, not a barrier* to God. His method is always that of order, although neither science nor religion can affirm just what that order must be. We must realize also the various levels of being, and that higher levels bring new possibilities and a higher order. The crucial matter is: have we a living God who can work freely toward his ends? Is the order of nature for him (as for us) a means to be used or a barrier to action? Has he less freedom than means? Is the expression of his rational nature to be found merely in the uniformities of nature?

3. *As to biblical miracles*

(1) Biblical miracle accounts must be studied historically and critically. We must distinguish between fact and interpretation, and between first-hand accounts and those

of later date or at second hand. We must recognize a tendency to multiply marvels and to objectify or externalize spiritual experience.

(2) We must apply a religious test. We are concerned only with that which has significance as a worthy manifestation of the spiritual.

V. *The Problem of Evil*

Consult *Christianity*, chapter 18

From Geo. MacDonald: "This is a healthy, a practical, a working faith. First that a man's business is to do the will of God. Second, that God takes upon himself the care of that man. Third, and therefore, that a man ought never to be afraid of anything." (In Robert Falconer)

VI. *The Providence of God*

By the providence of God we mean his control and direction of the world to secure his ends of good.

1. As to *"general providence"*. Here we recall

(1) The method of God, discussed above, by which his world is so ordered as to make possible the achievement of the highest ends.

(2) The active presence of God in the world as sustaining energy, ordering purpose, and indwelling Spirit of love and truth and righteousness.

2. As to "special providence". Is there a providence of God which is more than a general order? Is there a special and active relation to particular events and individual lives?

(1) We must not think of the order of nature as separating us from God or as having only meaning for the whole. It should express to us directly his love and purpose. Matt. 5:45.

(2) Further, we should think with Jesus of an immediate

and personal presence of God with each of us, of a love and concern for each of us, of our individual fellowship with him. Matt. 6:6; 10:29-31; Luke 15:1-10.

(3) What then should we pray for individually, and what expect? (a) In the spiritual world; grace, strength, guidance, comfort, God's Spirit, a life of personal fellowship. (b) As to the material and natural world: nothing can separate us from God; with a right attitude on our part all things will work together for good; the acceptance of all goods as a gift from God; the spirit of trust which will bring all needs of every kind to God and will leave all things with God; the recognition of higher ends transcending our individual life; the devotion of life and acceptance of toil and pain for the advancement of these ends.

VII. *A Christian Doctrine of Nature and of History*

The foregoing discussions indicate the need of a Christian doctrine of nature and history. Basic for both is the conception not only a transcendent God who is creator of nature and ruler of history, but of an immanent God who is actively and redemptively present in both.

1. By nature we mean the finite and visible universe of things and men.

(1) Its source is God as creator; its order is God's reason in action on this level.

(2) It reveals everywhere an urge or drive or impulse to self-maintenance and self-achievement, involving an aspect of contingency or "freedom".

(3) Within this, God works not only as sustaining energy and encompassing order, but as directing purpose and ordering power, creating by bringing into right relation, by the "whole-making" which brings forth the new and higher.

(4) Ethically considered, the natural world is the condition for the bringing forth of the spiritual, the school for its development, at once a help to man and a temptation to man, once a revelation of God and a veiling of God.

2. By history we mean the ordered and ongoing life of man as united in social relations and as continuous through the social heritage. It is the new level that is reached with the appearance of a creatures who is at once a part of the process of nature and yet can transcend it and transcend himself. This he can do by rational, moral, and religious insight apprehending a higher world, and by relating himself to this higher world in faith and obedience.

(1) Prophetic faith sees God working in history, revealing, judging, redeeming. It sees him working through a people of God (the Church) toward the kingdom of God as his goal.

(2) It sees history as the sphere of man's activity, as well as God's, an activity in which man may work with God, or in which he may as sinner revolt against God and bring judgment and destruction.

(3) Because the finite is imperfect and transitory, and because sin brings judgment, history looks to a salvation of God which is beyond history, just as its whole understanding of history is through faith in a God who, working in history, is yet more than history.

As to a Christian phil. of history

God is in history and works in and through history
Man, rational, free responsible, is an essential factor.
But not man simply as individual — man in groups — family, community, state, industry, international realms, religious assn., the indiv. depth and at same time contributory.
a continuity, an increasing purpose, a growing achievement.
The meaning and place of the church here — nature, function
The meaning of the kingdom of God.
The kingdom beyond time.

B. "WHICH WAY THEOLOGY?"

By Harris Franklin Rall

The Garrett Tower, Jannuary, 1935

The teacher of religion is faced with perplexing questions today, and of late it has seemed that even the leaders did not know where they stood. So the query has been raised by more than one of our friends: "where does Garrett stand?" Is there a swing back to the theology? Is liberalism dead? Has authoritarianism come back? Is Methodism turning to Calvin by the way of Karl Barth? Are we going back to individualism in theology? Shall we give up individualism and limit ourselves to a social gospel? What has the church to say on social matters? And what about God: Is he Person or Process? Is he absolute or finite?

None of these questions raises new issues. The difference is that increasing numbers of our pastors are waking up to the fact that such questions have to be faced, and that a ministry which has no clear convictions and no convincing message of faith is leading a losing cause. No one man has a right to speak for Garrett here. The finest thing about Garrett is the way in which she holds the true Christian union of faith and freedom: faith that in Jesus Christ God has revealed himself and the way of life; freedom to follow the truth and set forth what is meant by this faith. I can simply express my own convictions, though I think I am at one with my colleagues in broad outline. Space compels brief and categorical statement. If it sounds dogmatic, it is not so intended.

1. Are we going back to Calvin by the way of Barth? No. A divine determinism that fixes every event, including

the fall of man and the damnation of the non-elect, a God who is arbitrary will and authority before he is moral goodness, the denial of human freedom and responsibility— we are not ready for these. We are not ready for Karl Barth: for the dogmatism that marks his method, for the agnosticism that leaves God finally unknowable, for the dualism that sets God and man so sharply against each other that God cannot really enter into human life, that rules out a real doctrine of the indwelling and transforming Holy Spirit and denies Methodism's insistent belief in salvation as moral renewal, nor for its assertion that religion has no message for the social order and can furnish no power for its renewal.

2. Is the old theology coming back? "Old theology" is as meaningless a phrase as "new theology." Neither represents a single definite, consistent system. The story of the "old theology" is one of constant change and difference. Back of the question lurks the supposition that you can have a complete, unchanging, absolute system of doctrine which a man can accept on authority and take as a whole. Many would like to do that in order to be relieved of thinking and get a comfortable certainty. There lies the appeal of the Roman Church to many minds. That is impossible for us. There are old doctrines that cannot come back: verbal infallibility of the Bible, old theories of creation and the old pictures of the earth and the heavens, mechanical and unethical doctrines of penal substitution, theories of total depravity that deny obvious facts and of original sin which make it a physical inheritance rather than a moral fact, speculations about God which are no part of the gospel.

3. Is liberalism dead? No. Ideas which individual liberals have held have been found imperfect or unsound, alike in theology, economics, and politics, exactly as in the case of conservatives. But liberalism itself is not a system of doctrine; it is an attitude, a faith, a method. It is the conviction that men must keep an open mind and follow where truth

leads, that we cannot accept an external authority which compels submission without conviction, that human freedom belongs to the highest human life. The ideas which liberals have held demand constant criticism, and liberalism by its principles calls for this. Liberalism represents not simply a right but a duty. It has been won at great cost. It is threatened today by a new autocracy in fascist and communist states, and by authoritarianism in religion; and it is being depreciated by unthinking liberals, while it is attacked by reactionaries and radicals. Liberalism by itself is, of course, not enough. Religion means finding and not merely searching; we need more than the open mind. It is the truth that makes us free, not simply the search for it. But a free and forward looking spirit in religion is still needed.

4. Have tradition and authority any place in religion? Yes, and large place which is being more recognized. We run to extremes. Men fought against external authority which repressed, and demanded free search. But there is an authority that is not external; it is the authority of right and truth as they win the conviction of mind and soul. Then they have the right to command; then comes the highest freedom, not that of search but that of obedience when we have found. The open mind remains, but the truth that has found us sets us free. So we Christians have found God in Jesus Christ; rather, he has found us, and we have answered and given him authority over our life. And always we must remember that our individual search and finding is a very limited matter. High tradition represents the experience of the race, particularly of its great spirits, coming to us especially through the Bible and the Church. We are not to accept it unthinkingly; that would be traditionalism. But we need its help to inform and inspire and bring to us God. The temptation of liberals, prizing their freedom, is to depreciate the past. There is today an increasing appreciation of its treasures. We will have to revise and restate, but we are seeing now values in old

truths that were too lightly passed by, and especially in the Bible itself.

5. Does religion mean salvation as well as duty and service? Yes, and the fact in its full meaning is being recognized anew. We have had a constant emphasis on organization and activity and service, on the ethical and human side of religion. There was urgent need of that. Too often religion had been merely a matter of otherwordly hopes, or of luxuriating in pious emotions, or of dependence upon some mechanical or magical process of salvation. The reaction from that has been extreme. Man discarded vital truths together with outworn theories. But there is something more in religion than ideas and organizations and efforts; there is a living God who comes into saving fellowship with men. There is a deep need of man to be delivered from doubt and fear, from uncertainty and futility, from his weakness and sin; and there is a God who meets that need. God gives men peace and power by bringing them into a living fellowship with himself. We must bring that word to this confused and doubting and very needy day. But we cannot do it by simply trying to galvanize old phrases and doctrines into fictitious life. A clear, and convincing, and adequate doctrine of salvation is urgently needed in order to a truer and more effective preaching.

6. Do we need a realistic theology? Yes. Christianity is a realistic religion, if by that you mean a religion that keeps close to the concrete facts of life and faces its stern realities, including that of evil. Such realism will move away from the dogmatic on the one hand, from the speculative on the other. It will set itself against the danger of believing according to our wishes, or of trying to make man the measure of all things. We must make central a God who is revealed and yet transcends our knowing; we must recognize the fact of evil, though we can never fully understand it. But we must remember, too, that religion is idealistic; it is insight into meaning that does not appear

on the surface; it is faith in the unseen and a conviction that the unseen is good; it is faith that the final reality is Spirit, not things.

7. Which way are we moving in our thought of God? Just now that concerns especially three matters:

(1) Is God transcendent or immanent? But these are not opposites. One concerns the faith that God is more than his world, and that needs and is receiving new emphasis. The other asserts the intimate presence of God in his world. When transcendence, as with Barth, is of such a kind as to exclude the living, saving presence of God in history and human fellowship, then we have not just an emphasis on transcendence, but a misconception as to what it means.

(2) Is God personal, or is he some cosmic order or process, producing personality and even moral values but not himself personal? I do not think the impersonalism of Wieman, or of Whitehead and Dewey whom he follows, can meet the facts of life when we recognize that moral and religious life and experience are as valid as our experience of the physical order. Only, remember that a personal God does not mean a magnified man; it means One who is not less than the highest we know in reason and purpose and goodness, and with whom we can have fellowship as we cannot with things and beasts.

(3) Is God finite or infinite? omnipotent or limited? No mere yes or no will answer this question. I think we are moving away from the old absolutisms which were abstract and unmeaning and expressed philosophical speculation rather than religious faith. For faith, God is not sheer power, or absolute in that he is the power on which all depends, the goodness which commands utter trust and devotion. But he is also purpose, a goodness that is creative and works toward ends. His character of goodness and reason and his purpose of good will are the dominant facts, and these condition his power in all that he does. Unless we recognize such conditions and limitations, evil

will contradict faith. For the sake of honest thought and religious faith, it is time we got away from the emphasis on sheer and unlimited power, which presents God more as physical force or as oriental monarch than as redemptive and creative good will working at cost of pain and toil as love and truth must work.

The problem of the social message remains, but Dr. Schermerhorn's admirable discussion in the last issue concerned itself with this.

C. Pastoral Prayers

We thank thee, O Lord, that in thy grace and mercy thou hast called us this morning to join in the hymn of praise unto Thee, Our Father, and unto Our Lord Jesus Christ, in whom thou hast given thyself unto us and through whom thou hast made known to us thy love and thy mercy. And our songs here are but a part of the hymn of praise which today is circling with its melody and with its adoration and with its incense of thanksgiving this world that thou hast made. From lives that have not been free from sorrow or from misfortune; from places of oppression and darkness even, there is rising this day the song of thanksgiving to Him who made them and redeemed them. We too have reason to join in this praise toward Thee. Praise for this day and for the beauty and brightness of the sunshine; praise for thy glory, thy brightness and thy beauty, of which the most glorious day of life is but a reflection, a suggestion, a shadow. Praise to Thee, O Father, for thine ownself, in that love and mercy which can enter into every heart, into every life, into every oppression, every darkness, if we but let Thee in and put our trust in thee; to make it glorious and to make it light.

And so, O Father, as we begin our hour of worship, we pray that thou who are in our midst, very near to each one of us, waiting at each heart's door, wilt Thou O God speak to each of us this morning, do thou help us by thy grace that the door of that heart may be open to thee. Let no distraction of thought, no dissipation of our interest; let no burdening care that is trying to stay with us from the days of the past week; let no darkness or burden of sorrow; let no weakness of flesh or discouragement from failure; let no sin or sense of our misdeed, close that door, but do thou O God, who dost receive all thy children, however they come, with whatever burdens and with whatever needs and with whatever past failure, do Thou help us Lord to bring all to Thee and lay all before thee.

O Thou God of Light, thou hast light for every heart and for every life in thy presence. Shine in upon us. Shine in upon the discouraged hearts this morning. And if there are hearts that have known anything of thee but feel that they have lost something of thy presence, do thou fill them with a new sense of thy presence and with a new radiance of thy beauty this morning. Shine in upon hearts that sorrow, that they may realize, O Father, that deeper than any grief, any burden of sorrow, that thou dost bring us, is the measure of thine own love and mercy; and that where we as friends often stand by in helpless desire to be of some use in the ministry of comfort, thou canst enter in with all the knowledge of all the need and bring grace and help and strenght. And if there are those here who have never known thy presence, speak thou to them this morning: chase the shadows of night away, turn their darkness into day. And so O God may we in thy presence this morning rejoice in the sense of thy goodness and of thy love.

We confess before Thee, O Father, the weakness and imperfection, yes, the sin, the wrong-doing in our life. We have not been as diligent in service as we might have been; we have not been as thoughtful in thy service as we might have been. Forgive us. Forgive us our negligence and remissness. We have not been as true in our hearts as we should have been; we have not loved thee as constantly, as warmly as we should. We have not been toward our fellow-man as kindly and compassionate, as merciful, as charitable in thought and judgment as we should have been. Wilt thou forgive us. And wilt thou take these lives of ours, with all their imperfections, with all their sin, and purify them and make them true. O God help us to serve thee not only with lips, not only with deeds, but with our hearts, with pure love, with true loyalty, with simple childlike faith. Cleanse the thoughts of our hearts by the inspiration of thy holy spirit, that we may perfectly love thee and worthily magnify thy holy name.

And now, Father, may all our worship this morning be blessed of thee. The entrance of thy word giveth light; may it give light and life. Thy word is bread for our souls; may we be fed this morning, and may thy spirit so direct the word that is spoken and so prepare our hearts that it may be for us a message that shall bless us and help us through the week.

We pray for thy churches in this city. Where thy people meet together may thy blessing rest upon them. May the ministers of thy Word have thy guidance; may thy people be found ready in thy day to serve thee. Let thy kingdom come among us. Grant us a life that in all churches shall be pure and true. In all civic activities, and in all our political life as a city may we be clean and righteous. Grant thy blessing upon us as a state (and upon the Governor and the supreme legislative body now in session.) May righteousness in judgment as well as wisdom in council rule there. And so we pray that upon us as a nation, upon all those whom thou hast placed in authority, let thy blessing rest; that we as a people may serve thee; that we may be cleansed from iniquity, from unrighteousness; that we may be made pure as a people in all our life.

And as we thank thee for material blessings, O God we pray grant us that without which no nation can live, without which we shall be poor indeed — clean and pure and true lives in thy sight.

Let thy blessing rest upon the nations of the earth. We pray thee especially for that land which at the close of awful warfare now has a warfare within its own borders. Grant to heal the passions of the hearts of men. Grant to give strength and wisdom to those who are trying to stay and direct the course of rule; may there be righteousness in their council and may there be strength in all their ways. And do thou grant that men who have dishonored thee by their savagery toward those whom thou hast made in thy image, grant that they may come better to know the Father and so to live better with their brethren of all kinds, of all names, of all colors and from all lands; with those who are still our brethren because they are children of one Father.

Hear us in our petitions. Grant us thy blessing upon our homes. Grant thy mercy to all those who are dear to us. Grant to quicken thy work in our midst; and so guide us in our life, so strengthen us in service, so maintain our faith and quicken our love that when we shall have lived our allotted life here and thou shalt call us, we shall hear and shall answer in trust and in rejoicing, and shall go home to be with thee and with those whom thou hast called before us; through Jesus Christ our Lord.

• • •

December 17, 1905, morning prayer

O God, holy and mighty, Creator of all things, Ruler of heaven and earth: we thank thee for that greater name with which Christ has taught us to come to thee. We call thee Father. Give us the courage to believe that thou art indeed Our Father. Help us to believe that thou art here in our midst this morning, that there is not one heart here whose deepest thoughts are not open to thee, not one life whose needs thou dost not know, not one of us whom thou dost not wait to help.

Draw near to us as we draw near to thee. Quicken our minds this morning that we may know thy truth. Kindle high desires within us. Forgive us for being contented with ourselves.

We bring our lives to thee. Thou hast made us. Thou dost know our faults and failures: forgive them. Create within us clean hearts and renew a right spirit within us. Give us quietness and confidence and strength.

We give thee thanks for all thy gifts. Give us joy as we use them. Give us humility as we remember our unworthiness. Give us courage and trust in thee as we face the future. For our land we thank thee. Deliver us from pride and boasting, from self-satisfaction and selfishness. Help us to remember the lands that are in need, the many that cry for food, that lack shelter, the myriads driven out from their homes. May we give of that which thou hast given to us.

Direct this land of ours in ways of justice and service and peace. May thy kingdom come in our own hearts, in our land, and in all the earth. Give thy blessing to this church, to its pastor and those who labor with him. Bless thy church in all. Make it more truly one in faith and fellowship and fit it for the work to which thou hast called it. Direct us in the further worship of this hour and help us as we pray together:

O God of infinite grace and goodness, who through all the ages hast sought to give thyself unto thy children, thou who hast led mankind by many paths that they might know thee and share thy spirit, give us thy help this morning as we seek thee. Be thou the praise in all our song, be thou the light by which we shall see, be thou the deep desire that shall quicken our hearts, may thy Spirit be the life that shall move in all the worship of this hour.

O God, who hast not left us without help, we thank thee for all those heroes of life and faith who have climbed a little nearer to the heights and have made it easier for us to see thee and believe in thee. We thank thee for all saints and seers, and for all patient searchers who have discovered to us something more of thy truth and thy world. Most of all we thank thee this morning for those whose lives of patient toil and steadfast loyalty have made this world a place in which it is better to live and easier to believe in thee.

O God of all majesty and glory, whose wisdom is seen in all the world and whose glory shines in all the heavens, whose power is beyond all our knowing and whose depths of being no man can by thought search out. We thank thee for the common gifts of life in which we see thee, for sunlight and beauty of sea and land, for the faces of little children and the love of friends, for the work that comes with each day and the strength that comes with the task. We thank thee that thou art the God of the common days and the common ways, the God whose love and help is given to the common folk for the common needs.

Grant us thy forgiveness, O God, where we have walked our common ways and have not seen thee. We have thought ourselves lonely when we had thy presence at our side. We have been weak when we might have been strong in thee. We have followed foolish ways of our own when thy light was waiting to show us the path. Forgive us where we have failed in the common ways of our life, in the daily tasks, in the simple demands of patience and sympathy, of kindliness and loyalty.

O God of all grace and mercy, who of thine infinite love didst send our Lord Jesus Christ to bring thy word and thy help to men, draw near to us as we draw nigh to thee, and give to us thy grace and peace in this our morning hour of worship.

We worship thee as the God of all nations and remember thee as a nation today. We adore thee as the God of all righteousness and truth, the God of light in whose light we see all our life. We praise thee as the source of all life, in whom all things have their being, and through whose life this world is having its rebirth of beauty in this season of spring.

Quicken us, we pray thee, as we draw nigh to thee. We have so little to offer thee as we come: these bodies worn with the work of the week, these minds too often dull and distracted, these hearts burdened and distressed, stained with our sins, discouraged with the sense of defeat. And so we offer thee our needs, that thou mayest supply all our wants. Let no heart go forth from this hour of worship that shall not have felt the quickening breath of the divine. Forgive our sins, cleanse the thoughts of our hearts by the inspiration of thy Holy Spirit and renew us in every purpose that is right and good.

We pray thee for all that are sick, for the aged and infirm, for those who sit in loneliness of sorrow, for those to whom disaster and desolation have come by flood or famine or disease, but most of all for men and women who have not seen thy light or known thy presence in their life. Draw near to all such with thy help and healing.

We give thee thanks this day for our land. Especially would we remember those who have given their lives to it in service. We remember those who went forth in time of war and counted not their lives dear unto themselves. We think of those who lie buried on fields of battle, and of those who returned from service. And we remember those who gave their lives in ways of peace, who bore hard burdens in quiet faithfulness: the pioneers who dared the danger of wilderness, whose ploughshare first plowed these prairies, who laid the foundations of our cities. We thank thee for the faithful wives and mothers of our nation's yesterday, for preachers of thy word, for devoted teachers of the young, and for all who gave their service. Their names are unknown to history, but not unknown to thee. We reap from fields where we did not sow and drink from wells that we did not dig. They have labored and we have entered upon the fruits of their labor. In grateful memory we recall them all today, and give thanks to thee who art the inspiration of all service, and the guide of all peoples. Help us to rededicate ourselves this day in love and devotion to our land.

* * *

Memorial Day, May 29, 1927
May 17, 1942

O God, the Rock of Ages, who hast been the dwelling place of men in all generations: the heaven of heavens cannot contain thee, but the cry of the least of thy children reaches thy ears, and it is Thou that hast taught us to say, Our Father. Thou art the strength of our weakness, the light of all our seeing. Thou art the peace by which our hearts are healed, the love that redeems, our lives from littleness and bitterness and strife. Without thy Spirit we are desolate, without thy aid we cannot even cry to thee.

In this place of prayer, soon to be dedicated to Thee, we lift our hearts in adoration. We would forget all else but thee. Teach us to pray. Inform our hearts with thy Spirit that our lives may be conformed to Thy will. May we dedicate to Thee, not alone these walls of stone, but the deepest thoughts and affections of our hearts.

O God, from whom every good gift cometh, we thank Thee for those through whom thy gifts of love are mediated to men. We thank Thee for these friends, who, joined in that life which death cannot destroy, have given this oratory of the soul for the service of men.

We thank Thee for this School, and for all those whose prayers and gifts and toils have conspired through the years to make it a servant of men in the gospel of Jesus Christ. We thank Thee for those who have given their lives as teachers of the truth and who have lived the truth which they taught. We thank Thee for those who have come here to study and gone forth to serve, whose line is gone out through all the earth and whose work to the end of the world. We thank Thee for the never-ending company of those who are pressing on to take their place.

We pray for all those who through the years to come will wait and worship at this shrine. May this become a place of help to men who have become weak in the conflict of life. Within these walls may the high purposes of soul be confirmed and the faith of men grow stronger.

> May struggling hearts that seek release
> Here find the rest of God's own peace;
> And, strengthened here by hymn and prayer,
> Lay down the burden and the care.

And let the beauty of the Lord our God be upon us; and establish Thou the work of our hands upon us; yea, the work of our hands establish Thou it. Through Jesus Christ, our Lord. Amen.

• • •

Prayer offered by Dr. Harris Franklin Rall at the Dedicatory Service of the Frank W. Howes Memorial Chapel, January, 1937.

O Thou God, infinite and eternal, in whose mercy is our hope, in whose will is our peace, once more we gather in this place, hallowed by sacred memories. Once more we bring our worship, our confession of sin, our grateful thanksgiving. Thou art our Father. Thou knowest each one of us. Our secret thoughts, our deepest needs, our cares and sorrows are all known to thee. Draw near to us with thy help and make us deeply sensible of thy presence.

We thank thee for thy Church, the Church of the living God. We thank thee for this church, for all that it has meant to us in the ministry of thy servant whom thou hast taken from his labors. We thank thee for truth faithfully proclaimed, for inspiration and courage which have come to us through his word. We thank thee for the fellowship which we have found here. We thank thee for the many who have labored and worshipped here in the years past, whose faith and devotion have made possible our privilege. Help us, we pray thee, here to dedicate ourselves anew to the unfinished task, to carry on their work, and thy work, in this place.

Bless us in the worship of this hour. If we have been careless, summon us to a new devotion. If we have sinned, bring us to repentance and grant us forgiveness. Strengthen the weak, the tempted. Comfort and help the troubled and sorrowing. Grant to us all thy joy and peace.

Bless our nation and give it guidance in these troubled days. Bless the United Nations organization and help all men everywhere who are seeking to bring our world into unity and peace. Bless thy Church in all lands and make her a faithful witness to the way of Christ, alike in word and life; through Jesus Christ our Lord. Amen.

• • •

September 18, 1949-Harris Franklin Rall

O Thou God of all the earth, whose power is in all the heavens and whose mercy reaches unto all creatures that draw the breath of life, teach us something of the wideness of the divine compassion. Deliver us from all narrowness of sympathy and hardness of heart. Give us that understanding of men that was in the heart of Jesus. Help us to look beneath the outer garb, the form of speech, the color of skin. Help us to see in all men the children of our Father. And by all our need of thee, by all the love undeserved that thou dost bear to us, help us that we may see and own all men as our brothers.

Give us, we pray thee, a truer understanding of ourselves. If we have been complacent in our self satisfaction, teach us a true humility. Help us to discover in ourselves the unsuspected evils that must be rooted out. Give us a better appreciation of those goods of life which are highest in thy sight. And grant us true patience and high faith, and unfaltering devotion as we follow after them.

Teach us as a people wherein our greatness lies. Deliver us from pride of possession, from lust of power and from greed of wealth. May we covet a greatness of spirit that shall match the wideness of these lands with which thou hast so richly endowed us. Help us in our relations to other peoples that we may have the self mastery that should go with strength, the devotion to justice that belongs with a faith in the God of all nations, and that goodwill which alone can make of us a Christian people and secure peace upon earth. •

• • •

A Prayer of Thanksgiving

O Thou God of grace and mercy, from whom come all the good gifts of life, grant us, we beseech Thee, the spirit of thanksgiving. We confess before thee our sins of thoughtlessness and ingratitude and indifference. We have seen the glory of the stars with hearts unstirred by wonder. We have watched the morning sun bring its daily miracle of light and have not remembered the God who makes his sun to rise on the evil and the good. We have had comfort and joy and peace in the unselfish love of the home and we have not lifted our hearts to him from whom every family in heaven and on earth is named. Help us now to bring thee our prayer of thanksgiving.

We thank thee for the beauty of earth that waits our eye each day: for the beauty of unnoticed things, the soft morning light, the flush of dawn, the glory of the sun that rides on high, for the hush of evening, for the solemn splendor of the distant stars.

We thank thee for the spirit of kindness and love that thou hast put in the hearts of men; for friendly greetings as we go down the street, for children that smile up at us, for the kindness of strangers who have answered our questions and met our needs or helped us in extremity, for the deeps of human compassion that have flowed forth to reach the farthest shores of human need and minister to the tragic suffering of our day, for friends who know us and yet love, us, for fellowship that binds in deep interests and high ideals and common loyalties, for the love of home which gives and asks not in return, which multiplies joys as it shares them and lightens burdens by a common bearing.

We thank thee for the fellowship of the church of our Lord Jesus Christ, for the worship that quickens our dull souls and lifts them anew to God, for the Word that speaks to our sins and brings the God of help and mercy, for hymns and prayer that voice confession and need and praise, for the fellowship of faith and love that rises above the strife of class and nation and makes us one with the followers of our Lord throughout the earth, for the family of God that takes in earth and heaven and joins us to those who have gone on before.

And for thyself we thank thee most of all, for thy love revealed in Jesus Christ, for thy mercy undeserved which heals and saves, for thy power which is mightier than sin and selfishness, than hate that corrodes, and fear that enslaves, and war that destroys, for thy saving presence as thou dost give thy Spirit to men, and for thy saving purpose that shall yet bring thy rule of thruth and justice and love and peace upon earth.

Open our eyes, O God, to thy beauty and glory and goodness and power. Deliver us from the dullness that does not see and the ingratitude that fails of praise. Save us from the fear that has forgotten God. And to thee we give praise and grateful thanks, through Jesus Christ our Lord. Amen.

D. Anthology of the Cross

Nineteen hundred years ago the cross was nothing more than a pagan instrument of terrible death reserved by Rome for the lowest of criminal offenders. And then one day they hanged upon this cross a humble peasant whose death transformed it for all the centuries since. It is a symbol now, charged with many meanings. A few of these I want to bring to you in the words of others. I am not quoting Scripture or hymn or theology. Purposely I am turning aside from the broad highway of traditional Christian expression to note how the theme of the cross has again and again stirred the soul of poet and mystic and lover of men as they have dwelt on the dark places and the deep meanings of life.

I. The Cross in Human Life

The cross was in the world before Jesus suffered. Love has always meant pain. Life and death have ever been joined together. Sometimes suffering has seemed like stark unrelieved evil; yet out of it, and more especially out of suffering for others prompted by love, there have come the highest glories of mankind. If a man die, queried Job, shall he live again? Except a grain of wheat fall in the ground and die, it cannot live, said Jesus. Except a man lose his life, he shall not find it. Goethe said it in words that I find hard to translate.

> Till this word is made thine own,
> Die and live again.
> Thou art but a pilgrim lone
> In this world of pain.

Sarvapalli Radakrishnan, professor of eastern religions at Oxford University, is a Hindu, yet he finds in the cross something common to both worlds. These words are taken from his *East and West in Religion*:

"The mystery of life is *creative sacrifice*. It is the central idea of the Cross, which was such a scandal to the Jews and the Greeks, that he who truly loves us will have to suffer for us, even to the point of death. It is the truth central to all living religions. The victory over evil through suffering and death; we have it not only in the garden of Gethsemane, in the palace of Gautama, the Buddha, in the cell where Socrates drank the hemlock, but in many other unknown places. Only that which suffers is truly loving, truly divine. Blessed are those that suffer, is the cry of all religions. Suffering is the substance of spiritual life, the very flesh of reality, the blood that unites us all. The Cross signifies that evil, in the hour of its supreme triumph, suffers its decisive defeat by the force of patient love and suffering."

Walther Rathenau was a German and a Jew who worked with Stresemann for a new Germany. In his unselfish and brave devotion, he showed the spirit of that other Jew that hung upon the cross. He was assassinated by the Nazis before Hitler came to power. Later, the Nazis tore down the tablet which had been placed in his memory. He wrote these prescient words some years before his death.

"Mankind will travel this Path of the Soul through hostility, contempt, and persecution; nor will its pioneers be exempt from that supreme test: the being assailed by those whom they are leading to redemption. They will be visited with bitter penalties, and condemned to vicarious sacrifice as evil-doers."

In a spirit which makes us think once more of him who spoke from his cross, his mother wrote to the mother of one of his assassins:

"In unspeakable grief I beg of you, unhappiest of women, that we may clasp each other's hands. Tell your son that I forgive him in the name and in the spirit of my boy, as I trust God may forgive him when he shall render a full confession of his guilt to his earthly judge, and repent before his heavenly judge a contrite sinner. Had he known my boy, the noblest man that ever trod the earth, he would sooner have turned the murderous weapon upon himself. May These words bring some peace to our soul."

Let me take one more illustration of this spirit of the cross which identifies itself with sufferers and sinners in the spirit of love if by any means it may serve some. Eugene Debs was a socialist, a man whose protest against America's entrance into the world war took him at last to prison. These words were spoken to the judge who sentenced him:

"Years ago I recognized my kinship with all human beings, and I made up my mind that I was not one with better than the meanest of the earth. I said then, and I say now, that while there is a lower class I am of it, while there is a criminal class I am of it, while there is a soul in prison I am not free."

II. The Cross in the Life of God

The cross as suffering and death is found outside the Christian sphere, yes, and as vicarious suffering, as love bearing another's pain. The Christian faith goes further: the cross belongs to God's life, not alone to man's. The cross of Christ is a revelation of what sin is and a judgment upon it; but it is more. In it we see God's own deed of love. It is a daring thought, this thought of a suffering God, but this is our faith: God is love, and without love this universe could not hold together. Creation itself and redemption most of all mean God giving himself, humbling himself, entering with toil and pain into his world. This time we turn to the poets, and first to the mystic, William Blake, in his *Jerusalem*.

"Wouldst thou love one who never died
For thee, or ever die for one who had not died for thee?
And if God dieth not for Man, and giveth not Himself
Eternally for Man, Man could not exist, for Man is Love
As God is Love. Every kindness to another is a little death
In the Divine Image, nor can Man exist but by brotherhood."

Not his miracles but his love, says Alfred Noyes in his *Watchers of the Skies,* shows Jesus as divine.

"While one dear humble heart,
Beating with love for man between two thieves,
Proves more than all his wounds and miracles
Our Crucified to be the Son of God."

and then, in *The Last Voyage, carries* the thought further:

"Did his creation, then, involve descent,
Renunciation, sacrifice in heaven,
A Calvary, at the inmost heart of things,
Wherein the eternal Passion still enacts
In an eternal world what mortal eyes
Saw dimly on one shadowy hill of Time?"

Kagawa, at once mystic and apostle of social justice, speaks out of a life which has itself known the suffering of the cross.

"Without awakening to this full Cross-consciousness
The social revolution is absolutely futile.
It is the adventure of ultimate Love.
It is the consummate Art of the Universe.
                    The Cross is
The whole of Christ, the whole of Love.
God speaks to man through the Cross

Of Love's mysteries concealed in the Divine Bosom.
These who have no love of humanity
Have no way of knowing the Love of God.
Without the Cross there is no victory."

III. The Cross as Power

The cross is light on human life, alike on the lot of pain, the darkness of sin, and the glory of love. The cross is a vision of God. But in Christian faith it is one thing more, as Paul saw long ago: it is the greatest power in the world. That is hard to believe in a day when the whole world is in terror before the new dictators with their air planes and bombs, or is still putting its trust in the old materialisms and imperialisms. But when lying propaganda has defeated itself, when the mighty have perished by the sword which they seized, when selfishness of men or nations brings the inevitable death, then the cross with its judgment on sin and its reconciling love goes winning men's hearts and transforming their lives and slowly changing the kingdoms of greed and force into the kingdom of God. Still its folly is the wisdom of God and its weakness is God's power.

This time, looking once again to unconventional sources, we turn to the dramatists, and first to some words from Ibsen's *The Emperor Julian*, where the apostate ruler speaks.

"I dreamed of him lately, I dreamed that I had subdued the whole world. Then I looked down at my own earth, from which I had driven out the Galilean. But, behold, there came a procession by me. There were soldiers, and judges, and executioners at the head of it, and weeping women followed. And lo! in the midst of the slow moving array was the Galilean, alive, and bearing a cross on his back. Where is he now? What if *that* at Golgotha was but a wayside matter, a thing done, as it were, in passing, in a leisure hour? What if he goes on and on, and suffers, and dies, and conquers, again and again, from world to world?"

And then there is the familiar scene from *The Terrible Meek* of Charles Rann Kennedy, with the Roman captain speaking.

"I tell you woman, this dead son of yours, disfigured, shamed, spat upon, has built a kingdom this day that can never die. The living glory of him rules it. The earth is *His* and he made it. He and his brothers have been moulding and making it through the long ages; they are the only ones who ever really did possess it: not the proud: not the idle, not the wealthy, not the vaunting empires of the world. Something has happened up here on this hill today to shake all our kingdoms of fear and blood to the dust. It can't last: it never has lasted, this building in blood and fear. Already our kingdoms are beginning to totter. Possess the earth! We have lost it. We never did possess it. We have lost both earth and ourselves in trying to possess it."

E. Selections from *The Christian Advocate* "We Believe" and "Dr. Rall Answers"

We Believe: "Theology for Everyman" - February 6, 1941

Here is a query to begin with: What can Christians hope for today?

All around this world men and women are in distress and anxiety and fear, looking out on a world at war and wondering about tomorrow. Christian men are wondering, too; and it seems almost harder for them than for others. Why such a world as this if there be a God in heaven?

Among the fifty questions or more that I have already received from people who were told about this column, this question, in one form or another, comes again and again.

Has not God all power? Is he not deeply concerned? Shall we ask him to kill the dictators and militarists? (One church woman suggested to a group that they arrange for meetings at which people would pray God to kill Hitler.) Shall we expect God by sheer power to overthrow the evil and give victory to the good? Or is the Lord to return very soon, make the world over all at once, and bring history to an end?

First, we must not expect that we can escape the consequences of wrongdoing. "Whatsoever a man soweth, that shall he also reap." And that applies to nations. There is an order of God in history as truly as in nature. We see it in God's judgment on our day. By what they have done, and what they have failed to do, the nations have been preparing this day.

And who will say that we have been without blame? We needlessly affronted a proud people (the Japanese, by the form of the exclusion act); we refused to help when, twenty years ago, there was the chance for a new world order; we furthered the rising nationalism by building trade walls against other peoples, while expecting them to buy from us; we joined in the scramble for prosperity and pleasure.

We cannot hope that God will enter this war with supernatural power and destroy the forces of evil. What God wants is truth and love and justice. No act of force, not even from God, can establish these upon earth. No destruction of armies can overcome evil. This is not the order of God or the method of God. Are we forgetting Christ and his cross?

We can hope for the coming of God's rule on earth. Christ is not deceiving us when he bids us pray: "Thy kingdom come, thy will be done on earth as it is in heaven." We hope for this because we trust God.

But are we then left to wait some one divine deed in an indefinite future? No, God is here now and is working now. Evil destroys itself in the end — that is God at work as judgment. The Church is here, bearing witness, still joining

in one fellowship the men of many lands — that is God's mercy his living presence. God is working in men, men of faith and good will.
We Believe: "Theology for Everyman" - February 13, 1941

How Shall I Picture God?

It would be easy to answer: "Do not picture God. Pictures are of things visible and physical, and God is spirit and is unseen. To picture God is to drag him down to our level."

But that is not quite true. We are always using pictures to help us understand what is unseen .That is especially true of religion and poetry and love. When we find that which is too great and wonderful for us to define or describe, we use a sign or symbol or picture for it. Sometimes, as in religion, men forget that these are only pictures and take them literally. Sometimes they use crude pictures or wrong ones. Sometimes they keep the pictures of childhood when they should move on to something better. But pictures or symbols we must use if we speak of things of the spirit.

The simplest answer to our question is: Use the highest that you know to picture what God is, but never forget that God is higher than any picture man can form.

The men of the Bible never try to define God in words of reason or logic, any more than they try to prove God; but they are always trying to tell what God means to them and they use numberless pictures in so doing. Some of the Old Testament words are not up to the highest New Testament level. When they would set forth the power of God they use such pictures as captain, king, Lord of hosts, and man of war. But how many noble and appealing symbols they bring when they tell what God means to men. He is a refuge, a dwelling place; he is light, strength, salvation. He is a shepherd; he pities like a father, and men feel beneath them, upholding them, "the everlasting arms."

Yet they do not forget that he is infinitely above man in holiness and glory and power.

What picture shall we use? No one picture will do to bring our God before us. Science tells us of power, of one energy that in many forms moves in all things; God is this all-sustaining power. There is an order that holds the universe togther and makes it one; the God of truth and wisdom is that order. But he is far more than power and reason. In man at his best we find goodness, justice, mercy. And in one Life lived here on earth, that mercy and goodness was without fault or stain. Jesus showed us what God was like and gave us a name for him.

We will still think of him as the Power that bears up a universe, as the Presence that reaches its every part, and as the Holiness that is above all that is finite and sinful. But we will picture him as Father. That does not mean physical form or features; it does mean spirit and character. It means infinite Power that gives strength to my weakness, a God of holiness who is near with his mercy, a Father whose care reaches me and whose help touches my life, and it means a personal spirit, a God who knows and speaks, and to whom in prayer we can speak.

Dr. Rall Answers: "Questions on Beliefs - On Salvation as Life" - March 5, 1942

"Degrees of salvation?" a reader writes, referring to a comment of last May, "positively not." In this case it seems to be a difference as to meaning of words, and the word that we need to understand first is "salvation."

For many people, in the Church as well as without, I fear salvation has become a vague word, without clear meaning. Part of the difficulty is due to the way in which we have narrowed it and clung to old and often unconvincing phrases and theories. Part of it is because people do not understand.

So we need to state the simplest fundamentals of the idea first. Salvation means life by the help of God.

"Life" is the first word here. Salvation is something positive. True, it means being saved from something — from ourselves and our sin and selfishness, from defeat and despair, from empty and meaningless lives, from enmity with men and separation from God, from lives that are out of right relation with ourselves and our whole world. To live thus is to be lost.

But you cannot really know what being lost means until you know what it means to be saved. No paragraph, no volume, can tell that; but if we are to take a single word to suggest the right meaning, it would be the word "life." To be saved is to "have life," to "enter into life." "You did He make alive" is Paul's suggestive phrase. To be alive in this sense is more than to escape death and destruction. It is more than merely to exist. To be saved concerns the whole man: body, mind, spirit, will, imagination, affections. It takes in every relation of life: God in heaven and our neighbor here on earth, the world of things which we own and use (or which may own us and make slaves of us), the world of spiritual values, of truth, and beauty and love, all the human fellowships, of life, even a man's relation to himself.

At every one of these points there may be loss, suffering, and death if, through ignorance or folly or selfishness or any form of sin, we are out of right relations. In such case we cut ourselves off from our world, and that means death because we live for things, death to physical and moral and — death to love because of selfishness, death to the spirit spiritual well-being because of weak and wicked self-indulgence, death to peace because of anger and hate and bitterness.

The real trouble, of course, lies beneath all this. Man makes himself the center and that throws everything out of relation. Seeking to save his life, he loses it. And there is only one way — the true center of our life, and the world's life, is God. To find him, to be repentant for sin, in trust and obedience to make him central, and then to see our life in his light and live it by his help — this is to be saved.

Dr. Rall Answers - "Mysteries of God" - January 24, 1952

In I Cor. 4:1 Paul speaks of himself as servant of Christ and steward of the mysteries of God. What does he mean by "the mysteries of God"? asks a friend.
What are "the mysteries of God"?

In New Testament times there were a number of religions which had "mysteries" and made a great deal of them. Their mysteries were special religious rites (one consisted of a kind of blood baptism), which were hidden from the people and revealed only to a selected few. Men thought of these rites as giving them secret knowledge, uniting the worshiper to the hero god, giving him assurance of the life beyond.

The apostles spoke to these people who were searching for light and life. We have the answer to the mysteries of life, they said, to the dark mystery of death, the mystery of suffering, and above all else the mystery of God. The answer is Christ. There is darkness in the world, but now "the light shines in the darkness" and that light is Christ. The answer to the mysteries of life is God, the God who is mightier than death and all evil, the God who rules, to whom the future belongs, the God whose love and saving help are revealed in Jesus Christ.
Are there mysteries for us today?

Are there still dark places for man despite all his knowledge of science? Yes, there are mysteries still and they concern the deepest matters of life. So far as the world of things is concerned we are not troubled by our limits. There is much to learn, but science moves on.

But when it comes to the higher life of man, to the world of the spirit, the old problems are all there. Why is evil here and why is it so mighty? Why does it descend on the innocent and guilty alike? What of the tragic fact of death? Is that the end of our love and joy and hope when the lifeless form is laid in the cold earth? And is the story of mankind on earth a tale of endless struggle, of war and oppression, of ignorance and cruelty? Is there a God? Where is he? Does he care for men? If so, what is he doing? And how may we know him and have his help?

Where then is the answer?

God has made it known in Christ. Much is still hidden from us. But God has given us in Christ, not the answer to all our questionings, but all the answer that we need. The Bible is not an encyclopedia of knowledge, but it brings us the light that we need for life. Back of time and change, greater than suffering and death, mightier than all evil is the eternal God whom Christ has revealed. In Christ he enters our life, to give us faith, to join us to himself.

What then is the stewardship of the mysteries of God?

There is more than one kind of mystery. Over against the mysteries of life, the dark and tragic mysteries suggested above, there is the "mystery" of God. The New Testament speaks of it also as the mystery of the kingdom of God and the mystery of Christ. This mystery is not one of darkness and fear, but of light and hope; it is a revealed mystery.

The Lord of heaven and earth, the infinite God, knows us and loves us and takes us to himself. Only God by his Spirit can help us to believe this wonder. "God was in Christ," God was in the humble, loving, serving, suffering life of the man from little Nazareth, the life that ended in the shameful death on the cross, a death more glorious than any conqueror's victory. Here is the mystery of God's infinite love, to many a stumbling block, to us the power of God and the wisdom of God.

And we have the stewardship of this mystery; the treasure is intrusted to us. Here is stewardship at its highest, to proclaim to all the God of saving love ("the mystery of Christ") and his saving purpose ("the mystery of the kingdom of God").

Dr. Rall Answers — "What is Christian Perfection?" — May 1, 1952

Recently received letters have raised questions about the meaning of holiness, sanctification, perfection, and being filled with the Spirit. The questions belong together. For the present I should like to consider what we mean by Christian perfection.

These great words, holiness, sanctification, perfection, are not heard so often from Methodist pulpits as they once were. The words are not what matters. What they stand for is vital.

Our religion has three great meanings. It is a faith with which we look up to God, a life which God gives us, and a way of life which we are to follow. The second of these we call salvation. It is a rich word. It stands for all the light and life and peace and hope which God brings as he enters our life. At its center is the fact that when God comes in he makes new men of us. "If any man is in Christ, he is a new creation."

What is "being a new man"?

What does this mean, this being a new man? The New Testament expresses it in several different ways. We are to be children of our Father. We are to be like Christ, to have his spirit rule our life, to have Christ live in us and be formed in us. It is nothing less than being perfect.

We draw back from these old words — holiness, sanctification, perfection. We say: this is for the few, the saints, but not for us common folk. Not so. Jesus put it plainly. We are to be sons of our Father. That means being like him. "You, therefore, must be perfect, as your heavenly Father is perfect."

But that is impossible, you say; we are finite, human, imperfect. We need daily to pray, forgive us our trespasses. True, the New Testament does not show us perfect men. Paul declares that he has not attained, is not perfect. What he does say is that this is his goal and that he is pressing on so that he may "lay hold on that for which also I was laid hold on by Christ Jesus."

Paul sets up a simple and searching test for the Christian: to be a Christian means to set a goal and then to follow after it. And that goal can be nothing less than the highest — perfection, a life ruled by the spirit of Christ.

Original meaning of perfection

Look a little more closely at the words perfection and sanctification. The word perfect in the original New Testament Greek comes from a word meaning goal or end. Perfection is the goal to which we press on. Sanctification (holiness) stands for two things: belonging and being made over. That is holy which has been dedicated to God. That is man's side. That is holy which has been made over. And that is God's side.

These two sides of this matter both need emphasis today. There is only one standard for Christians, only one goal — perfection, the life wholly given to God, aiming at nothing less than the highest.

The Christian, as Christian, gives himself to the highest when he gives himself to the Most High. It may be well to drop the old words which are so often misunderstood, but we must hold to the truth.

The other side is equally needed. There is a saving power of God which sanctifies men who give themselves thus to him which makes them holy. Here, too, simpler words might be better. Let us say, God waits to make us over, to make new men whose life shall be ruled by the spirit of love and faith.

That brings up other questions on which Christian men have differed. How does God work to make men over? What is the road by which we move on to perfection? Answering a specific question sent in by a young man, I wish to discuss that next week. Here, if anywhere, we need an open mind, a willingness to learn. We must distinguish between God's power by which he thus makes men over and delivers them from ignorance and imperfection and sin, and the way in which God does this work.

F. SPEAKING SCHEDULE (Selected)

1893

8/23	C. A. Thomas, Camp meeting, Riverside Park	Psg. 9:17
8/24	O. Rall, Camp meeting, Riverside Park	Mark 11:24
8/24	O. Hansen, Camp meeting, Riverside Park	Is. 40:30
8/24	W. Horn, Camp meeting, Riverside Park	Luke 19:1-10
8/25	Bünde, Camp meeting, Riverside Park	Luke 5:18-26
8/25	Winous, Camp meeting, Riverside Park	Is. 65:2
8/25	W. Horn, Camp meeting, Riverside Park	Acts 4:12; Matt. 1:21
8/26	O. Beck, Camp meeting, Riverside Park	John 16:8
8/26	Nolte, Camp meeting, Riverside Park	I Thess. 5:23,24
8/26	Sostz, Riverside Park Camp meeting	John 1:27
8/27	W. Horn, Camp meeting, Riverside Park	Con. 2:1
8/27	T. C. Meekel, Camp meeting, Riverside Park	Phil. 3:20
8/27	L. Scherer, Camp meeting, Riverside Park	John 14:6
8/28	W. Horn, Camp meeting, Riverside Park	1 Cor. 11:24
8/28	Bishop Horn, Camp meeting, Riverside Park	Ps. 40:1-3
8/31	O. Rall, Cedar Falls	I Pet. 1: 8,9
9/3	O. Rall, Cedar Falls	Rom. 8:6
9/10	Dr. Sory, Des Moines	2 Pet. 3:18
9/10	Dr. Sory, Des Moines	2 Pet. 2:6
9/17	Rev. Srs, Henry, Des Moines	Ex. 25:40
9/24	J. L. Sory, Des Moines	Phil. 8:20
9/24	J. L. Sory, Des Moines	Con. 2:15
10/8	Rev. Weaver, Des Moines	Matt. 5:17
10/15	Dr. Sory, Des Moines	Jn. 17:22

1900

August 5	Mark 5:4		
Sept. 23	Ezek. 27:10	Psalm 1	Hymn 21, 567
	Heb. 12:17	Psalm 2	Hymn 92, 17, 488
Sept. 30	I Cor. 1:23-24	Psalm 3-4	Hymn 88, 213, 204
	Mark 2:14	Psalm 5	Hymn 182, 426, 197
Oct. 7	Communion Talk		
	I Cor. 10:16	Psalm 7	Hymn 14, 837, 851
	Chinese Question		
	I Cor. 12:9	Psalm 6	Hymn 140, 51, 28
Oct. 14	Heb. 11:29		
	The Crown of Failure	Psalm 9	Hymn 95, 66, 596
Oct. 21	Mt. 28:7		
	He goeth before you	Psalm 10	Hymn 106, 72, 90
	Chinese question	Psalm 11, 12	Hymn 144, 943, 917
Oct. 28	Rom. 15:20		
	2 Cor. 19		
	I Thess. 4:11	Psalm 14, 15	Hymn 8, 162, 587
	Praise Service	Psalm 115, 133	Hymn 56, 136, 140
Oct. 29	Heb. 12:16 Esau, Special Services		
Nov. 4	Communion Talk		
	Col. 1:24	Psalm 16	Hymn 137, 836
Nov. 9	Heb. 12:16 Esau,	Psalm 18:1-24	Hymn 117, 99, 344
	St. Andrews		
Nov. 11	(My Church) The		
	Church Mt. 16:15	Psalm 18	Hymn 135, 768, 765
Nov. 18	Bishop Goodall	2 Sam. 24:24	Hymn 109, 6, 581
Nov. 21	Epworth Church		
	1 Sam. 21:6		
Nov. 25	Bishop Hurst		
	Gal. 4:4	Psalm 19	Hymn 3, 61, 788
Nov. 29	Thanksgiving Union		
	Service	Psalm 1:1; 150:6	
Dec. 2	Com. Service		
	Mt. 27:24	Psalm 24	Hymn 789, 837
Dec. 9	The Place of Habit		
	in Relig. Life		
	Acts. 10:30	Psalm 25	Hymn 136, 166, 459
Dec. 16	2 Cor. 8:7	Psalm 27	Hymn 130, 781, 159
	Lu. 5:28-30	Psalm 28	Hymn 421, 196, 108
Dec. 23	The Signs of the		
	Shepherds		
	Lu. 12	Psalm 2	Hymn 192, 190, 782

1904

April 17	I Cor. 2:2	Lesson I. Cor 1:18-31	Hymn 72, 743, 248
	Paul's Ambitions Rom 15:20; 2 Cor. 5:9; I Thes. 4:11		Hymn 1, 292, 102
April 24	"God's Army" Ezek. 27:10	Lesson: Ezek. 27:1-4	Hymn 6, 279, 608
	Hard Sayings of Jesus The Door of the Empty Room Luke 11:24-26		Hymn 17, 93, 587,
May 1	Com. Service Talk on Jn. 6:75 "Hard Sayings "The Law of Unequal Reward Luke 19:26		Hymn 14, 160, 491, 116
May 8	The Garden of the Lord, Jn. 18:1,2		Hymn 136, 485, 760
	Hard Sayings III The Place of Hatred in the Life Luke 14:26		Hymn 109, 135, 581
May 10	Baltimore S.S. Assn. Address on the Teacher's Elements of Power		
May 15	A Christian and His Debts, Rom 1:14		
	I. Cor. 9:15-27		Hymn 88, 17, 605
	A Man, Is. 32:2		Hymn 21, 919, 608
May 22	The Other Self, Gal. 2:20		Hymn 81, 521, 491
	Praise Service-"The Right to Worship" (N. H. Spencer in autobiogr.)		Hymn 330, 743, 697, 94
May 29	A.M. Children's Day Service P.M. "Hard Sayings"		Hymn 6, 149, 518

1927

May 8	The Intolerance of Jesus	Hymn 30, 394, 408
May 15	The Growing God	Hymn 3, 475, 81, 577
May 22	The Abiding God	Hymn 2, 29, 446
May 29	The Man that Stood by	Hymn 25, 388, 704, 706
June 12	The Marks of a Man	Hymn 41, 34, 7, 445
June 19		Hymn 11, 76, 88, 409
July 3	The Faith of the Fathers	Hymn 5, 704, 706, 707
July 10	The Empty Rooms	Hymn 21, 39, 431, 396
July 17	Dividing Lines	Hymn 78, 41, 82, 545
July 24	Second Hand Religion	Hymn 7, 45, 435, 197
July 31	Lost and Found	Hymn 10, 494, 438, 293
Aug. 7	Messiahs, New and Old	Hymn 30, 26, 145, 475
Aug. 14	The Ministry of Reconciliation	Hymn 6, 29, 421, 133
Aug. 21	The Religion of the Commonplace	Hymn 30, 42, 438, 411
Aug. 28	I Know God	Hymn 37, 128, 82, 197

1934

1/9	Garrett Chapel: "Earth is not Enough"
	Church night, Ist Church "What Is Religion?"
	first of series on What Can We Believe?
1/10	Jimetkka Community Church, "What Is Religion"
1/16	Church night: How Should We Think About God?
1/21	Wilmette M.E. Men's Class
1/23	Church Night: Problem of Evil
1/25	LaSalle, Ill., Union Sun. Eve. Club, 1st M.E. Church: Intolerance
1/30	Church Night: Immortality
2/2	Lebanon, Ill. Area Conference: Our Faith and Our Message
2/5	Evang. Preachers Assn.: Salvation
2/6	Church night: The Church in Germany
2/11	First Church, Wilmette, The Religion of Nationalism
2/14	First Church, Oak Park, Area Meeting, Our Faith and Our Message
2/22	Inter. Seminary Union of Chicago: The Minister's Theology
2/25	First Church, Wilmette, Men's Class: The Christian Ethics
2/27	Church Night: How Men Can Know God
3/11	Woodstock, Ill., Messiahs New and Old
3/13	Church Night: Religion and Recovery
3/21	Wheaton Church: Windows
4/15	Wilmette H.S. Group: Religion in the Headlines
4/22	Wilmette Men's Class: Science and Religion
4/25	N. Univ.: Harris Hall and Thorne Hall: Dialogue with Haydon on Can We Believe in God?
5/6	Austin M.E.: Messiahs, New and Old
	Walls and Windows
5/11	St. Paul: 80th Anniversary Hamline Univ. "Who Is the Educated Man?"
5/13	Edgebrook Community Church: Walls and Windows

1944

7/4	Silver Lake, N.Y. Pastor's School
	On Salvation (1) Relgiion as Salvation (2) Salvation through Right Relations (3) Salvation in History
	7/4: "I am a Liberal, Catholic, Evang., Methodist
7/14, 18, 19, 20	Took Nels Ferre's class at Garrett on Reason and Rev.
7/18	Garrett Chapel: Freedom

8/6	First Church Ev.: The First Freedom
8/18	Woodlawn Church Freedom
9/11	Cleveland Minist. Assn. (auspices Fed. Council) Our Gospel for Today
10/10	GBI 90th anniversary — spoke on progress in theol. study at Garrett
10/12	Garret Chapel "Marching Feet"
10/30	Read report of sub-com. at session of Com. II on Just and Durable Peace (Cleveland)
12/20	Nashville Board of Education staff on God

1956
received-earned
50 Adv.
75 Bd. Mis. Art. World Outlook
50 Adv.
20 Art. Assoc. Encycl.
50 Adv.
75 Waterloo
50 Art. Meth. Publ. H.
25 Address Champaign
50 Meth. Pub. H. Adv. Arts.
25 Meth. Pub. H. Adv. Arts.
50 Meth. Pub. H. Adv. Arts.
75 Meth. Pub. H. Adv. Arts.
25 Meth. Pub. H. Adv. Arts. Together
25 Meth. Pub. H. Adv. Arts. Together
25 Meth. Pub. H. Adv. Arts. Together
—

FOOTNOTES

CHAPTER I

1. Jameson Jones. "A Brief Vita," *The Garrett Tower*, Volume 40, Number 1, December, 1964, p. 4. On October 15, 1964, a memorial service for Dr. Rall was held in the First Methodist Church, Evanston, Illinois. This issue of *The Garrett Tower* includes in addition to Jameson Jones' article, the prayer offered at the Memorial Service by Horace G. Smith, president-emeritus of Garrett, an interpretive article by him on the influence of Rall, an appreciative survey of his theology by Georgia Harkness, an article on Rall and his leadership in Methodist social concerns by Professor Murray H. Leiffer, and a tribute by Professor Paul A. Schilpp, who began, "Most 'of what I am or ever hope to be I owe' to Harris Franklin Rall." (p. 27)
2. *Ibid.*, p. 5.
3. Cf. Frank Hugh Foster. *A Genetic History of the New England Theology*. Chicago: The University of Chicago Press, 1907. Interesting also is the general exclusion of Yale theologians from standard contemporary anthologies of Theology in America: Smith, L., Handy, R. and Loetscher, L. *American Christianity*, 2 Vols., New York: Charles Scribner's Sons, 1963; Sydney Ahlstrom, ed. *Theology in America*. Indianapolis: Bobbs Merrill, 1967.
4. Roland H. Bainton. *Yale and the Ministry, A History of Education for the Christian Ministry at Yale from the Founding in 1701*. New York: Harper and Brothers, Publishers, 1957, pp. 161ff.
5. Cf. *The Philosophical Basis of Theism*. New York: Charles Scribner's Sons, 1883; *The Self-Revelation of God*. New York: Charles Scribner's Sons, 1887; *God, the Creator and Lord of All*. 2 Vols. New York: Charles Scribner's Sons, 1896.
6. Dumas Malone. (ed.) *Dictionary of American Biography*. New York: Charles Scribner's Sons, 1932, Volume VIII, pp. 319-320.
7. Foster, *op. cit.*, p. 424.
8. *Ibid.*, pp. 427ff.
9. Bainton, *op. cit.*, p. 173. Quoted from *The Kingdom of Christ on Earth*, (Andover, 1874), p. 255.
10. *Ibid.*, p. 179.
11. Cf. notably, *The Pauline Theology*. New York: Charles Scribner's Sons, 1892, 1918; *The Johanine Theology*. New York: Charles

Scribner's Sons, 1894; *The Theology of the New Testament*. New York: Charles Scribner's Sons, 1899; *The Teaching of Jesus*. New York: The Macmillan Company, 1901.
12. Bainton, *op. cit.*, p. 180. Quoted from *The Christian Doctrine of Salvation*. New York: Charles Scribner's Sons, 1905, p. 131.
13. *Idem.*
14. George B. Stevens, "Horace Bushnell and Albrecht Ritschl, A. Comparison," *The American Journal of Theology*. Vol. 6, Number 1, January, 1902, p. 36.
15. *Ibid.*, p. 40.
16. *Ibid.*, p. 47.
17. *Ibid.*, p. 56.
18. Merle Curti, *The Growth of American Thought*, Third Edition. New York: Harper and Row, Publishers, 1964, p. 566. Cf. his excellent bibliography on this chapter, "Scholarship and Popularization of Learning." Cf. also Henry A. Pochmann. *German Culture in America, Philosophical and Literary Influences, 1600-1900*. Madison: The University of Wisconsin Press, 1957, pp. 304ff.
19. Harris Franklin Rall. *Der Leibnizsche substanzbegriff mit besonderer beziehung auf seine enstenung and sein verhältnis zur körperlehre*. Halle a.s. Druckvon E. Karras, 1899.
20. Cf. the excellent series "Makers of Modern Theology," Jaroslav Pelikan, ed. New York: Harper and Row, Publishers, 1966. - for individual treatments of Ritschl, Schleiermacher, and Harnack. Also, cf. Claude Welch, *God and Incarnation, In Mid-Nineteenth, Century German Theology, G. Thomasius, I. A. Dorner, A. E. Biedermann*. New York: Oxford University Press, 1965. To my knowledge, no comparable material has been published on Kaftan and Pfleiderer.
21. David L. Mueller. *An Introduction to the Theology of Albrecht Ritschl*. Philadelphia: The Westminster Press, 1969, p. 28. Quoted from Otto Ritschl, *Albrecht Ritschls Leben*. Freiburg I. B. and Leipzig: J.C.B. Mohr-Paul Siebeck, 2 Vols., 1892, 1896, II, p. 385.
22. *Ibid.*, p. 28. Quoted from Cajus Fabricus, *Die Entwicklung hei Albrecht Ritschls Theologie von 1874 bis 1889 nach den verschedenen Auflagen seiner Hauptwerke dargestellt und beurteilt*. Tübingen: J.C.B. Mohr, 1909, p. 16.
23. W. P. Paterson. "Kaftan's Dogmatik," *The Critical Review*, 1898, Volume VIII, Number 4, p. 407. Von D. Julius Kaftan. *Dogmatik*. Freburg, i.b.; J.C.B. Mohr; London and Edinburgh: Williams and Norgate, 1897, 8 Vol., pp. 644.
24. *Ibid.*, p. 408.
25. *Ibid.*, p. 409.
26. *Idem.*

27. *Ibid.*, p. 417.
28. Otto Pfleiderer. *Christian Origins*. Daniel A. Huebsch, tr. New York: B. W. Huebsch, 1906, pp. 4ff.
29. *Ibid.*, p. 21.
30. *Ibid.*, pp. 24-5.
31. Otto Pfleiderer. *Evolution and Theology and Other Essays*. Orello Cone, London, Adam and Charles Black, 1900. P. 85.
32. *Ibid.*, pp. 100-01.
33. *Ibid.*, p. 104-105.
34. H. Richard Niebuhr. *The Kingdom of God in America*. New York: Harper Brothers, Publishers, 1937, p. 193.
35. Cf. G. Wayne Glick. *The Realty of Christianity, A Study of Adolf von Harnack as Historian and Theologian*. New York: Harper and Row, Publishers, 1967. Also, John Dillenberger and Claude Welch, *Protestant Christianity*. New York: Charles Scribner's Sons, 1954, esp. chs. IX, X.; Paul Tillich, *Perspectives on 19th and 20th Century Protestant Theology*. New York: Harper and Row, Publishers, 1967, ch. V. Professor Glick notes that the *Festschrift* for Harnack's seventieth birthday was presented on behalf of 215 theologians of all countries and specific vocations; and of these 155 had studied with Harnack. Among American scholars were included: William Adams Brown, Shirley Jackson Case, Edgar Goodspeed, Eugene Lyman, Arthur McGiffert — and I would add Harris Franklin Rall. (p. 36, Fn. 2).
36. Glick, *op. cit.*, pp. 36-7. Quoted from Agnes von Zahn-Harnack. *Adolf von Harnack*. Berlin: Hous Bott, 1936, pp. 82-83.
37. *Ibid.*, p. 37; p. 80.
38. Tillich, *op. cit.*, pp. 222-23.
39. Some scattered analyses and reviews appear in American theological journals; one of interest is by Professor George B. Stevens of Yale, *op. cit.* The following books represent the earliest attempts at presenting Ritschl to America. James Orr. *The Ritschlian Theology and The Evangelical Faith*. London: Hodder and Stoughton, New York: Thomas Whittaker, 1897; Alfred Ernest Garvie. *The Ritschlian Theology, Critical and Constructive; An Exposition and an Estimate*. Edinburgh: T. & T. Clark, 1899, Charles M. Mead. *Ritschl's Place in the History of Doctrine*. Hartford: Hartford Seminary Press, 1895; John K. Mozley. *Ritschlianism*. London: James Nisbet and Company, 1909; Albert T. Swing. *The Theology of Albrecht Ritschl*. London and Bombay: Longmans, Green, and Company, 1901.
40. Horace Greeley Smith. "Harris Franklin Rall, As An Adviser," *The Garrett Tower*, Volume 40, Number 1, Henry E. Kolbe, ed., December, 1964, p. 8.

41. Cf. Emory Stevens Bucke, gen. ed., *The History of American Methodism*. 3 Vols. New York - Nashville: Abingdon Press, 1964. Also, Robert E. Chiles, *Theological Transition in American Methodism: 1790-1935*. New York - Nashville: Abingdon Press, 1965.
42. Harris Franklin Rall. "Ninety Years of Theology at Garrett," Unpublished Manuscript, 1944.
43. *Idem.*
44. *Idem.*
45. *Idem.*
46. *Idem.*

CHAPTER II

1. Private unpublished manuscript now located in the library of Garrett Theological Seminary, Evanston, Illinois. Throughout this chapter I have preserved in large measure the first person address found in the manuscript, perhaps a pedagogical style identified with Professor Rall, although not limited to him in those years. Afterward noted as *Rall Manuscript*.
2. *Ibid.*, n.p.
3. *Ibid.*
4. *Ibid.*
5. Felix Adler, *Creed and Deed* (New York: G.P. Putnam's Sons, 1877). Pp., 1, 2ff, 38.
6. *Rall Manuscript*, p.8.
7. *Ibid.*, p. 34.
8. *Ibid.*, p. 35.
9. *Idem.*, p. 35-36. Percy Gardner *Exploratio Evangelica* (New York: G.P. Putnam's Sons, 1900).
10. *Idem.*, p. 36.
11. *Idem.*, pp. 2-3.
12. *Idem.*, n.p.
13. *Idem.*, p.4
14. *Idem.*, p.6. What Rall has in mind by the history of "Hegelian Theology in Germany" he nowhere states. Cf. Claude Welch (ed. and trans.) *God and Incarnation In Mid-Century German Theology*, (New York: Oxford University Press, 1965). Also cf. Emil L. Fackenheim, *The Religious Dimension in Hegel's Thought* (Bloomington: Indiana University Press, 1967).
15. *Idem.*, pp. 10-12.
16. Included in Rall's notes is the following outline of the Ritschlian Position. The Ritschlian Position involves:
    1. A definite conception of the nature of religion as ethical and

practical. Its supreme interest is not ideas but ideals, that is, ethical values.
2. The truths with which it is concerned are therefore practical-judgments of value. It asks not about God as absolute — as separate from his world — but God as related to us in his purpose and grace. This does not mean that religion is indifferent to the real existence of these objectives of value. It is rather a protest against arguing speculation and intellectualism (orthodoxism-rationalism).
3. The method of knowledge
1) Sense perception 2) a mode of theoretical knowledge by use of logical principles (mode of specific reason). But other organs of knowledge as well if usual method in whole value of personal and ideal; are sense of values (are appreciation; beauty, truth, love, right) an inner conviction of reality (as well as worth), a trust and action, deepened convictions and enlarged knowledge through action.

III. THE NATURE AND LIMITS OF RELIGIOUS KNOWLEDGE

I. Ritschl's Theory of the Nautre of Religious Knowledge.
 1. It is not theoretical knowledge.
 2. It concerns judgments of worth, (this not a denial of objetive knowledge).
 3. Its ground is in experience.
 4. It includes an element of obedience.

II. His conclusions as to theological method draw from this position.
 1. No metaphysics! — application to doctrine of God — phenomenalistic tendency.
 2. No philosophy or theoretical considerations! — empiristic tendency.

III. His Philosophical Theory of Knowledge.
 1. Its place in Ritschl's system. Practical realism and philosophical scepticism.

IV. Critical and Positive Considerations.
 1. The relation of faith and knowledge.
  (1) The practical nature of belief — the theoretical element.
  (2) The theory of a practical knowledge — its validity — James, Ward, Gardner.
 2. The relation of philosophy and theology.
  The place of metaphysics — the right to theoretical consid-

erations — the right to construe a philosophy — the practical grounds of a theistic philosophy.

17. *Rall Manuscript,* p. 30. Julius Kaftan, *Dogmatik,* (Tübingen, 1897).
18. H. Richard Niebuhr, *The Kingdom of God in America* (Harper & Row, 1937).
19. *Rall Manuscript,* p. 27ff.
20. *Idem.,* p. 30. William James, *The Will to Believe* (New York, London, Bombay: Longmous, Green and Company, 1898) [c. 1896].
21. *Idem.,* p. 38.
22. Percy Gardner, *Op. Cit.*
Auguste Sabatier, *Outlines of Philosophy of Religion* (New York: James Pott and Company, n.d.). *Vitalities of Christian Dogmas* (Christen tr. New York: Macmillan, n.d.). *Rall Manuscript,* Idem., pp. 38ff.
23. *Idem.,* p. 6.
24. *Idem.,* n.p.
25. *Idem.,* p. 32.
26. *Idem.*
27. *Idem.,* p. 39.
28. *Idem.,* pp. 49-50. "Fleshly Jesus" refers to the first historical quest.
29. W. Bornemann, *Unterricht im Christentum* (Göttingen, 1890).
30. *Rall Manuscript,* pp. 20-21.
31. Andrew Martin Fairbairn ,*The Place of Christ in Modern Theology* (New York: Scribner's, n.d.).
32. *Rall Manuscript,* p. 17.
33. *Idem.,* pp. 31-32.
34. *Idem.,* p. 10.
35. *Idem.,* pp. 18-19. Julius Kaftan, *The Truth of the Christian Religion,* 2 vols. (New York: Scribners & Son, n.d.).
36. *Idem.,* pp. 27-30. Johann Georg Wilhelm Herrmann, *Christian Communion With God.* German title: *Der Vekehr der Christen Mit Gott,* (Stuttgart, 1886).
37. *Idem.,* p. 32. Rall quotes directly from Harnack in the manuscript, but fails to document the specific source. The sentences might well have been from *What Is Christianity?* Thomas Bailey Saunders, tr. (New York: G. P. Putnam's Sons. London: Williams and Norgate, 1901). German Litle: *Das Wesen des Christentums* (Leipsig, J. C. Hinricks, 1901) or *History of Dogma,* 7 vols. Neil Buchanan, tr. et. al. (3rd German edition; London: Williams and Norgate 1896-1899).
38. *Idem.*
39. Horace Bushnell (1802-1876), pastor of North Congregational Church, Hartford, Connecticut: cf. the volume of his writings in the *Library*

of *Protestant Thought*, H. Shelton Smith (ed.), both for the articles and the bibliography listed there.
40. Robert William Dale (1829-1895), English pastor of Carr's Lane Chapel, Birmingham, the Lyman Beecher Lecturer, 1877. *Christian Doctrine* (New York: Armstrong & Son, n.d.). Dale has an impressive list of titles.
41. Frederick William Robertson (1816-1853), pastor Trinity Chapel, Brighton. Several published volumes of sermons and addresses.
42. Phillips Brooks (1835-1893), Episcopal bishop, Trinity Church, Boston. Numerous collections of sermons and addresses.
43. I understand a thesis is now being pursued at Yale University under Professor Sydney E. Ahlstrom which will focus on the issue of the dependence of Albrecht Ritschl upon Ferdinand Baur relative to the interpretation of the continuity and authority of doctrinal development.
44. *Rall Manuscript*, pp. 36-38.
45. Robert William Dale, *Op. cit.*
46. Horace Bushnell, *The Character of Jesus* (New York: Schibner's & Son, 1886). E. Ullmann, *The Sinlessness of Jesus* 2 vols. (Columbus, Ohio: Lutheran Book Concern, n.d.).
47. *Rall Manuscript*, pp. 39-42. James Orr, *The Christian View of God and the World* (New York: Anson D. F. Randolph & Company, 1893).

CHAPTER III

1. Harris Franklin Rall, *New Testament History* (New York: Abingdon, 1914); *According to Paul* (New York: Scribners & Son, 1944).
2. Harris Franklin Rall, "The Attitude of the Church Toward New Truth" *The Mid Year Assembly of the New York East Annual Conference* (Marmaroneck, New York, October 27-28, 1902, n.p.).
3. *New Testament History*, p. 10.
4. Philip Hefner, *Faith and The Vitalities of History A Theological Study Based on the Work of Albrecht Ritschl* (New York: Harper & Row, 1966).
5. *New Testament History, op. cit.*, p. 9.
6. Cf. Sydney E. Ahlstrom, "Continental Influence on American Christian Thought Since World War I," *Church History*, XXVII, 3 September, 1958), pp. 256-72. Also, my dissertation, "Theology of the Methodist Episcopal Church, During the Interwar Period, 1919-1939" (Yale University: 1960), a portion of which has been published as "American Methodist Thought and Theology, 1919-1960," in *The History of American Methodism* (New York: Abingdon, 1964) Vol. III, pp. 261-327.

7. Karl Barth, *The Epistle to the Romans 1919* (6th ed. London: Oxford University Press) tr. by Sir Edwyn C. Hoskyns, 1933.
8. Anders Nygren, *Agape and Eros* (London: Society for Promoting Christian Knowledge. New York: The MacMillan Company, 1932-39) tr. by A. G. Hebert and Phillip Watson.
9. A review of Walter Lowrie, *Our Concern With the Theology of Crisis,* Garrett Tower, Vol. III, No. 1 (January, 1933), p. 15.
10. "The Idea of God in Recent Literature," *Religion in Life,* Vol. I, No. 1 (Winter, 1932), pp. 66-67.
11. *Christianity* (New York: Charles Scribner's Sons, 1940), p. 152.
12. "The Teaching Ministry and Evangelism," *Evanston Series,* 1933, p. 50.
13. *Garrett Tower,* Vol. XII, No. 1 (November, 1936), p. 14.
14. "Which Way Theology?" *Garrett Tower,* Vol. X, No. 2 (January, 1935), p. 1.
15. *According to Paul, op. cit.,* pp. 146-47.
16. *Ibid.,* p. 187.
17. *Iibid.,* pp. 241-42.
18. Cf. John Broadus Watson, *Behavior* (New York: Holt, 1914); *Behaviorism* (New York: Norton, 1925); *Phychology From the Standpoint of a A Theoretical Basis of Human Behavior* (2nd ed. New York: Lippincott, 1924). Albert P. Weiss, *A Theoretical Basis of Human Behavior* (2nd ed. Columbus, Ohio: R. G. Adams & Company, 1929).
19. Harris Franklin Rall, ed., "Faith in God in an Age of Science," *Christianity Today,* (Nashville: Cokesbury, 1928) p. 135.
20. *Ibid.,* p. 137.
21. Cf. John Fiske, *Outlines of Cosmic Philosophy* (Boston: Houghton, Mifflin & Company, 1874 2 vols.). Also, c. Richard Hofstadter, *Social Darwinism in American Thought* (Philadephia: University of Pennsyvania Press, 1944).
22. *Christianity Today,* pp. 150-51. A poem by William H. Carruth, 1859-1924, was extremely popular during these years and used extensively by Rall and others in sermons, meditations, etc.

EACH IN HIS OWN TONGUE

A fire-mist and a planet,
A crystal and a cell,
A jelly-fish and a saurian,
And the caves where the cave-men dwell;
Then a sense of law and beauty,
And a face turned from the clod, —
Some call it Evolution,
And others call it God.

> A haze on the far horizon,
>   The infinite, tender sky,
> The ripe, rich tint of the cornfields,
>   And the wild geese sailing high;
> And all over upland and lowland
>   The charm of the golden-rod, —
> Some of us call it Autumn,
>   And others call it God.
>
> Like tides on a crescent sea-beach,
>   When the moon is new and thin,
> Into our hearts high yearnings
>   Come welling and surging in:
> Come from the mystic ocean
>   Whose rim foot has trod, —
> Some of us call it Longing,
>   And others call it God.
>
> A picket frozen on duty,
>   A mother starved for her brood,
> Socrates dinking the hemlock,
>   And Jesus on the rood;
> And millions who, humble and nameless,
>   The straight hard pathway plod, —
> Some call it Consecration,
>   And others call it God.

23. "Theology and the Historical Method," *Methodist Review*, LXX, No. 1 (March, 1910), p. 194.
24. *Ibid.*, pp. 194-95.
25. *Ibid.*, p. 195.
26. *Ibid.*, p. 196.
27. *Idem.*
28. *Ibid.*, p. 197.
29. *Ibid.*, pp. 198ff. Wilhelm Heitmüller, "Im Namen Jesu," *Eine sprach- und religiongeschichtliche Untersuchung zum Neuen Testaments, speziell zur altchristlichen Taufe* (Gottingen: Vandenhoeck and Ruprecht, 1903). Hermann Gunkel, *Zum religiongeschichtlichen Verständnis des Neuen Testaments* (Gottingen: Vendenhoeck and Ruprecht, 1903).
30. *Ibid.*, pp. 201-02.
31. *Ibid.*, p. 203.
32. *Idem.*
33. *Ibid.*, p. 204.

34. *Ibid.*, pp. 205-06, Gunkel, *op. cit.*
35. *Ibid.*, p. 205.
36. *Ibid.*, p. 207.
37. *Idem.*
38. *Ibid.*, p. 210.
39. William P. King, ed., "What Does Behaviorism Mean for Religion,?" *Behaviorism; A Battle Line* (Nashville; Cokesbury, 1930), pp. 288-306.
40. *Ibid.*, p. 291.
41. *Ibid.*, pp. 298ff.
42. Julian Kaftan, *The Truth of the Christian Religion* Vol. I (Edinburgh: T. & T. Clarke, 1894) p. 15. Cf. also, Lewis Stearns, *Evidence of Christian Experience* (New York: Scribner & Sons, 1890).
43. *Working Faith* (New York: Abingdon, 1914), p. 41.
44. *Christianity, op. cit.*, pp. 145ff.
45. *The Christian Faith & Way* (New York: Abingdon, 1947) pp. 16-17.
46. Phillip Hefner, *op. cit.*, p. 28.
47. *Ibid.*, p. 59.
48. *Ibid.*, pp. 76-77.
49. *Ibid.*, p. 79.
50. *Ibid.*, p. 114.

CHAPTER IV

1. *Religion As Salvation* (New York: Abingdon-Cokesbury, 1953), p. 204.
2. *Christianity* (New York: Scribner's & Sons, 1940), p. 3.
3. *A Faith for Today* (New York: Abingdon, 1936), pp. 28-29.
4. *Christianity*, p. 5.
5. *Idem.*
6. *Ibid.*, p. 7. Rall credits here the following books as formative in his thinking: Rudolf Otto, *The Idea of the Holy* (London: Oxford University Press, 1923), German title: *Das Heilige* (Breslau: Trewendt und gramor, 1922); Nathan Soderblom, *Des Werden des Gottesglauben* (Leipsig: J. C. Hinrichs, 1926); Robert R. Marett, *The Threshold of Religion* (London: Methuen and Company, 1900).
7. *Idem.*
8. *Ibid.*, p. 10. W. E. Hocking, *The Meaning of God in Human Experience* (New Haven: Yale University Press, 1912).
9. *Idem.*, p. 11. Rall's source is Harald Hoffding, *The Philosophy of Religion*, B. E. Meyer tr. (New York: Macmillan Company, 1906), p. 113.
10. *Ibid.*, pp. 12-13. The quotation is found in *Science and the Modern World* (New York: Macmillan Company, 1928), pp. 267-269.

11. *Ibid.*, p. 13. Joseph Wood Krutch, *The Modern Temper* (New York: Harcourt, Brace & Company, 1929): Possibly p. 249, "Ours is a lost cause and there is no place for us in the natural universe, but we are not, for all that, sorry to be human. We should rather die as men than live as animals."
12. *Ibid.*, p. 16.
13. *Ibid.*, p. 25.
14. *Ibid.*, p. 27.
15. *Ibid.*, p. 28.
16. *Ibid.*, p. 42. Friedrich Heiler, *Prayer*, Samuel McComb, ed & tr. assisted by J. Edgar Park (London: Oxford University Press, 1932), German title: *Das Gebet,* (5th ed. 1923), Appendix, p. 617.
17. Cf. especially Muller's *Anthropological Religion,* The Gifford Lectures of 1891 (London: Longmans, Creen and Company, 1892); Tylor's *Primitive Culture* (London: J. Murray, 1871); and Frazer's *The Golden Bough* (London: The Macmillan Company, 1890-1937). The entire issue of the origin and impact of comparative religion in the United States has been carefully delineated in Sydney E. Ahlstrom's *The American Protestant Encounter with World Religions,* The Brewer Lectures on Comparative Religion (Beloit College: Beloit, Wisconsin, 1962).
18. "The Religion of the Bible in the World Today," Study IX, *The Institute,* IX, No. 9 (June, 1925), p. 133.
19. *Ibid.*, p. 134.
20. *Ibid.*, p. 143. Of interest is the set of questions Rall lists at the conclusion of this brief article. In themselves they indicate the tenor of the discussion of religion and theology in that decade.

   1. Is the idea of a creative God rendered impossible by our modern theory of development?
   2. Have we come to any loftier or more commanding conception of God than that which Jesus brings?
   3. Does this biblical idea of God make room for our thought of the indwelling God?
   4. How far does the Bible teaching meet our need for a religion that is through and through ethical, that has social idealism and social dynamic, that is universal in its outlook, that is not tied to forms of ritual or institution?
   5. Have we transcended the ethical ideal that is furnished by the spirit of Jesus?
   6. What are some of the broad areas of our human life, especially of our associated life, in which this is still waiting to be put into effect?
   7. How far does this religion of the Bible meet the needs and the

ideals of the modern movement of democracy taken at its best?
8. What of the value of its conception of man: (a) of human personality as sacred, (c) of man as rational and responsible, (c) as a being who can be trusted, (d) as made for a life of freedom?
9. What about its conception of the relation of God and man as personal and free, and of its idea of God's method with man and with the world, dealing as the Spirit of truth and justice and good will, and not as an autocrat with compelling force?
10. What of the value of the social outlook of this religion, its idea of the kingdom of God, for the social hope of today?
11. Considering the Christian grounds for the belief in immortality, have they been strengthened by "scientific" demonstrations of spiritualism?

21. *Christianity and Judaism Compare Notes* (with Samuel Cohen) (New York: Macmillan, 1927) p. 31.
22. *Christianity, op. cit.*, pp. 70-71.
23. *Ibid.*, pp. 73-74.
24. *Idem.*, p. 71. Quoted from Adolf Harnack, *Dogmenschichte*, I, 71: "'It is the person, the deed of his life, that is new, and that creates the new.'" Rall concludes his footnote, See Adolf Deissmann, *The Religion of Jesus and the Faith of Paul* (London: Hodder end Stoughton Ltd., 1923), p. 150. Cf. the comment of a modern Jewish writer, Rabbi Hyman Enelow in his *A Jewish View of Jesus* New York: The MacMillan Company, 1924), p. 15 'Wherever we find true personality, we have originality. Supreme personality is greatest originality.' Elsewhere he quotes from Hazlitt: 'This is the test and triumph of originality, not to show us what has never been and what we may therefore very easily never have dreamt of, but to point out to us what is before our eyes and under our feet, though we have had no suspicion of its existence, for want of sufficient strength of intuition, of determined grasp of mind, to seize and retain it.' p. 15.
25. *Ibid.*, p. 72.
26. *Ibid.*, p. 73.
27. *Ibid.*, p. 74.
28. *Ibid.*, p. 78. H. R. Mackintosh, *Types of Modern Theology* (London: Nisbet and Company, Ltd., 1937), p. 215. Rall suggests also, N. Soderblom, *Natürliche Theologie und allgemeine Religiongeschichte* (Stockholm: Albert Bonnier; Leipzig; J. C. Hinrichs, 1913), pp. 82-86, and Sidney Cave, *The Future of Christianity*, James Marchant, ed. (London: J. Murray, 1927), pp. 17-25.
29. Andrew Seth Pringle-Pattison, *The Idea of God in the Light of*

Recent Philosophy, The Gifford Lectures of 1912 and 1913 (London: Oxford University Press, 1917); *Studies in the Philosophy of Religion,* The Gifford Lectures of 1923 (Oxford, The Clarendon Press, 1930); *Two Lectures on Theism* (New York: Charles Scribner's Sons, 1897).

30. Frederich Carl Eiselen, Edwin Lewis, David G. Dawney, eds., *The Abingdon Bible Commentary* (New York: Abingdon-Cokesbury Press, 1929).
31. Edwin Lewis, "From Philosophy to Revelation," *Christian Century,* LVI, 24 (June 14, 1939), p. 764.
32. Edwin Lewis, *God and Ourselves* (New York: Abingdon Press, 1931), p. 237.
33. William E. Hocking, ed., *Re-Thinking Missions* (New York: Harpers, 1932), p. 50.
34. Edwin Lewis, "From Philosophy to Revelation," *Christian Century,* LVI, 24 (June 14, 1939), p. 764.
35. Edwin Lewis, "The Re-Thought Theology of Re-Thinking Missions," *Drew Gateway,* IV, 3 (April, 1933), p. 4.
36. *Ibid.,* p. 5.
37. "The Authority of Our Faith," *International Review of Missions,* XXIX, Winter Issue, (January, 1940), p. 130.
38. *Ibid.,* p. 130-31.
39. Henrik Kraemer, *The Christian Message in a Non-Christian World* (London: Published for the International Missionary Council by the Edinbrugh House Press, 1938).
40. "The Authority of Our Faith," *op. cit.,* p. 136.
41. *Idem.*
42. *Ibid.,* pp. 136-37.
43. *Ibid.,* p. 137.
44. *The Obligation of Methodism,* (pamphlet) (Baltimore, Maryland, 1910), p. 10.
45. *Idem.,* pp 11-12.
46. Rall played an instrumental role in the formation of this creed:
The Methodist Church stands —
For equal rights and complete justice for all men in all stations of life. For the principle of conciliation and arbitration in industrial dissensions. For the protection of the worker from dangerous machinery, occupational diseases, injuries, and mortality.
For the abolition of child labor.
For such regulation of the conditions of labor for women as shall safeguard the physical and moral health of the community.
For the suppression of the 'sweating system.'
For the gradual and reasonable reduction of the hours of labor to the lowest practical point, with work for all; and for that degree of leisure for all which is the condition of the highest human life.

For a release from employment one day in seven.
For a living wage in every industry.
For the highest wage that each industry can afford, and for the most equitable division of the products of industry that can ultimately be devised.
For the recognition of the Golden Rule and the mind of Christ as the supreme law of society and the sure remedy for all social ills.
The Doctrines and Discipline of the Methodist Episcopal Church, 1908 (New York: Eaton and Mains; Cincinnati: Jennings and Graham), pp. 479ff.

47. "Do We Need a Methodist Creed?" *Methodist Review,* LXXXIX, (1907), pp. 225-26.
48. *Ibid.,* p. 228.
49. *Ibid.,* p. 230.
50. "Making a Methodist Theology," *The Methodist Quarterly Review,* (October, 1925), p. 581.
51. *Ibid.,* p. 584.
52. *Ibid.,* p. 584-85.
53. *Ibid.,* p. 585.
54. *Ibid.,* p. 587.
55. *Ibid.,* pp. 586ff.
56. *Ibid.,* p. 590.
57. *Idem.*
58. *Ibid.,* p. 591.
59. *Ibid.,* p. 596.

CHAPTER V

1. Harris Franklin Rall and Samuel S. Cohen. *Christianity and Judaism Compare Notes.* New York: The MacMillan Company, 1927, pp. 43-44. Quoted from Alfred North Whitehead, *Religion in The Making.* New York: The MacMillan Company, 1926, pp. 67-68. The full quotation reads: "To-day there is but one religious dogma in debate: what do you mean by 'God?' And in this respect, to-day is like all its yesterdays. This is the fundamental religious dogma, and all other dogmas are subsidiary to it."
2. Rall Manuscript, p. 9.
3. *Ibid.,* pp. 10-11.
4. *Ibid.,* p. 13.
5. Cf. Kenneth Cauthen. *The Impact of American Religious Liberalism.* New York and Evanston: Harper and Row, Publishers, 1962, for the delineation of liberalism specifically on the American scene. John Dillenberger and Claude Welch in *Protestant Christianity, Interpreted*

Through Its Development New York: Charles Scribner's Son, 1954, define liberalism as resting on a duality of interest: it was open to all the prevailing thought-currents of the nineteenth century while at the same time it was the product of a resurgence of religious vitality connected with the missionary movement in particular, and in application of Christianity to social problems. Following, in part, the thinking of H. P. Van Dusen, a contributor of such liberalism in America in his presidency of Union Theological Seminary, New York, in his *The Vitality of the Christian Tradition* (ed. by G. F. Thomas), New York: Harper, 1945, Dillenberger and Welch list some nine themes of such liberalism: (1) the liberal spirit; (2) respect for science and the scientific method; (3) tentativeness as to the possibility of achieving certain knowledge of ultimate reality; (4) emphasis upon the principle of continuity; (5) confidence in man and his future; (6) the authority of Christian experience; (7) the centrality of Jesus Christ; (8) criticism of the tradition from within; (9) social idealism. pp. 211-217. I choose to depend upon the excellent analysis of the theological nuances of liberalism of the late nineteenth and early twentieth centuries by Langdon Gilkey, *Naming The Whirlwind: The Renewal of God-Language*. Indianapolis and New York: The Bobbs-Merrill Company, 1969, especially chapter two, "The Theological Background of the Present Crisis."

6. *Ibid.*, p. 74. Cf. also two delightful personal reminiscences in William Newton Clarke. *Sixty Years With The Bible: a record of experience.* New York: Charles Scribner's Sons, 1912 and Harry Emerson Fosdick. *The Living of These Days.* New York: Harper, 1956.

7. *Ibid.*, pp. 74-75. Gilkey adroitly includes in his discussion of this shift the striking observation of Auguste Sabatier that if one *part* of an absolute authority is shown to be in error, then that authority has in effect been judged by a criterion beyond itself to which validity has been given thus damaging if not destroying the absoluteness of the authority on its own grounds. Cf. Auguste Sabatier, *Religions of Authority and the Religion of the Spirit.* London: Williams and Norgate, 1904, pp. 255-60. Interestingly, it is precisely at this point that the emerging liberalism vs. conservatism debate (wrongly attributed as the fundamentalist-modernist controversy) will center.

8. *Ibid.*, p. 75. Later in his book, Gilkey differentiates between such theological outlooks of liberalism and contemporary radical/secular Christian theologies. On the face of it, the latter's basic assertions — "the denial of the transcendent, absolute God, the acceptance of the authority of secular thought and norms, the principle of personal and intellectual honesty as against all appeals to authority, the emphasis on the historical Jesus, the rejection of all supernatural

entities, and the emphasis on creative action rather than correct belief" — "appear to be warmed-over early twentieth century American liberalism." Gilkey acknowledges that in reality, these *are* the formative principles of the earlier era. The difference rests in the very different context for theology than that of the earlier decades. The ground of the distinction for him locates precisely in the role of the divine, and so of religion itself, in life generally, and from a very different understanding of the meaning of secularity then and now. Then, the divine was immanent in all of developing reality and thus human existence and the divine principle were held in creative continuity. Hence, "... the God known in specifically religious experience could also be found — by philosophical, social, historical, moral, or scientific analyses — as the source of creativity in the general experience of men." Secular culture was embraced, then, not because it was "religionless," but it was within a developing secularity that the divine power in religious experience increasingly manifested itself. "Liberalism was, therefore, founded on a belief in the universality of a relation to God, a relation that could in principle appear everywhere and that filled with increasing value every form of human life... liberalism had no great difficulty with God-language." Now, Gilkey observes and records, the heart of modern secularity, "... is that human experience, secular or religious, is devoid of relation beyond itself to any ground or order, and that there is no form of human thought that can by speculation come to know of such a ground or order.... Clearly, for such a view, the philosophical sources of liberal religion, be they moral or religious experience, metaphysical speculation, or an analysis of either cosmic or human history, are as moribund as is the revelation which was the basis of Christianity's older dogmatic formulation." (pp. 184ff.)

9. William Newton Clarke, *An Outline of Christian Theology*, Fifth Edition: (Edinburgh: T. & T. Clark, 1899), p. 15; First Edition: (Cambridge: J. Wilson and Sons, 1894).
10. Olin Curtis, *The Christian Faith, Personally Given in a System of Doctrine*. Lithoprinted, Grand Rapids, Michigan: Kregel Publications, 1956, pp. ix-x; original edition New York: Eaton and Mains, Cincinnati: Jennings and Graham, 1905.
11. *Ibid.*, p. v, vii.
12. Clarke, *op. cit.*, pp. 139-40.
13. Curtis, *op. cit.*, p. 259.
14. Rall *Manuscript, op. cit.*, p. 9. Compare with footnote 5 *supra*.
15. *Ibid.*, p. 10.
16. *Ibid.*, pp. 11-13. The Dr. Gladden in the quotation is Washington Gladden (1836-1918), pastor of First Congregational Church, Columbs, Ohio. He, with Walter Rauschenbusch (1861-1918) pro-

fessor of church history at Rochester Seminary, are held to be the lonely prophets of the social gospel era within American Protestantism. Cf. Robert T. Handy, *The Social Gospel in America*. New York: Oxford University Press, 1966.
17. *Ibid.*, pp. 11, 13.
18. Rall and Cohen, *p. cit.*, pp. 26-27.
19. Rall, *Christianity*, op. cit. p. 224. Rall notes in particular the books by Wieman: *Religious Experience and Scientific Method*. New York: The MacMillan Company, 1926; *The Wrestle of Religion with Truth*. New York: The MacMillan Company, 1927; *Growth of Religion* (especially Chapter 1) with Walter Marshall Horton. Chicago — New York: Willett, Clark & Company, 1938. Cf. also Bretall, Robert Walter, ed. *The Empirical Theology of Henry Nelson Wieman*. New York: The MacMillan Company, 1963.
20. *Idem.*
21. *Ibid.*, p. 225.
22. *Ibid.*, p. 228.
23. *Ibid.*, p. 229.
24. *Ibid.*, p. 231.
25. James Gustafson, "Context Versus Principles: A Misplaced Debate in Christian Ethics," *New Theology No. 3*, Martin E. Marty and Dean G. Peerman, eds. New York: The MacMillan Company, 1966, pp. 69-102.
26. Rall, *Christianity*, op. cit., p. 233.
27. Rall asserts that the type of modern idealism of the type of Walter Lippmann will provide a welcome context for such argumentation. Cf. Walter Lippmann. *Preface to Morals*. New York: The MacMillan Company, 1929.
28. Rall, *Christianity*, op. cit., pp. 236-7.
29. Rall. "The Nature of Revelation." Address presented to the Fourth Biennial Meeting and Conference of Theological Seminaries and Colleges in the United States and Canada at Garrett Biblical Institute, Evanston, Illinois, June, 1924.
30. H. Richard Niebuhr. *The Meaning of Revelation*. New York: The MacMillan Company, 1952, pp. 60-61.
31. In his lecture in 1924, Rall illustrates the older concept with reference to Charles Hodge and Princeton Theology and his statement, "Inspiration in itself has no sanctifying influence." p. 27. (no reference to source).
32. *Ibid.* p. 28.
33. Rall. *The God of Our Faith*. New York: Abingdon Press, 1955, p. 105.
34. *Ibid.* p. 110.
35. Claude Welch. *In This Name, The Doctrine of the Trinity in Con-

temporary Theology. New York: Charles Scribner's Sons, 1952, pp. 59-60.
36. Lecture notes of 1936, on file at the library of Garrett Theological Seminary, Evanston, Illinois.
37. Rall, op, cit., p. 81.
38. Ibid., p. 120.

We believe in one God, the Father Almighty, maker of heaven and earth, God of holiness and power, God of righteousness and love. All things are from him; he is our trust and our hope. To him belongs our utter obedience. He is the living God, the God that works; creation, rule, redemption, the final salvation — all are from him.

We believe in Jesus Christ as the supreme revelation of this God. We believe that God has come to us in him, revealing his character, his will for man's life, his purpose in the world, his way of saving help. We see Christ's word and work as the word and work of God. But Christ was more than one who spoke God's word as a prophet and who did God's work as his servant; he was one with God. Born a man among men, wholly dependent upon God, he was one with God in spirit and life. He was God incarnate so that to see him was to see the Father. But he was not less man by being wholly filled with God.

We believe in God as indwelling Spirit. The holy and transcendent God dwells in his world, himself works in his world, not as a ruling force, but as spiritual presence and power, as a life of love and truth and righteousness, the true life of man given to him of God. This is more than an influence from without; it is the work of a self-giving, indwelling God. This is God as Holy Spirit, present and working in the soul of man, in the Church, in history. (p. 119)

39. Rall, *A Working Faith*, op. cit., p. 51.
40. Rall, *A Faith For Today*, op. cit., p. 67.
41. Ibid., p. 68
42. Rall, *Christianity*, op. cit., p. 95.
43. Rall, *A Faith For Today*, op. cit., pp. 110-11.
44. Rall, *The God of Our Faith*, op. cit., p. 139.
45. Ibid., p. 94.
46. Rall, *Christianity*, op. cit., p. 313f.
47. Ibid., p. 337
48. Ibid., p. 344.

CHAPTER VI

1. Cf. *supra*, Chapter III, Chapter V, for Rall's judgments on Barth and Wieman. Also, cf. Appendix B, "Which Way Theology?"

2. Rall refers in this instance to the general research into the "lives of Jesus" or *Leben-Jesus-Forschung* of the nineteenth century. He acknowledges that in one aspect and another, "...the question has been touched upon by many writers." He notes the works of Wilhelm Hermann and Martin Kähler, [did he mean, Kähler's *Der sogenannte historiche Jesus und der Geschichtliche, biblishe Christus*, Leipzig: A. Deichert, 1892, 1896, (*The So-Called Historical Jesus and the Historic, Biblical Christ*), recently translated and edited by Carl E. Bruten, Philadelphia: Fortress Press, 1964?] or, *Die Erlösung durch Jesus Christus und die Wessenschaft*, 1898, by Herman, or David W. Forrest, *The Christ of History and of Experience* (The Kerr Lectures of 1897), (Edinburgh: T & T Clark, 5th Ed., 1906, or David Somerville, *St. Paul's Conception of Christ*. New York: Charles Scribner's Sons, n.d. (1900 Yale Lectures). Cf. also Albert Schweitzer, *The Quest of the Historical Jesus*. W. Montgomery tr. London: A. & C. Black, 1910. James M. Robinson, *A New Quest of the Historical Jesus*. London: SCM Press, 1955; Claude Welch, ed. tr. *God and Incarnation; In Mid-Nineteenth Century German Theology*, Library of Protestant Thought New York: Oxford University Press, 1965.
3. Rall might have had in mind any of three publications by Edmond L. Stapfer (tr. Louise Seymour Houghton): *Jesus Christ Before His Ministry*. New York: Charles Scribner's Sons. 1896; *Jesus Christ After His Ministry*. New York: Charles Scribner's Sons, 1897; *The Death and Resurrection of Jesus Christ*. New York: Charles Scribner's Sons, 1898.
4. Rall, Yale Lectures, 1900, pp. 43-48. The last paragraph implies that Rall will deal with Christology within the development of his ecclesiology. Cf. Chapter IX.
5. H. H. Meyer and D. G. Downey, eds. *The Kingdom of God Series*. New York, Cinncinati: Methodist Book Concern, 1917, 1918, 1924. Rall also wrote *Teachers' Manuals* for these books.
6. Rall, *The Teachings of Jesus*, p. 10.
7. *Idem*.
8. Jerry Wayne Brown. *The Rise of Biblical Criticism in America, 1800-1870. The New England Scholars*. Middletown. Connecticut: Wesleyan University Press, 1969.
9. Erik Routley. *The Man For Others*. New York: Oxford University Press, 1964. Cf. also, J. A. T. Robinson, *Honest To God*. Philadelphia: The Westminister Press, 1963, especially Chapter 4 "The Man for Others," pp. 64-83.
10. Rall, *op. cit.*, p. 11.
11. *Ibid.*, pp. 15-16.
12. Cf. *supra*, Chapters II and III for an analysis of summary of Al-

brecht Ritschl's epistemology and Rall's response. Also, cf. there Rall's thoughts on Christology insofar as they form a construct of his theory of revelation and knowledge.
13. Rall, *The Teachings of Jesus, op. cit.,* p. 214.
14. *Ibid.,* p. 216.
15. New York *Christian Advocate,* September 10, 1925, p. 1103.
16. Rall, *A Working Faith, op. cit.,* pp. 151-52.
17. *Ibid.,* p. 152.
18. Rall, *A New Testament History.* New York: Abingdon Press, 1914, p. 141.
19. Rall, *The Teachings of Jesus, op. cit.,* p. 197. He does not identify his source.
20. *Idem.,* "The House By the Side of the Road", Sam Walter Foss, *Masterpieces of Religious Verse,* James Dalton Morrison, ed. New York and London: Harper and Brothers Publishers, 1948. Selection 1387.

There are hermit souls that live withdrawn In the peace of their self-content;
There are souls, like stars, that dwell apart, In a fellowless firmament;
There are pioner souls that blaze their paths Where highways never ran; —
But let me live by the side of the road And be a friend to man.
Let me live in a house by the side of the road, Where the race of men go by —
The men who are good and the men who are bad, As good and as bad as I.
I would not sit in the scorner's seat, Or hurl the cynic's ban; —
Let me live in a house by the side of the road And be a friend to man.

I see from my house by the side of the road, By the side of the highway of life,
The men who press with the ardor of hope, The men who are faint with the strife.
But I turn not away from their smiles nor their tears Both parts of an infinite plan;
Let me live in my house by the side of the road And be a friend to man.

I know there are brook-gladdened meadows ahead And mountains of wearisome height;
That the road passes on through the long afternoon And stretches away to the night.

But still I rejoice when the travellers rejoice, And weep with the strangers that moan,
Nor live in my house by the side of the road Like a man who dwells alone.

Let me live in my house by the side of the road Where the race of men go by —
They are good, they are bad, they are weak, they are strong, Wise, foolish — so am I.
Then why should I sit in the scorner's seat Or hurl the cynic's ban? —
Let me live in my house by the side of the road And be a friend to man.

21. *Ibid.*, p. 205.
22. *Ibid.*, p. 209, unidentified source for the poem.
23. 1936 Lecture notes, p. 108.
24. *Ibid.*, pp. 108-09.
25. *Ibid.*, p. 109. Quoted from Olin A. Curtis. *The Christian Faith Personally Given in a System of Doctrine*. New York: Eaton and Mains, Cincinnati: Jennings and Graham, 1905, pp. 246, 235.
26. *Idem.*
27. *Ibid.*, p. 110.
28. *Ibid.*, p. 111.
29. *Idem.* The reference is to *Foundations: a Statement of Christian Belief by Seven Oxford Men*, B. H. Streeter, A. Brook, William Temple and others. New York: The MacMillan Company, 1912, p. 214.
30. *Ibid.*, pp. 111-12.
31. *Ibid.*, p. 113. Reference is to P. T. Forsyth, *The Person and Place of Christ*. London: Independent Press, Ltd., 1909, p. 313.
32. *Idem.* Reference is to Dean William Ralph Inge, *Oustpoken Essays*, 5th Edition. London, New York: Longmans, Green and Co., 1920, p. 135.
33. *Ibid.*, p. 114.
34. Rall. *Religion As Salvation*. Nashville: Abingdon-Cokesbury, 1953, pp. 131-32. Reference is to William Blake, *Jerusalem*.

CHAPTER VII

1. James Orr, general editor, J. L. Nuelsen, Edgard Y. Mullins, assistant editors. *The International Standard Bible Encyclopedia*. Chicago: The Howard-Severance Company, 1915, pp. 2681-85.
2. *Ibid.*, pp. 2683ff.

3. Undated Manuscript, typed on the back of a letterhead of the Methodist Federation of Social Service, of which Rall was secretary; letter dated October 15, 1911.
4. *International Standard Bible Encyclopedia, op. cit.,* p. 2684.
5. *Ibid.,* p. 2685.
6. Cf. *supra*, Chapter XI. re: Rall's relationship to the Methodist Federation of Social Service and his involvement in the social action of The Methodist Episcopal Church. The Social Creed of 1908 was the first social-institutional pronouncement of any church in America. In 1909 the delegates of the Federal Council of Churches of Christ in America adopted it as a credal statement of that body. Cf. Chapter IV, footnote 46.
7. Private correspondence, letter dated January 3, 1957.
8. Rall, *A New Testament History.* New York: Abingdon Press, 1914, p. 74.
9. "The Social Ministry of Jesus", Harry F. Ward, ed. *The Social Ministry.* New York: Eaton and Mains; Cincinnati: Jennings and Graham, 1910, p. 41.
10. *Ibid.,* p. 43ff.
11. Rall, *A Working Faith.* New York: Abingdon Press, 1914, pp. 192-3.
12. Northwestern *Christian Advocate,* January 21, 1920, p. 106. The activities of the churches following the First World War are in process of documentation for a forthcoming manuscript.
13. "Industry Tomorrow; A Test for Christianity," *Epworth Herald,* November 26, 1921, p. 1167. Rall preached a sermon by that title at the Hennepin Avenue Methodist Church, Minneapolis, Minnesota, on September 4, 1921. Cf. Appendix for representative sermon titles.
14. *Ibid.,* p. 1169.
15. Church bulletin, Hennepin Methodist Church, Minneapolis, Minnesota, dated August 28, 1921.
16. *Idem.*
17. Unpublished Manuscript, p. 1.
18. *Ibid.,* p. 8.
19. Hans Hoffman. *The Theology of Reinhold Niebuhr.* tr. by Louise Pettibone Smith. New York: Charles Scribner's Sons, 1956.
20. Rall, review. "Non-Critical Interpretation," *Interpretation, A Journal of Bible and Theology,* Volume X, Number 4, October, 1956, pp. 457-58.
21. *Ibid.,* p. 458.
22. *Ibid.,* p. 459.
23. *Religion as Salvation, op. cit.,* p. 24.
24. *Ibid.,* p. 204.

25. Edwards in reply to the trustees of the College at Princeton, displayed hesitation to accept their invitation to him of the presidency of that institution. After citing his disqualifications for the position, he wrote: "'Beside these, I have had on my mind and heart, (which I long ago began not with any view to publication) a great work, which I call a *History of the Work of Redemption*, a body of diversity in an entire new method, being thrown into the form of a history.'" Perry Miller concludes of this work that its genesis was a series of sermons preached in 1739, to be published in 1786, and that its thesis is the unity of history, an over-all design as a steady progress from the fall of Adam to Christ, "... then a reversal of direction with the coming of the Saviour, and thereafter 'a finishing state,' where all is spent 'in finishing things off which before had been preparing, ... in summing things up, and bringing them to their issues.'" Perry Miller. *Jonathan Edwards*. New York: Meridian Books, 1959, p. 315; cf. pp. 304ff. Rall and Edwards, beginning from radically different theological bases, appear very similar in their soteriological **hypotheses.**

CHAPTER VIII

1. Harris Franklin Rall, "Brunner in Revolt," *The Christian Century*, Volume LVII, Number 1, January 3, 1940, p. 18. The review is of Emil Brunner, *Man in Revolt: A Christian Anthropology*. New York: Charles Scribner's Sons, 1939.
2. *Idem.*
3. Rall, *The God of Our Faith*, New York: Abingdon Press, 1955, p. 9.
4. 1936 Lecture, mimeographed, p. 1.
5. *Idem.*
6. *Ibid.*, p. 2.
7. *Religion As Salvation*, New York, Nashville: Abingdon-Cokesbury Press, 1953, p. 23.
8. *Ibid.*, p. 24.
9. *Ibid.*, p. 25.
10. *Ibid.*, p. 27.
11. *Christian Faith and Way*, New York, Nashville: Abingdon-Cokesbury Press, 1947, p. 40.
12. *Religion As Salvation, op. cit.*, pp. 34-35.
13. *Ibid.*, p. 36. The full quotation reads "From this original corruption, the eating of the forbidden fruit by Adam and Eve

whereby we are utterly indisposed, disabled, and made opposite to all good, and wholly inclined to all evil, do proceed all actual transgressions." Chapter VI. *Of the Fall of Man, of Sin, and of the Punishment Thereof.* From John H. Leith, Ed., *Creeds of the Churches,* Garden City, New York: Doubleday and Company, Incorporated, 1963, p. 201.
14. *The Coming Kingdom,* New York: Abingdon Press, 1924, p. 33.
15. *Ibid.,* p. 39.
16. Harris Franklin Rall, *A Faith For Today,* New York: The Abingdon Press, 1936, p. 153.
17. *Religion As Salvation, op. cit.,* pp. 46-7.
18. *Christianity, an inquiry into its nature and truth,* New York: Charles Scribner's Sons, 1940, p. 330.
19. *The Teachings of Jesus, op. cit.,* p. 60.
20. *Ibid.,* p. 494.
21. *Religion As Salvation, op. cit.,* p. 61.
22. *Ibid.,* p. 64. Quoted from Reinhold Niebuhr. *The Nature and Destiny of Man: A Christian Interpretation,* Volume I, *Human Nature.* New York: Charles Scribner's Sons, 1940, p. 208.
23. *Ibid.,* p. 82.
24. *Ibid.,* p. 67.
25. *Ibid.* p. 68.
26. *Ibid.,* pp. 68-69. Quoted from Karl Heim, *Leitfaden der Dogmatik; zum Gebräuch bei Akademischen Vorlesungen,* 2nd edit., (Halle: a. S., M. Niemeyer, 1916-21), 2 volumes in 1, p. 47.

CHAPTER IX

1. *The Christian Faith and Way.* New York: Abingdon Press, 1914, p. 85f.
2. *A Working Faith.* New York: Abingdon Press, 1914, p. 196.
3. *Ibid.,* pp. 198-99.
4. *Ibid.,* p. 202.
5. *Ibid.,* p. 207.
6. *Ibid.,* pp. 217-18.
7. *Ibid.,* p. 220.
8. *Ibid.,* p. 223.
9. *Ibid.,* p. 241.
10. *A Faith For Today.* New York: Abingdon Press, 1936, p. 211.
11. *Ibid.,* p. 213.
12. *Journal of the General Conference of The Methodist Episcopal Church,* 1916. New York, Nashville: The Abingdon Press, pp. 15, 135-39, 152-54.

13. Thomas B. Neeley, *The Revised Ritual of 1916*. Philadelphia: The Methodist Episcopal Book Store, 1920, pp. 97-98.
14. "Making a Methodist Ritual," *The Christian Advocate*, James R. Joy, ed. Volume XCV, Number 16, April 15, 1920, p. 529.
15. "Making a Methodist Ritual," *The Christian Advocate*, James R. Joy, ed. Volume XCV, Number 17, April 22, 1920, p. 561.
16. *Religion As Salvation*. New York: Abingdon-Cokesbury, 1953. p. 163.
17. *Ibid.*, p. 169.
18. "What About Our Ministry?" *The Methodist Review*. May-June, 1924, CVII, p. 406.
19. *Ibid.*, p. 410.
20. Professor Rall represented The Methodist Episcopal Church at the Second World Conference on Faith and Order, convened at Edinburgh in 1937. "That gathering prepared a remarkable statement on 'The Grace of Our Lord Jesus Christ,' prefaced with the judgment, 'There is in connection with this subject no ground for maintaining division between Churches.' But with respect to 'The Ministry and Sacraments' very deep differences were revealed, pointing to the matters that needed further illumination. Yet the generalization seemed generally accepted that in the doctrinal realm, the agreements between the churches cover eighty-five per cent of the ground." William Walker. *A History of the Christian Church*. Revised by Cyril C. Richardson, Wilhelm Pauck, and Robert T. Handy. New York: Charles Scribner's Sons, 1959, pp. 541-42.
21. "The Methodist Conception of the Church," private manuscript, n.d., p. 3.
22. *Ibid.*, p. 6.
23. *Ibid.*, p. 8.
24. *Ibid.*, pp. 8-9.
25. "The Ethical Element in Methodist Preaching as Related to the Concept of the Church," private manuscript, n.d., p. 4.
26. "Edinburgh, 1937," *Sunday School Journal*, Lucius H. Bugbee, ed. December, 1937, Volume LXIX, Number 12, p. 621.
27. "The Church Given or Gathered?" *Christendom*, Spring 1939, IV, p. 165.
28. *Ibid.*, p. 169.
29. "After Edinburgh". *Religion in Life*, Winter, 1938, VII, p. 29.
30. *Ibid.*, pp. 32-3.
31. *Ibid.*, pp. 34-5.

CHAPTER X

1. The fuller development of these paragraphs on John Wesley and Premillenialism can be founds as an appendix to *Modern Premile-*

nialism and the Christan Hope. New York: The Abingdon Press, 1920. Reprinted as pamphlet and distributed in the thousands as *Was John Wesley A Premillenialist?* Toronto: Methodist Book and Publishing House, 1921.
2. Private Manuscript, n.d., p. 44.
3. "Premillenialism, I. The Issue," *The Biblical World,* Shailer Mathews, ed., New Series LIII, July, 1919.
4. *Modern Premillenialism and the Chrstian Hope, op. cit.,* p. 253.
5. Albert Schweitzer, *The Quest of the Historical Jesus, op. cit.*
6. *Modern Premillenialism and the Christian Hope, op. cit.,* p. 69.
7. *Ibid.,* p. 95.
8. "Methodism and Perillenialism," *Methodist Review,* Fifth Series, ed. Jan-June, William Kelley; July-Dec., George Elliott, Vol. 36, 1920, p. 219.
9. "Premillenialism and the Work of the Church," *Zion's Herald,* ed., L. O. Hartman, Vol. 94, No. 6, February 9, 1921, p. 170.
10. *Idem.*
11. *Idem.*
12. *Idem.*
13. "The War and the Second Coming," *The Christian Century,* Charles Clayton Morrison, ed., Volume 60, Number 33, August 18, 1943, pp. 941.
14. *Ibid.,* p. 942.
15. *A Faith For Today,* New York: The Abingdon Press, 1936, pp. 250-51.
16. *Ibid.,* p. 257.
17. *The Coming Kingdom,* New York: The Abingdon Press, 1924, p. 109.
18. "What About Judgment and Hell?" An address presented at the Hennepin Avenue Methodist Episcopal Church, Minneapolis, Minnesota, in the series, *Plain Talks for Puzzled People,* August 7, 1921.
19. *Religion as Salvation,* New York, Nashville: Abingdon-Cokesbury Press, 1953, p. 237.
20. *Ibid.,* p. 240.

CHAPTER XI

1. To cite recent studies which forced this opinion upon me I list Henry F. May, "Shifting Perspectives on the 1920's," *The Mississippi Valley Historical Review,* Volume XLIII, June, 1956 to March, 1957, pp. 405-427; Barton J. Bernstein, ed., *Towards a New Past, Dissenting Essays in American History.* New York: Random House, 1967.
2. Hubert Saal. "Burt Bacharach, The Music Man 1970," *Newsweek,* Volume LXXV, Number 25 (June 22, 1970), pp. 50-54.

3. Dwight MacDonald, "Masscult and Midcult," *Against The American Grain.* New York: Random House, 1952, p. 3.
4. *Ibid.,* p. 37.
5. Franklin L. Baumer, "Intellectual History and Its Problems," *The Journal of Modern History,* XXI (September, 1949), pp. 191-203. Also, cf. Charles A. Barker, "Needs and Opportunities in American Social and Intellectual History," *Pacific Historical Review,* XXI (February, 1951), pp. 1-9; John L. Greene, "Objectives and Methods in Intellectual History," *The Mississippi Valley Historical Review,* XLIV (June, 1957), pp. 58-74; John Higham, "American Intellectual History: A Critical Appraisal," *American Quarterly,* XIII (Summer Supplement, 1961), pp. 219-33; Rush Welter, "The History of Ideas in America: An Essay in Redefinition." *The Journal of American History,* LI (March, 1965), pp. 599-614, R. Richard Wohel, "Intellectual History: An Historian's View," *The Historian,* XVI (Autumn, 1953), pp. 62-77.
6. Professor Claude Welch has just received the Bross Prize for his forthcoming book on 19th century Protestant Theology. Harper and Row have announced the publication of a three volume set dealing with theology of the early 20th century, under the editorship of Professor Jaroslav Pelikan of Yale University.
7. Robert S. and Helen M. Lynd. *Middletown.* New York: Harcourt, Prace and Company, 1929; *Middletown in Transition.* New York: Harcourt, Prace and Company, 1937.
8. Timothy L. Smith. *Revivalism and Social Reform in Mid-19th Century America.* Nashville: Abingdon Press, 1957.
9. I might add at this point that the historian and scholar should also study in similar fashion William Porcher DuBose (Episcopalian), Edgar Young Mullins (Southern Baptist), et. al. denominational theologians.
10. Cf. the incisive essays of Sidney E. Mead, *The Lively Experiment, the Shaping of Christianity in America.* New York: Harper and Row, 1963; also, his article-analysis "In Quest of America's Religion" (How My Mind Has Changed), *The Christian Century,* LXXXVII, 24, June 17, 1970, pp. 752-56.
11. Murray H. Leiffer, "Dr. Rall and Methodist Social Concerns," Henry E. Kolbe, ed. *The Garrett Tower.* Vol. 40, Number 1, December, 1940.
12. *New Testament History and Modern Pre-Millenialism* and *The Christian Hope.* Cf. *The History of American Methodism,* Vol. II, Ch. 24, for a fuller treatment of the Course of Study.
13. *The History of American Methodism,* Volume III, p. 272. Quoted from Harold Paul Sloan. *Historic Christianity and the New Theology.* Louisville: Pentecostal Publishing Company, 1922, p. 37.

14. Robert Moats Miller. "Methodism and American Society, 1900-1939." *The History of American Methodism, op. cit.,* Vol. III, p. 395. Quoted from *The Daily Christian Advocate,* the Methodist Episcopal Church, May 16, 1908, p. 8. For a fuller analysis of the Methodist Federation of Social Service, cf. Robert Moats Miller, *American Protestantism and Social Issues 1919-1939.* Chapel Hill: The University of North Carolina Press, 1958.
15. Editorial. *The Social Questions Bulletin,* Volume 27, Number 6, June, 1937, p. 4.
16. Miller, *op. cit.,* p. 396.
17. Joseph Haroutunian, "Theology and American Experience," *CRITERION,* Volume Three, Number Two, Winter, 1964, pp. 3-11.
18. *Ibid.,* pp. 3-5.
19. *Ibid.,* pp. 8-11.
20. Walter Lowrie. *Our Concern with the Theology of Crisis.* Boston: Meador Publishing Company, 1932, p. 36. Cf. especially his analysis of American evangelical liberal theology, pp. 29-30, the numbers indicating the points that the Theology of Crisis specifically addresses itself to:
(1) Of all the religions of mankind, Christianity, we are sure, is the highest; (2) for we regard it as the climax of a long evolutionary process, (3) in which the people of Israel, because they were a race especially gifted for religion, played a conspicuous part, while above this level of human attainment towered (4) the Founder of our religion, (5) a religious genius so unique that men may well hesitate to deny that (6) in some sense he was divine. (7) We acclaim him as the Master, in appreciation of the fact that his (8) religious consciousness, as manifested in precept and example, is in some degree normative for us — in spite of the fact that the movement to which he gave impetus (9) has resulted in clearer conceptions of the divine and of the human than was possible at the beginning. We still envisage the moral task in the figurative terms which Jesus proposed, as a (10) 'building up of the Kingdom of God!' which we understand as (11) the realization of a perfect human society, having no doubt that (12) man is equal to such a task, (13) because man is inherently a child of God and therefore essentially good. We cannot ignore the fact that this great end is (14) more remote than Jesus seems to have conceived, and that the chief obstacle is something that used to be called sin. But we are confident that (15) at long last the evolutionary process will eliminate (16) this organic defect of our brute inheritance. And if ever we reflect how great a dose of resignation is required of us in laboring for a utopia in which we shall personally have no part, we are consoled by the Christian belief in (17) the immortality of

the soul, which we associate with the 'kingdom of heaven!' (18) By this faith in the continuity of the here and the hereafter, of time and eternity, we have (19) robbed death of its terror, and even of its apparent significance. Jesus purified religion by teaching us to see (20) that God is our Father, and therefore can be approached without fear and without the sense of awful distance. (21) For God is essentially near, immanent in his world and therefore discoverable in it — (22) especially in the depths of the human heart, in a more or less mystical experience. (23) Experience is therefore the foundation of faith, (24) though Jesus of Nazareth as an historical person, in whom we see realized the (25) ideal of humanity, is none the less necessary to give a note of (26) authority to our intuitions. (27) Therein lies the supreme value of the Gospels. But a unique religious value attaches to the whole Bible; to the (28) Old Testament, because it is a record of the most significant evolution of the religious ideas (what may be called by analogy the vertebrate line of development); and (29) to the New Testament, because it is the record of the experience of the first generations of Christians, which we cannot but regard as the classical experience, (30) since the disciples who in line were nearest to the initial thrust must have experienced it more vividly, though they naturally could not understand its significance so adequately as we who view it from a position immensely more remote.

21. William R. Hutchinson, ed. *American Protestant Thought, The Liberal Era*. Harper Torchbook. New York and Evanston: Harper and Row, Publishers, 1966, p. 7.
22. H. Shelton Smith, Robert T. Handy, Leffer A. Loetscher, *American Christianity, An Historical Interpretation with Representative Documents*. 2 Vols. New York: Charles Scribner's Sons, 1963, Volume II, p. 256.
23. Cf. Karl Barth. *Protestant Thought from Rousseau to Ritschl*. New York: Harper and Row, Publishers, 1959; John Dillenberger, Claude Welch. *Protestant Christianity Interpreted Through Its Development*. New York: Charles Scribner's Sons, 1954, pp. 198-200; Hugh Ross Mackintosh. *Types of Modern Theology; Schleiermacher to Barth*. London: Nisbet and Company, Ltd., 1937, pp. 138-180; H. Richard Niebuhr, *The Meaning of Revelation*. New York: The Macmillan, Company, 1941, pp. 25-33.
24. Philip Hefner. "A. Ritschl and His Current Critics," *Lutheran Quarterly*. Vol. 13, 1961, p. 105.
25. *Idem.*
26. *Idem.*
27. *Ibid.*, p. 108.
28. Cf. the still-classic Albert K. Weinberg. *Manifest Destiny, A Study*

of *Nationalist Expansionism in American History*. Baltimore: The John Hopkins Press, 1935; also, Ernest R. May, *American Imperialism*. New York: Atheneum, 1968, *Imperial Democracy*. New York: Harcourt, Brace and World, 1961; Sidney Mead, *op cit.*, esp. Chapter IX: Smith, Handy, Loetscher, *op. cit.*, Vol. II, Chapter 19; and selected sources in Nelson R. Burr, *A Critical Bibliography of Religion in America*. Princeton: Princeton University Press, 1961. Allied with these are H. Richard Niebuhr's, *The Kingdom of God in America*. New York: Harper Brothers, Publishers, 1937 and the recent book, Winthrop S. Hudson, ed. *Nationalism and Religion in America, Cancepts of American Identity and Mission*. New York: Harper and Row, Publishers, 1970, especially Chapter 3.

29. Edwin Scott Gaustad. *A Religious History of America*. New York: Harper and Row, Publishers, 1966, p. 177. Quoted from Philip Schaff, *America: A Sketch of Its Political, Social, and Religious Character*. Cambridge: The Belknap Press of Harvard University, 1961, p. 135.

30. Michael Novak, ed. *American Philosophy and The Future*. New York: Charles Scribner's Sons, 1968.

31. Kenneth Hamilton. *Revolt Against Heaven*. Grand Rapids: William B. Erdmans Publishing Company, 1965, p. 86. Of particular interest is Hamilton's footnote:
    39. Barth, oddly, belittles Ritschl's influence, describing his teaching merely as a reaction, a return to the Enlightenment (*Protestant Thought from Rousseau to Ritschl*, pp. 390-97). Brunner describes him as 'the second milestone' in nineteenth century theology (Eng. trans. *The Mediator*, London: Lutterworth Press, 1934, p. 56). Kenneth Cauthen in *The Impact of American Religious Liberalism* (New York: Harper and Row, 1962), mentions Schleiermacher and Ritschl together as 'tremendously influential' (p. 19).

    Hamilton is quite correct!

32. Arthur Cushman McGiffert. *The Rise of Modern Religious Ideas*. New York: The Macmillan Company, 1915, p. 139.

33. Wohl, *op. cit.*

34. Cf. e.g. Charles H. Hopkins, *The Rise of the Social Gospel in American Protestantism*. New Haven: Yale University Press, 1940; Aaron I. Abell, *American Catholicism and Social Action: A Search for Social Justice, 1865-1950*. Garden City: Doubleday, 1960; *Urban Impact on American Protestantism, 1865-1900*, Cambridge: Harvard University Press, 1943; Henry F. May, *Protestant Churches and Industrial America*, New York: Harper and Brothers, Publishers, 1949; Robert T. Handy, ed. *The Social Gospel in America, 1870-1920*. New York: Oxford University Press, 1966.

35. Sydney E. Ahlstrom, ed., *Theology in America.* Indianapolis: The Bobbs-Merrill Company, Inc., 1967, p. 531.
36. Sydney E. Ahlstrom, "Theology in Americas: A. Historical Survey." James Ward Smith, A. Leland Jamieson, ed., *The Shaping of American Religion.* Princeton: Princeton University Press, 1961, pp. 295f.
37. C. M. Mead, "Ritschl's Place in the History of Doctrine," *Hartford Seminary Record,* Vol. 5, 1894, p. 161ff.
38. *Ibid.*, p. 162.
39. Cf. the standard treatments: Frank Hugh Foster. *The Modern Movement in American Theology; Sketches in the History of American Protestant Thought from the Civil War to the World War.* New York: Fleming H. Revell Company, 1939; Richard Hofstadter, *Social Darwinism in American Thought.* Philadelphia: The University of Pennsylvania Press, 1944, esp. ch. 3., "The Reception of Evolution by Theologians;" Stow Persons, ed. *Evolutionary Thought in America.* New Haven: Yale University Press, 1950, esp. his chapter, "Evolution and Theology in America."
40. Cf. *supra*, III, pp. 25-26.
41. Virgillus Ferm, ed. *Contemporary American Theology,* Volume II, New York: Round Table Press, 1933, pp. 248-249.
42. Jaroslav J. Pelikan. "Methodism's Contribution to America," *The History of American Methodism,* Emory Stevens Bucke, gen. ed., New York: Abingdon Press, 1964, Volume III, p. 597.
43. *Idem.* Quoted from Philip Schaff, *America, op. cit.,* p. 136.
44. Cf. Robert C. Chiles, *Theological Transition in American Methodism: 1790-1935.* New York: Abingdon Press, 1965, esp. ch. V, "From Free Grace to Free Will."
45. Colin W. Williams, *John Wesley's Theology Today,* Nashville: Abingdon Press, 1960, p. 154f. Quoted in Pelikan's article.
46. *The History of American Methodism, op. cit.,* Volume III, p. 615.
47. Harris Franklin Rall. "The Methodist Church," R. Newton Flew, ed., *The Nature of the Church,* New York: Harper and Brothers, 1952, p. 329. Quoted by Gerald O. McCulloh, "The Theology and Practices of Methodism, 1876-1919," *The History of American Methodism, op. cit.,* Vol. II, p. 599.
48. Virgilus Ferm, ed. *Contemporary American Theology.* Volumes I and II, New York: Round Table Press, 1932, 1933. These theologians were Benjamin Bacon, Edgar Brightman, John Buckham, Shirley Jackson Case, Winfred Garrison, Walter Marshall Horton, Rufus Jones, Albert Knudson, J. Gresham Machen, Douglas Clyde Macintosh, Ernest F. Scott, Henry Nelson Wieman, Edward Scribner Ames, John Baillie, William Adams Brown, Eugene W. Lyman, Daniel McGregor, Shailer Mathews, Frank Chamberlin Porter,

William L. Sullivan, Luther Weigle, William Kelley Wright, and Harris Franklin Rall.
49. *Ibid., Second Series,* p. 249f.
50. *Ibid.,* p. 251.
51. *Ibid.,* p. 252.
52. *Ibid.,* p. 271.